The Wonderful Food
of Provence

THE WONDERFUL

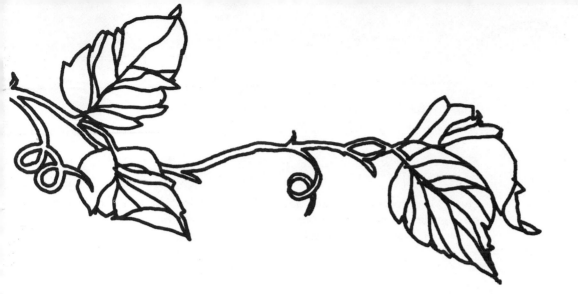

FOOD OF PROVENCE

Jean-Noël Escudier and Peta J. Fuller

with decorations by Ron Becker

PERENNIAL LIBRARY

HARPER & ROW, PUBLISHERS, New York

*Cambridge, Philadelphia, San Francisco, Washington, London, Mexico City,
São Paulo, Singapore, Sydney*

Note: *The commentary and interpolations printed in boldface type throughout this book, as well as the preface and the entire text of Chapter III, are the work of the American co-author and translator, Peta J. Fuller.*

This book was originally published in France by Editions Gallia under the title *La Véritable Cuisine Provençale et Niçoise,* copyright 1953 by Editions Gallia. A hardcover edition of *The Wonderful Food of Provence* was published in the United States in 1968 by Houghton Mifflin Company, Boston.

First PERENNIAL LIBRARY edition published 1988.

LIBRARY OF CONGRESS CATALOG CARD NUMBER: 87-45612
ISBN: 0-06-097131-2

88 89 90 91 92 RRD 10 9 8 7 6 5 4 3 2 1

Introduction to This Edition
by PAULA WOLFERT

YOU ARE HOLDING in your hands one of my favorite cookbooks, a book I have treasured through the long years that it has been out of print. Now I am delighted to see it republished, particularly in such a lovely new edition.

The Wonderful Food of Provence first came out in its translated version in 1968. I recall reading it with that same excitement and sense of discovery that I felt when I first read Elizabeth David's books in the late 1950s. The book spoke to me in the most extraordinarily poignant and insightful way of the wonderful, pure, simple basic cooking that everyone now associates with Provence. At that time, haute cuisine was in vogue, nouvelle cuisine did not exist, and notions of simplicity were out of fashion.

Moreover, the book spoke to me of the Provençal way of life, of which its cuisine is both a symbol and a reflection. My rereading of *The Wonderful Food of Provence* has confirmed my memory: the book contains recipes, but like all the best regionally based cookbooks, it is really about falling in love with a place and its food. And who can visit Provence without falling in love with it—its rocky outcroppings spotted with wild thyme, lavender, and rosemary, its cooking that is at once rustic, refined, and lush? Provençal cooking utilizes all the good things from the earth and sea—good fish, good oil, fresh vegetables, delicate lemons, fragrant herbs. Who can visit this land, taste this cuisine, and not say: "I want some of this in my own life, too"?

In a real sense this cookbook is a statement about the good life. Jean-Noël Escudier, known in France as "M. Provence," loves his region and shares his love with his readers. His recipes stun by their simplicity and honesty—they all work, they are do-able, the ingredients are available, and best of all, they will make you happy. But the reader of the English-language edition gets an added treat denied to readers of the original. I am referring to the vivid notes by the translator, Peta J. Fuller, who writes of how she fell in love with this book and resolved to create a translation that would do it justice. Clearly, she tested every recipe, and from time to time she has noted her observations in the most charming way.

The Wonderful Food of Provence was ahead of its time in this country. For fifteen years now it has lain in obscurity. Iconoclastic, knowledgeable, passionate, real, it is refreshing compared with the many cookbooks that have appeared over the past decade, books about fashionable food invented by fashionable chefs—food without history, without truth. For this is a truthful cookbook written in a personal style. M. Escudier felt no need to rethink or recreate existing recipes, nor was he interested in showing off his brilliance. He simply gathered what existed, wrote it down, and by so doing revealed the cooking of a region.

What recipes he found! Barbouiado, a casserole of fresh favas and artichokes with just a hint of cinnamon for "an element of pleasant surprise." "One-eyed" bouillabaisse, made with poached eggs, fennel, and saffron. Myriad things to do with fish. Numerous superb mussel dishes. The delicious, original version of salad Niçoise that is not only simplicity itself but also state-of-the-art.

This book will make you want to cook, and it will make you want to travel. It may also scent your dreams with mimosa and wild herbs.

Preface

IN 1953, when *La Véritable Cuisine Provençale et Niçoise* by Jean-Noël Escudier was first published, the French press received it jubilantly. "The best thing you can do is to buy it quickly for your wife," they wrote, and "It should be in everybody's home." Never before, it seemed, had there been an anthology of authentic Provençal recipes.

Not surprisingly, the little book became a standard reference work for other food writers, some of whom, with rather unsportsmanlike disregard of poaching rules, have served up generous helpings of the text in their own pages.

The Wonderful Food of Provence is the English language version of the parent book and has been prepared with the full endorsement of Jean-Noël Escudier. Except for a very few deletions, it contains all the original material, revised, annotated, and supplemented by the translating partner in this collaboration.

Every dish presented here is truly Provençal and has some specific regional characteristic, either in the ingredients or in the method of preparation. There has been no attempt to modify recipes to suit the so-called American taste. Unfortunates who don't like (or, as is oftener the truth of the matter, don't know they *do* like) garlic, or who feel no shame in inability to distinguish between fine olive oil and a substance favored by boll weevils, may decide they're in the wrong book. Everyone else, though, should have a wonderful time.

The translation actually began several years ago in the kitchen library of Felice Merton, a knowledgeable friend, although I was big with book, so to speak, long before any of us realized what had happened. Felice's library, incidentally, is a real library, not a mussy little scatter of cookbooks with debonair titles behind which people explain, ever so amusingly, how, with a can opener and ten minutes to spare, you can pretend to make something.

Inheriting an intemperate curiosity about anything anybody anywhere is cooking — or even saying about cooking — makes one an incurable food snoop. Thus it was while blissfully snooping that I spotted that first little white paper-bound *"La Véritable"* — as my husband and I began to refer to it at home. Riffling its pages, I moved into a new territory, gastronomically speaking. And what a lift for the spirits! For here, in our dissatisfied, complaining times, was one Jean-Noël Escudier, delighted by his world, animated by sweetly unaggressive chauvinism, and sustained by the thought that the Provençal — that peerless male — is a creature of unique and superior endowments who, understandably, has chosen to inhabit a uniquely superior place. Here was "a cuisine that reflects the sensitive intelligence, the lucidity, wisdom and verve with which all Provence is blessed," wrote this happy man. "This beauty, this joy, this most harmonious blend in the world, exemplifies the fantastic idealism which is the mark of the man of Provence."

"*Why?*" he was to exclaim later in genuine astonishment when a trip to New York was proposed. "*Why?* when everything is *here?*"

La Véritable, once I got it home (for, of course, I borrowed it) turned out to be full of surprises even in a household as unapologetically alliophile as ours. Who'd have imagined, for example, that 40 cloves of garlic could be so unassertive, or a scrap of orange peel so lively? The creative cook, once initiated in Provençal techniques, discovers a new dimension for all her cookery. For my husband and me, the book marked the beginning of a culinary adventure that was to lead, eventually, through the attractive pages of *Gourmet* magazine and across the Atlantic air to adorable Toulon and, at last, to Monsieur Provence himself.

"Monsieur Provence." That is how people in southern France (and far beyond) sometimes affectionately refer to Jean-Noël Escudier, the man who was to become my friend and collaborator. And no wonder. Because it is unlikely that any other person knows more than Jean-Noël Escudier about what has made Provence Provençal. He is, for one thing, a specialist in the Provençal language which even the Portuguese understand better than most French people do. He is also founder, director, and publisher of the monthly *Journal d'Aix-en-Provence* and the bimonthly *Provence, Côte d'Azur.* He is founder-president of the Compagnie des Gastronomes de Provence; president of the Association des Anciens Combattants de Toulon; vice-president of the Société des Amis de l'Art Vivant and of l'Académie Poétique de Provence; Grand Prévôt of the Ordre Illustré des Chevaliers de Meduse (a bacchic brotherhood dedicated to the thoughtful investigation of vintages — Provençal vintages, of course); member of the board of directors of the Académie de Moustier; master of ceremonies of the Confrérie des Chevaliers de l'Étoile, and of the Comité de la Société des Chevaliers des Palmes Académiques. He was awarded the Croix de Guerre with four citations, and the Médaille Militaire, and is a Chevalier de la Légion d'Honneur.

Provence has never had a better friend.

PETA J. FULLER

Acknowledgments

FOR THIS English language version of Jean-Noël Escudier's *La Véritable Cuisine Provençale et Niçoise,* the American half of the partnership, transposing from an idiom unfamiliar even to most French people, drew heavily on the knowledge and patience of family, friends, and strangers. I want to thank first and last, my husband, James Fuller, who, without excessive protest, and even cheerfully, survived the seemingly endless alarums and excursions the project involved; Joyce Hartman and Dale Warren at Houghton Mifflin Company for encouragement; Mary Ann Fell who, bless her, turned up, unbegged, from time to time, to soothe and type; Susan Rowe, who read copy with an ear sensitively tuned toward questions less sophisticated readers might ask; Richard Koch for many valuable clues to sources of information; Simone Daumen for clarification of obscure Provençal terms; the Basançons, Père et Fils, at the Deauville Market in Manhattan, who so amiably interpreted and demonstrated for me the French cuts of meat; wine authorities Julius Wile and Fernande Garvin for helpful comments about Provençal wines; and Waverley Root who surely knows as much about the cuisine of *all* France as any man alive, and whose book *The Food of France* holds all the wonder of French kitchens within its covers.

My very special gratitude goes to Henri Fluchère, designer, illustrator, writer, wine connoisseur, neighbor, friend, Provençal, and son of a great cook, for indulgently letting me interrupt his work again and again with questions . . . and for always having the answers.

PETA J. FULLER

Contents

I

The Heritage

A CUISINE is all of a terrain and its whole past. And that of Provence lies deep in antiquity. On her coasts, the scent of a tuft of thyme, the sun on the sea, the chant of the cicadas, all become part of a fragrant bouillabaisse, of an *aïoli* (that incomparable golden pomade!), or of a platter of fish grilled and flamed with fennel. A regional dish is a whole countryside. But this cuisine is not, of course, solely the reflection of things Provençal and Mediterranean. Much of it represents traditions established over the course of centuries.

Provence, Hellenized first in the sixth century, B.C., then Romanized toward the end of the year 1 B.C., drew inspiration from highly refined and vigorously seasoned Greco-Roman dishes. This was fare that could be easily adapted, since most of the aromatics loved by the Romans were to be found in abundance in Provence. It was equally easy to produce there the two ingredients most essential to Roman cookery: olive oil and wine.

Thus a great number of recipes which were indigenous to a people were saved from extinction. Clearly, Provençal cuisine was richly dowered by several Mediterranean civilizations and, in turn, has of course strongly influenced French eating habits. Many great nineteenth-century chefs, having been born in the Midi, learned there how to lighten and "relieve" the heavy northern dishes. They developed those knowledgeable syntheses of olive oil, anchovies, garlic, wine, and spices that became the prototype of Mediterranean food.

The specialties of Provence are so original, so different from those of other regions that they astonish and sometimes actually disconcert those who come upon them with no warning. The boldly declarative flavor of *aïoli,* for example, holds a shock for timid tasters although it swiftly makes converts of all but baby-food addicts. Then too, in Provence, one is frequently transported by a kind of *joie de vivre* that makes everything there seem superlative. "If the cuisine is superior," wrote Pierre de Pressac, "it is surely because it is identified with the Rhône, the blue sea, the olive groves, the acropolises of the Ventoux, Sainte-Victoire, and the Coudon, the horizon of the Maures, the sparkling porphyries of the Estérel, the splendor of the shores of the Côte d'Azur."

Provence possesses a culinary wealth that includes some four hundred indigenous dishes. It uses the best of natural products: the tender early fruits (eaten young, and not, as in the United States, left to grow older, tougher, and more profitable to the vendor); the delectable olive oil which no peanut can ever replace; the twenty "aromates" (herbs and spices, fresh or dried); the sixteen "fruits of the sea"; the forty-six species of fish peculiar to the shores of "la Gueuse Parfumée" ("the Perfumed Trollop"); and the grapes that the hot sun brings to perfection from Châteauneuf to the hills of Var and Nice, to be gathered into an imposing gamut of excellent vintages. Provence must be, surely, the most sumptuous of gourmand regions. To the substantial and charming gifts with which nature has been so prodigal, the gods add the blessings of imagination, a sharp sense of beauty, and a zest for life. This beauty, this joy, and this diversity are all part of the art that extracts the best from the products of the region and makes the most harmonious blend of tradition and evolution, exemplifying the fantastic idealism that is the mark of the man of Provence.

Haute cuisine is always an indication of a high level of cultural development, and that of Provence is in the top rank of our time. For there, says Gonzague Truc,* where the luscious olive is queen, it makes of even a simple vermicelli soup, sprinkled with grated Gruyère and Dutch cheese, an original dish in which the delicate vegetable flavor of olive oil enchants and astonishes the palate. It is a pure triumph, neither commonplace nor crude.

Out of the enormous variety of natural products provided by the earth and sea, Provençal kitchens have created the regional classics. But Provence also puts its stamp on many others. A stuffed shoulder of lamb, for example, or a slice of braised mutton will seem quite different dishes as served in Toulon and in Paris. Nor can we think of anything more delicious than a fish caught at dawn, cleaned, rinsed with sea water, and put on a grill with a branch of fennel in its flanks and, while browning, basted with a little bouquet of thyme dipped in olive oil. The Provençal, savoring this simple delicacy, sees again his blue sea, his beaches, his pine forests, and his coves.

The Greeks ate soberly, the Romans somewhat grossly. The *Provençaux* feast with finesse. One rarely finds among them the rapacious appetites common at Flemish revels, Alsatian wedding suppers, or Norman banquets; they prefer the exquisite to the copious.

Provence considers itself the habitat of a unique people who ally sobriety with refinement, high flavor in food with digestibility, good humor with permanent lucidity of mind. The light, savory dishes abundantly set off by the olfactory excitement of aromatic plants and, above all, by garlic; the crusty bread made of fine flour; the wines, clear and full-bodied from the flinty banks of the Rhône and the Var — these are what characterize Provençal fare, stimulate the appetite on warm days, and protect congeniality from excess and disenchantment. This cuisine corresponds, in its special way, to the intelligence, the lucidity, wisdom, and verve with which, blessedly, the Provençaux continue to be endowed.

* *La Provence* by Gonzague Truc.

II

The Essence of Provençal Cuisine

OLIVE OIL, GARLIC, AND HERBS: from these natural marvels whole worlds of culinary splendor have been evolved. Among them, the most indispensably Provençal is the oil.

Olive Oil

> The oil that is extracted here from the most beautiful olives in the world replaces butter. I had great misgivings about this substitution. But I have tasted it in sauces and, truthfully, there is nothing better.
>
> — Jean Racine, *Lettres d'Uzès,* 1661

For the dedicated connoisseur three hundred years later, the only oil fine enough for the subtleties of *haute cuisine* is olive — but olive oil, it must be understood, which has been neither cut nor emasculated, an oil young and ruddy, fragrant and fruity, retaining the exquisite flavor of the crushed pulp. It is not enough, however, for the oil to be pure olive. The quality and the *kind* of olives, and their degree of maturity are important factors in producing an oil that is fresh to the taste, soothing to the throat, pleasing to the palate, and *discreetly* fruity. It is imperative, moreover, not to confuse fruity oil with strong. The best is bland. The gentle, high-quality oil produced by the "Country of the Sun" is what gives the famous regional dishes their special cachet. Where there is prejudice against cooking with olive oil, the resistance usually turns out to have had its sources in bad examples, poor cooking methods, or second-rate oil. Perhaps all three. The good oil of Provence has never been known to upset a delicate stomach.

Garlic

Against garlic, the pervading genius of invigorating fare, the bias is more firmly fixed and not so easily traced. People are rarely of two minds about it. "All powerful garlic, marvelous seasoning, thou art the essence, the incense, that raises and exalts," quoth one Gustave Coquoit, and, warming up to his exalting subject, "Thou art the thorn that excites, stimulates. Garlic! Thou art the supreme appetizer, the sole condiment, the glorious, the sovereign extract of the earth!"

In olden times it was believed that the consumption of generous amounts of garlic assured long life. Indeed, one Annibal Camous, a *Marseillais* who lived to be 104, maintained that it was by eating garlic daily that he kept his "youth" and brilliance. When his eighty-year-old son died, the father mourned, "I always *told* him he wouldn't live long, poor boy. He ate too little garlic!"

"No garlic, no true Provençal cuisine," say the *Provençaux*. But it was nonetheless an acquired taste, originating in ancient Mediterranean civilizations. The early Egyptians held it in high esteem. According to Herodotus, they used it as a stimulant for the slaves who built the Great Pyramids. Its insinuations were noted at the famous feasts of Plato. Mention is made of it in the Old Testament. The Greeks used quantities of it (and still do). The Gauls spiked many a dish with garlic — a custom that survived even the Dark Ages. In modern times the use of garlic has greatly increased, particularly in Provence where "the poor man's truffle" plays a major role.

Brought to maturity, uprooted, dried in the sun on the spot, its dry stalks woven into braids, it is suspended in long tresses in the storeroom of the house. Though at least *some* olive oil goes into almost every Provençal dish, the same can't be said for garlic. Its use is certainly frequent, but never without discrimination. Except for certain dishes to which it gives the master touch, and others where its point should definitely be more discreet, garlic should never dominate or extinguish the other flavors but, on the contrary, merely reinforce and intensify them. Provençal cuisine properly finds its perfection in harmony that no dissonance may shatter.

Provençal garlic, curiously enough, seems to be not at all the brutal and bad-mannered condiment that, in northern countries, fortifies the postprandial breath of happy diners. It never produces an unpleasant, acrid flavor but is pure and delicate, like a verse by Mistral. It may be eaten without anxiety and digested without distress. Better still, it fills one's dreams with oleanders and silver olive trees.

How sad, then, that in the twentieth century, at least until the thirties, the word "garlic" was seldom found on an American woman's marketing list. Because of immigrant labor that had floated in on a pungent wave of (mostly) Neapolitan cookery, the magic clove became associated chiefly with the lower classes. Garlic, so the upper and middle classes decided, was not "refined," and anybody who was anybody was determined to be refined. Thus a great potential in American gastronomy was neglected.

The prejudice still exists of course, although, as with the olive oil, it is sustained for the most part by (1) gastronomic illiterates; (2) people of self-limited interests; (3) the bores who, without a shred of shame, boast that they "eat to live," and (4) the greater bores who, with the pleased air of one who has just hatched a fresh epigram, parrot, "I love garlic but garlic doesn't love me." Among true gastronomes today, to admit to a prejudice against garlic is something of an impropriety. For it is not by coincidence that the kitchens where food has been brought to its highest levels of subtlety and imaginative perfection are the French, Chinese, and Indian (usually ranked in that order) — kitchens where garlic is an honored staple, a daily familiar.

While it is not quite true that "there is no such thing as a *little* garlic," if the precious bud is boiled in liquid its powers are considerably diminished. A hostess with alliophobic guests can perform a good deed by confessing (after dinner—or, better, next day) that there was an undetected clove or two in the dish they liked so much.

The Aromatics

The term *aromates* has no English equivalent. It includes both herbs (dried or fresh) and spices, as well as the *zeste* (outer, colored, flavored skin) of citrus fruits. The distinction between herbs and spices is impossible to define. Dictionaries, both French and English, contradict each other and themselves. However, to most English-speaking people, a spice is a pungent, dried bark (example: cinnamon stick), a bud (cloves), root (turmeric), or seed (mustard, nutmeg, pepper, etc.), sometimes used whole, oftener ground. Herbs are fragrant leaves or stems, fresh or dried, of plants such as basil, bay, dill, fennel, savory, thyme, and the mints. The *herbes potagères* of France are potherbs to us, or "soup greens," in spite of the inclusion of yellow turnips and carrots. Actually, we don't think of these two as "herbs" at all.

"La Gueuse Parfumée" invokes rapturous alliances with the aromatic plants in which the south of France abounds. By the addition of these, her soups, sauces, wine stews, and roasts acquire style and finish. The volatile essences of such seasonings (basil, bay, capers, cloves, ginger, juniper, marjoram, rosemary, saffron, sage, savory, thyme, etc.), when released, blend with the nutritive properties of whatever is being prepared, increasing its merit and developing the ultimate degree of taste. With such abundant provender, how could Provençal fare be anything but varied and superior?

The art of using these essences is part intuition, part careful experimentation in choosing, apportioning, and blending them, with a thorough understanding of their intrinsic values — here a leaf, there a pinch, a sprig, a shred of *zeste* — to modify something that is too strong or perhaps chasten something that is too fibrous. In all Provence, there can be scarcely a kitchen without its gamut of fragrant herbs and spices, most of them home-packed. The diversity of blends is, of course, infinite. But although in practice each dish is usually individually seasoned, a typical all-purpose blend suitable for roasts might be approximately:

1 tablespoon coriander	3 tablespoons each of basil, nutmeg, rosemary, thyme
1 teaspoon lavender	
4 tablespoons powdered bay leaf	2 tablespoons each of clove, savory, white pepper

Small, inexpensive electric mills are now available in housewares departments of American stores. With these, spices may be pulverized in a flash, and the mills are also useful for grinding other dry ingredients such as bread, nuts, cheese, cereals, coffee beans (although a separate mill for coffee beans is recommended).

"If we spoke in musical terms," says my colleague, "we would say that herbs are the gastronomic half-tones, while the spice mixtures are the deep harmonies bordering on dissonance." But this is more description than guide to identification. Uncategorically speaking, the best course for the beginner seems to be just use and learn. Risking a few disasters is certainly more fun than settling for monotony and mediocrity.

III

Basic Recipes
and Procedures

FRENCH AUTHORS writing cookbooks for French readers take for granted a considerable familiarity with culinary practice. But even in France this is no longer entirely safe. And in the United States where people are, even today, somewhat in awe of French food, every prop for courage is needed. Although anyone who ever saw a wooden spoon probably knows how to make a cream sauce, there's always a first time for somebody, and even experienced cooks have absent-minded moments. Therefore, alphabetized for ready reference, we give here some of the basic directions essential to the success of your Provençal (and other) cooking.

Anchovies To freshen anchovies that have been packed in brine, rinse under the cold water tap to free them of salt. Then steep in warm (not hot) water for 15 minutes. Drain well.

Anchovies packed in oil are milder to start with, but are usually better for being rinsed and then re-covered with fresh *olive* oil.

Artichokes However they are to be used, artichokes must first be properly trimmed. The stems are broken off, and a slice taken from the bottom so they won't topple when set in the saucepan or, later, on the platter. Next, the tops are trimmed straight across like a privet hedge, and then the tips of the leaves cut off, one by one, all around, top to bottom. They are then cooked in plenty of boiling salted water for anywhere from 10 to 45 minutes, depending upon size and how they are to be used. Example: artichokes that are to be braised, or stuffed and baked, are usually simply blanched for 10 to 12 minutes. A large artichoke which is just to be boiled and then eaten with mayonnaise or other sauce may require 45 minutes' cooking or longer.

The chokes are removed *after* the artichokes are boiled. You reach right into the center leaves and pull out the chokes (whole, if possible).

Batter for Frying

1½ cups flour	1 whole egg, beaten with
½ teaspoon salt	2 egg yolks
4 tablespoons olive oil	Water

2 egg whites, beaten stiff

Sift flour and salt together. Combine beaten whole egg and yolks with the olive oil. Blend flour and egg-oil mixture well. Add enough cold water to make a soft paste. Fold in the beaten whites.

Béarnaise Sauce An acceptable "instant béarnaise" can be made by adding to a freshly made hollandaise (page 16) 1 tablespoon chopped fresh chervil or tarragon (or both), and ½ tablespoon minced shallots or scallions, plus a few drops of vermouth or Angostura bitters.

Béchamel Sauce This is what Americans call Cream Sauce or White Sauce and it becomes *Velouté* when veal or chicken stock is used for the liquid. The standard proportions are:

1 tablespoon melted butter blended with
1 tablespoon flour (This is called a *roux*)
1 cup milk or other liquid

For a thicker sauce use:

2 tablespoons butter   2 tablespoons flour
1 cup liquid

For very heavy sauce, such as is used in making soufflés:

3 tablespoons butter   3 tablespoons flour
1 cup liquid

The butter should be melted over medium heat, the flour stirred in with a wooden spoon, and this *roux* cooked for a few minutes. Many cooks insist that the milk, when added, be hot, but we think this step unnecessary. Cold milk, if stirred in, a little at a time, over low heat, makes just as smooth a sauce. Add a pinch of saffron to the *roux* to make Saffron Sauce.

Blanching

Blanching is a misleading term because, although some foods are blanched to firm and whiten (sweetbreads, for example), green, leafy vegetables are dropped into large quantities of rapidly boiling water to brighten color as well as to cook (at least to some degree of doneness). Other foods are "blanched" by being simmered for 5 or 10 minutes in a small quantity of water, a method by which salt pork can be coaxed to resemble the *petit salé* of France, which is the meat of chine of pork marinated briefly (about 12 hours) in a light brine.

Bouquet Garni

Bouquet garni may be almost any mixed green or dried herbs tied together, or dried herbs in a small cheesecloth bag. In Provence it consists of 1 bay leaf, 1 sprig of thyme, 2 or 3 sprays of parsley, and a small strip of orange peel. The bouquet is removed before the dish is served.

Brains and Sweetbreads

Recipes for brains and sweetbreads are more or less interchangeable, although sweetbreads are firmer than calves' brains and, of the brains, lamb and pork are firmer than those of the calf. All must be chilled, then blanched in a court bouillon, and chilled again. The membranes should be peeled off. For easier handling, the brains or sweetbreads should then be refrigerated for several hours, covered with a plate or platter topped by a weight. This simplifies subsequent handling.

Both brains and sweetbreads should be pretreated as soon as possible after purchase and used as soon as possible after that, for they do not keep well.

Butters **Anchovy butter** is made by blending unsalted butter with mashed, boned anchovies "to taste."

Brown butter is any butter heated until the froth just begins to color. It provides a delicious, professional touch to many dishes, especially cooked vegetables.

Snail butter was originally invented for use in cooking snails, but is now adapted to a number of uses. It is made by creaming ½ cup butter with 2 teaspoons minced mild onion, 2 peeled, mashed cloves of garlic, 2 tablespoons minced parsley, salt and pepper.

Court Bouillon is water boiled (covered) with herbs and other seasonings for 10 minutes, and then strained. The seasonings vary according to the use to which the court bouillon is to be put. Suggested combinations are:

For vegetables:

4 cups water	1 teaspoon thyme
½ cup olive oil	1 tablespoon chopped
Juice of 2 lemons	onion
Bouquet garni	Bay leaf
1 teaspoon dried or fresh	Piece of celery
fennel	½ tablespoon salt

plus the hard-to-find-but-delicious bit of parsley root.

For meat:

4 cups water	4 peeled, sliced or
Bouquet garni	quartered onions
8 peppercorns	4 cloves
2 scraped, diced carrots	½ tablespoon salt

Basil, chives, sage, savory, sorrel, tarragon, garlic, and allspice or other flavorings may be included at the discretion of the cook.

For fish:

1 quart water	1 small carrot, chopped
2 teaspoons salt	3 sprigs parsley
2 tablespoons lemon juice or vinegar	2 sprigs thyme
	1 bay leaf
1 tablespoon minced onion	1 teaspoon peppercorns

Bring all to a boil, then simmer for 15 minutes before putting the fish into it to cook.

For salmon, the court bouillon most often used is salted water in the proportions given above but seasoned only with thyme and a bay leaf.

Crème Chantilly

Crème Chantilly is whipped cream flavored with vanilla. This is also sometimes blended into softened cream cheese and used as a simple dessert — shaped into a cone, ringed with fresh fruits in season, and given a generous spill of sour cream.

Crème Patissière

4 egg yolks beaten with ¼ teaspoon salt	2 tablespoons flour
½ cup granulated sugar scant	1 cup light cream, heated
	1 teaspoon butter
	1 teaspoon vanilla

Beat the egg yolks with the salt until thick and smooth. Transfer to a saucepan with a thick bottom. Place over moderate heat. Sift in the flour, beating steadily (preferably with a wire whisk). Pour in the hot cream slowly, continuing to beat, and with special attention to the portion at the bottom of the saucepan. Do not allow it to adhere. When the mixture comes to a boil, reduce heat. Beat 1 minute longer, then add the butter and, last, the vanilla. To keep *Crème Patissière,* cover very tightly with plastic wrap and refrigerate. (Makes about one cup.)

Crumbs

For making bread crumbs we highly recommend the little electric mill (sometimes called a "Moulinex") sold in housewares departments for $9 or $10. These useful little machines grind nuts, spices, rice, coffee beans, and dozens of other (dry only) ingredients swiftly to the exact degree of pulverization needed.

Cracker crumbs, however, are best made by hand, because they clog an electric grinder. A simple method is to put them into a plastic sandwich bag and roll them with a rolling pin (or even a bottle). They can be kept for some time in a glass or plastic container. Rolled crackers of the Ritz or Waverly type are a convenience to have on hand.

Eggs For most recipes, eggs should be brought to room temperature before being cooked. Yolks are more yellow if beaten with salt.

Oeufs mollets (peeled soft-boiled eggs) may be substituted, in most recipes, for poached eggs, are easier to manage and, usually, more attractive. (See page 76.)

Fines Herbes is a term that, according to *Larousse Gastronomique,* usually means just chopped parsley, but there's no law that says the cook can't mix in any other herbs that suit his or her taste — chives, dill, marjoram, savory, tarragon, etc.

"French Dressing"

Pinch of salt
¼ teaspoon dry mustard
1 tablespoon vinegar or lemon juice

4 tablespoons good olive oil
½ teaspoon freshly milled peppercorns

Note: Don't make this dressing more than a few hours in advance of serving time. It should be chilled but should not be kept more than a few hours or it will develop the stale taste of bottled dressings.

Fumet is boiled-down stock (fish, chicken, etc.) and is usually made from the leftover parts of whatever is being cooked. For example, the skin, bones, head, etc., of a fish, cooked in water to cover and seasoned with salt, pepper, a bay leaf, and a pinch or two of any herbs that appeal to the cook. Sometimes onion, garlic, or a shallot is added. The stock is strained and simmered to reduce by half, producing a strongly flavored broth to be used in sauces.

Hollandaise Sauces **Standard hollandaise** (makes 1½ cups, scant)

4 egg yolks, beaten thick
½ teaspoon salt
¼ pound butter, diced

1 tablespoon cold water
2 teaspoons lemon juice
¼ teaspoon white pepper

Dash of cayenne pepper

Stir the salt into the beaten egg yolks in the top of a small double boiler over hot (but NEVER BOILING) water. Add the butter, a little at a time, stirring constantly. When all the butter has been absorbed by the yolks, turn off the heat. Combine water, lemon juice, white pepper, and cayenne and stir into the egg-butter mixture, a few drops at a time. Cook 2 minutes longer over very low heat.

If the hollandaise is to be held for some time before being served, add 1 teaspoon cornstarch to beaten yolks before adding the butter.

Blender hollandaise* (makes ¾ cup)

¼ pound butter	1 tablespoon lemon juice
3 egg yolks	¼ teaspoon salt
	Pinch of cayenne pepper

Heat the butter until it bubbles in a small saucepan. It must not brown.

Put the remaining ingredients into the container of the blender. Cover the container and turn motor to low speed. Immediately remove cover and pour in the hot butter in a steady stream. When all butter has been added, turn off motor.

Liver

Liver of any kind *must* be skinned either when it is bought or by the cook, and all the little tendons and arteries cut out (easiest to do with a pair of curved manicure scissors kept for that purpose). Liver should be cooked quickly by being put into hot butter at the moment when the froth of the butter has *just* started to color.

Mayonnaise

Mayonnaise is so easy to make, the wonder is that anyone buys the commercial substitute. An electric blender simplifies the production, of course. We give directions below for both methods. In either case, all ingredients should be cold.

Handmade mayonnaise

2 egg yolks	2 teaspoons lemon juice
¼ teaspoon salt	or vinegar
Pinch of cayenne	⅔ cup salad oil
½ teaspoon dry mustard	⅓ cup olive oil

Mix the egg yolks with the salt, cayenne, mustard, and vinegar. Beat thoroughly, then add the oil, 1 teaspoon at a time, stirring continu-

* From *The Blender Cookbook,* by Ann Seranne and Eileen Gaden (New York, Doubleday).

ously. When all the oil has been added, stir in a few more drops of lemon juice, to taste.

Blender mayonnaise

1 whole egg	2 teaspoons vinegar
¼ teaspoon salt	⅔ cup salad oil, mixed with
½ teaspoon dry mustard	⅓ cup olive oil

Put the egg, mustard, salt and vinegar into the blender container. Add ¼ cup of the oil. Cover and turn the motor to low speed. Immediately uncover and add the rest of the oil in a *thin,* steady stream.

Meat Extract   Real *glace de viande* is very hard to come by and impractical to make in a private kitchen. Fortunately, a good substitute is available in health food shops and in the diet food departments of big department stores such as Macy's in New York. Called Marmite, it comes salted and unsalted. A little goes a long way toward improving the flavor of certain gravies and sauces and casseroles.

Onions   When chopped or minced for use in flavoring a cooked dish, onions should always be sautéed in fat for a few minutes before being added to the other ingredients. *Exception:* if the onions are for a dish that should be kept white, mince them and then rinse them in cold water and press out the moisture by squeezing them in a cloth.

Orange Rind   is easy to peel with a vegetable parer. If it is to be grated, we recommend a little device sold for the purpose by the Hoffritz cutlery stores. The small tool is useful, also, for scoring cucumbers, melons, zucchini, etc., for decorative purposes.

Parsley   **Deep-fried parsley,** a popular European garnish for fried foods is, actually, just as appetizing with broiled or baked meat, poultry and fish, and is swiftly made. The stems should be left long. The parsley is rinsed and thoroughly dried in a cloth. A small, deep, heavy saucepan is half-filled with olive oil. When the oil is very hot (but not smoking) the parsley, held by the stems (and stand back!) is plunged, head first, into the hot oil and withdrawn almost immediately. It emerges, still green, and shattery crisp. Delicious!

Parsley tops should never be chopped when wet. They should first be squeezed dry in a clean cloth. If they are fresh, they are tougher than you think and spring right back.

Pâte brisée is "short" pie crust, that is to say, pastry that has a crumbly *Pastry* flake (in contrast to puff paste). The proportions for an 8-inch pie:

2 cups sifted flour	4 tablespoons chilled butter
1 teaspoon salt	3 tablespoons chilled lard
5 tablespoons ice water (about)	

A good technique is to chill the water in a glass salt shaker or a small flour dredge that has fairly large perforations in the top. This reduces the chances of dropping too much water in one part of the flour.

With a pastry blender or two knives, cut the chilled fats into the mixed flour and salt, working fast, until there are no lumps larger than a pea. Then shake the water, 1 teaspoon at a time, over the surface of the flour mixture, tossing aside the dampened parts of the flour with a fork as these take shape, and constantly flipping the dry parts to the top of the pile. Use only enough water to make the particles adhere when pressed together with the fingers. Form the dough into a ball, wrap in wax paper and chill 2 hours (or place in freezer for 45 minutes). Roll out the dough, using a lightly floured rolling pin and a lightly floured board, rolling outward from the center, turning the dough frequently to distribute it evenly.

Continental pie crust à la G. Mercier Doyle Koch. This recipe, contributed by a consistently successful American hostess, will, if followed carefully, result in perfect continental-type pastry of the kind that is flaky without being brittle or strudel-like. The ingredients in the proportions given below are enough for either three 8-inch, double-crust pies or two, depending upon how thin the dough is when rolled out.

3 cups flour, sifted twice	¾ cup butter
¼ teaspoon baking powder	¾ cup vegetable shortening
Pinch of salt	1 egg yolk
About ½ cup ice water	

Add the baking powder and salt to the twice-sifted flour and sift again. Using two silver or stainless steel knives, cut the butter and shortening into the flour, until no piece of floury fat is bigger than a pea. Stir in the egg yolk. Then add the ice water, a little at a time, until the dough leaves the sides of the bowl. Form dough lightly into a ball, wrap in wax paper, and chill overnight.

For three pies, divide dough into thirds. For one 2-crust pie, roll one of these pieces out very thin on a floured surface. *Now,* the important step: fold the dough first from one side and then the other, making three layers. Then fold down from the top and up from the bottom the same way, making five layers in all. Roll out this five-layer piece of dough and then repeat the whole folding and rolling process twice more (making three times in all).

To complete the pie, divide the dough, allowing slightly more for the top than for the bottom crust. Spread the bottom crust carefully in a pie plate. Put in the filling. Cover with the upper crust as usual, pinching the two crusts together around the rim. At this point in the procedure the imaginative cook likes to add little decorations made from strips of leftover dough. These, dampened slightly on their under sides, may be distributed here and there at whim over the top crust. Slash the top in a few places to allow steam to escape during the baking period. Brush a small amount of water over the top crust. Bake 15 minutes at 450°, then lower heat to 350° and bake 30 minutes longer.

Rouille   Half a teaspoonful of this fiery sauce will boldly heighten the flavor of fish dishes and soups.

Crush 1 red pepper, the very, very hot kind, fresh or dried,* and 2 peeled cloves of garlic in a mortar. When well-pounded, add 1 tablespoon of bread crumbs which have been soaked in water and pressed out. Then, slowly, stir in 4 tablespoons (generous) of olive oil. (See also page 69.)

* Not to be confused with the sweet bell pepper, this is the cayenne pepper known also, in France, by the charmingly apt name, *piment enragé* "enraged pepper."

Roux   *Roux* is flour and fat blended together into a paste, and cooked over medium heat for a moment to eliminate the raw taste of the flour, before being used as a thickening agent (in, for example, a béchamel sauce).

Salt Cod (Morue)   To freshen the kind of salt cod sold in a flat, dry, hard-as-linoleum piece, it must be soaked in cold water for at least 48 hours during which period the water should be changed three times. Then the fish must be boned.

Salt cod fillets, sold in ½-pound boxes, usually need only 2 or 3 hours of soaking, first in cold and then in lukewarm water.

Salt pork can take the place of the ubiquitous *petit salé* of French cookery (and has been so used in the recipes of this edition of *La Véritable*) if it is sliced and then blanched in boiling water for 10 minutes. ***Salt Pork***

To open clams, oysters, mussels, winkles, etc., heat with ½ cup water, covered, until the shells separate. This usually takes only a few minutes. Strain the broth through a fine-mesh sieve or two thicknesses of cheese-cloth. Save the broth! ***Shellfish***

Two tricks: (1) after beating the whites dry and stiff, stir thoroughly about ⅓ of them into the cheese-cream sauce base, then fold in the rest of the whites. (2) Don't be in too much of a hurry to take the soufflé from the oven. It needs to bake at least 45 minutes to "set" its crown. ***Soufflés***

Whether fresh, canned, purée, or paste, tomatoes should always be cooked in some kind of fat — butter, oil, bacon grease, drippings — for 5 to 10 minutes before being added to any sauce or cooked dish. The fat and the heat are necessary for modifying the sharpness of the tomato flavor. ***Tomatoes***

IV
Sauces

Aïoli gently intoxicates, charges the body with warmth, bathes the soul in rapture. In its essence, it concentrates the force and the joy of the sun of Provence. Around an *aïoli,* well-perfumed and bright as a vein of gold, where are there men who would not recognize themselves as brothers?

— Frédéric Mistral

Aïolis

LIKE BOUILLABAISSE, this dish symbolizes Provence and usually replaces a whole menu. For when one makes an *aïoli,* one eats nothing else, *needs* nothing else.

Coming upon its strange label, the uninitiated ask themselves what

this mysterious *aïoli* can be that everybody talks about but which, in its true form, is so little known outside of Provence? Quite simply, *aïoli* is a kind of garlic mayonnaise, surrounded by a whole gamut of ingredients cooked in water. We give below a rough idea of what these may be.

In Provence, an *aïoli* is eaten primarily on Fridays, and on certain special occasions — Ash Wednesday, for example. And at such times as the last day of local festivals, particularly in the Var and the Alpes-Maritimes, an immense table is set up in the public square, and the entire village assembles around a prodigious *aïoli*.

In preparing an *aïoli* it is most important to have the oil at the temperature of the room where the sauce is being made. If necessary, set it out ahead of time and let it unchill. Olive oil that is too cold will lead, relentlessly, to the ruin of an *aïoli*.

The number of cloves of garlic may be increased or decreased, depending on whether a strong or mild flavor is favored. For timid palates, a mayonnaise merely tinged with garlic might well be made, but this would only be a substitute. Here is the recipe for the authentic dish.

It should be noted here for the sake of Anglo-Saxon readers with their squeamish unease about garlic, that the magic bulb, as grown in Provence, is much less assertive than its American cousin. The quantities called for in these recipes may be safely cut to one-half, even one-third. However, it should be remembered that if garlic is to be cooked (as in some recipes that follow in other chapters), it will lose much of its vigor — so allowance should be made for this loss.

Aïoli

For 6 to 8 persons, pound fine 8 cloves of garlic in a mortar, add the yolks of 4 eggs, lightly beaten, with a pinch of salt; then, little by little, drop by drop, without ceasing to stir, and turning the pestle in the same direction and with the same rhythm, incorporate 2¼ cups good olive oil until you produce a thick mayonnaise. If the *aïoli* becomes too thick, add, before finishing, 2 teaspoons or more of tepid water. At the end, add a squeeze of lemon juice.

An "accident" can happen if the oil is too cool in contrast to the room temperature, or if it is poured in too fast. The oil will then rise to the surface and the *aïoli* will be spoiled. To reverse this disaster, pour the sauce into another bowl and clean the mortar and the pestle. Crush a garlic clove in the clean mortar with a little salt, add a few drops of water and the yolk of an egg, and start the operation over again by adding, in small spoonfuls, the first *aïoli* (the failure). Thus the sauce will be retrieved and your honor saved!

Boil separately: potatoes in their jackets, carrots, string beans, several beets, a cauliflower, one artichoke per person plus a few Jerusalem artichokes **[not to be confused with the ordinary, thistle type of artichoke]**, a hard-boiled egg per person, some desalted dry codfish, some snails or cockles, a blanched octopus, some winkles (*bigorneau,* or *"biou"* in Provence), and, traditionally, a fish cooked in court bouillon (see page 14), for example, *baudroie.** Needless to say, one may omit one or another of the items in the above list.

Serve the *aïoli* separately in the mortar itself or in a small salad bowl, and arrange the hot vegetables and fish attractively in bouquets on one or two large platters.

Some people profess that *aïoli* digests more easily if nothing but water is drunk with it. But are there many, above all in Provence, who respond enthusiastically to the thought of water-drinking at table?

As for the unfortunate who finds an *aïoli* too robust for his faulty digestive system, let him, like the ancient French, take the *"coù dôu mitan,"* or *"trou"* **[from *boucher un trou:* stop a gap or pay a debt]**, by way of a little glass of brandy in mid-feast. This, according to Dr. Raoulx, author of a valuable book on Provençal gastronomy, generates "the beneficial eructations that politeness obliges us to suppress in France and which, on the contrary, in Africa and Spain, proclaim by their sonority the magnificence of the repast."

---

* A Mediterranean fish, also called, because of its weight and ferocity, "sea devil." It is a rockfish, L. *lophius piscatorius* which resembles the American angler. Any white fish, such as a flounder or fillets of whiting, may be substituted.

Le Grand Aïoli

Besides the *aïoli* proper with the classic accompaniments such as are enumerated above, there once was served in Provence, on certain special occasions, something called *Le Grand Aïoli*. We say "was" because, alas, this dish is pretty much a thing of the past.

Codfish (salt) was an important part of it, of course, surrounded by boiled potatoes, then little blanched octopuses, haloed with rings of hard-boiled eggs. On another plate, there were beef and mutton from a *pot-au-feu à la provençale*. Then, boiled separately, green beans, artichokes, chick-peas. The dish was completed with snails or cockles cooked with a generous bouquet of thyme, bay leaf, sage, and wild thyme. All this was happily disposed on the plates around the mortar or bowl where gleamed the golden pomade, the whole ensemble being a harmonious and perfumed farandole.

Aïoli without Eggs (Aïoli sans Oeufs)

In certain Provençal families, *aïoli* is prepared without eggs. It is somewhat more difficult to achieve, but the pungency of the garlic is better developed.

Peel 4 cloves of garlic. Season with salt and pepper, and pound them in a mortar until they become a purée. Then incorporate 1 cup of oil, drop by drop, stirring without cease until a thick mayonnaise results.

You may, before blending in the oil, mix with the garlic several slices of well-chilled, mealy, boiled potatoes.

Anchovy Sauces

Anchovy Butter Sauce
(Sauce au Beurre d'Anchois)

Prepare anchovy butter as follows: crush ¼ pound freshened anchovy fillets [If tinned anchovies are used, buy the kind that are packed in olive oil and adjust the proportion of oil accordingly], and then pound them in a mortar with 1 cup olive oil or butter. Press mixture through a sieve. Slightly color 1 tablespoon butter over quick heat. Shake into this 1 tablespoon flour. Let this mixture take color, stirring over low heat, without letting it boil. Incorporate the anchovy butter a little at a time. Finally, sprinkle with a few minced leaves of tarragon or a minced basil leaf. This sauce is served with broiled meat.

La Bagna Caudo

5 tablespoons butter
5 tablespoons olive oil
3 cloves garlic
6 young artichokes, or
  12 artichoke hearts
A pinch of salt (careful!)
4 desalted anchovies
Celery stalks

This is a sauce, undoubtedly of Italian origin, which has become greatly honored in Provence.

Put the butter into a saucepan with the oil, garlic, and desalted anchovies (page 12), freed from their bones, and cut in strips, and a slight pinch of salt. [These are not, of course, tinned anchovies, but the kind sold in bulk from a barrel of brine in Italian and Greek shops.] Cook these ingredients over low heat without coloring the garlic which should remain very white. As soon as the anchovies are completely dissolved, the sauce is ready. Serve it hot, with raw celery stalks, or cooked, tender artichokes.

Hot Anchovy Sauce (Sauce Chaude aux Anchois)

Heat court bouillon slightly and then blend in the egg yolks. Add the oil and butter. Stir in anchovies. Mix well. Add a dash of pepper and a dash of lemon juice.

4 pounded anchovies
2 egg yolks
2 tablespoons oil
1½ cups fish court bouillon (page 15)
"Walnut" of butter
Pepper
Lemon juice

Oil of Anchovy Sauce (Sauce Huile d'Anchois)

Pound fine, in a mortar, a dozen freshened anchovy fillets with olive oil, and put through a sieve. (If a milder sauce is preferred, beat in more oil "to taste.")

Le "Saussoun"

This is an ancient recipe from the region of Roquebrune in the Var. Its composition may seem unusual, but this sauce, spread on slices of bread, produces in summer a delightful sensation of freshness.

Pound the almonds (shelled, blanched, and carefully picked over) in a mortar with freshened anchovies, a sprig of fennel, and the mint leaves. When all is well-crushed, mix it with an equal quantity of oil and water (half-and-half), to make a sauce. Salt it to taste and spread it on slices of bread. (Recipe from the collection of M. l'abbé Deschamps of Roquebrune-sur-Argens.)

1 cup almonds
2 freshened (page 12) anchovies
Water and oil — half-and-half
Sprig of fennel
4 mint leaves

Herb Sauces

Fennel Sauce (Sauce au Fenouil)

Clean, blanch (page 13), and drain the fennel; chop it fine. Heat 1 tablespoon tomato purée with the oil and half the fennel. Season with salt and pepper. Mix well and sprinkle the flour over it. When all this starts to color, add the other tablespoon of tomato purée and the rest of the fennel. Add the pinch of nutmeg. Blend well and let simmer, uncovered, over gentle heat for 10 minutes.

10 stalks fresh fennel
2 tablespoons tomato purée
Salt and pepper
2 tablespoons flour
2 tablespoons oil
Pinch of nutmeg

Herb Sauce I (*Sauce aux Aromates*)

1 cup bouillon
1 peeled, chopped medium-size onion
2 peeled, chopped shallots
1½ teaspoons marjoram
½ teaspoon dried sage
1 sprig thyme
4 peppercorns
1 tablespoon butter
1 tablespoon flour
1 tablespoon lemon juice
1 tablespoon chopped chervil and
    tarragon (or parsley), mixed
Salt and pepper

Pound the onion, shallots, marjoram, sage, thyme, and peppercorns fine in a mortar (or use a food mill). Add this mixture to the bouillon and simmer for a few minutes, skimming off any froth that rises to the surface. Strain and reserve the bouillon. Melt butter, add flour, and stir until smooth. Dilute with the bouillon infusion and stir over low heat until mixture thickens. Remove saucepan from the heat and add the lemon juice and the chopped chervil and either chopped tarragon or parsley. Salt and pepper to taste.

Herb Sauce II (*Sauce Verte des Martigues*)

2 mixed fresh herbs such as parsley,
    tarragon, or chervil
3 or 4 leaves of spinach
2 tablespoons capers
2 small gherkins, chopped
Salt and pepper
2 freshened anchovy fillets
3 hard-boiled egg yolks
"Walnut" of butter
¼ cup olive oil
A few drops of vinegar

Boil the mixed herbs and spinach leaves in water to cover for 1 minute. Drain well, and pound fine in a mortar with the capers, gherkins, and anchovy fillets. Add the egg yolks and butter. When all is smooth, add the olive oil, a little at a time, and a dash of vinegar. The quantity of oil may be varied according to how thin a sauce is needed. Season with salt and pepper to taste.

Herb Sauce III (*Sauce aux Fines Herbes*)

3 or 4 sprigs each of fresh tarragon,
    parsley, savory, thyme, dill
½ cup dry white wine
3 tablespoons butter (or more)
1 tablespoon chopped shallots
1 tablespoon flour
1 cup bouillon
Juice of ½ lemon
Salt and (optional) pepper

Remove and chop stems of the (washed) herbs. Set aside the leaves. Heat the wine and bouillon to the boiling point. Drop in the herb stems. Turn off heat and leave, covered, to marinate.

Meanwhile, simmer the chopped shallots in 2 tablespoons of the butter until soft, but not brown. Strain the herb-stem marinade into this saucepan. Discard the stems. Simmer the mixture until the liquid is reduced by half. Rub the flour into the remaining butter and stir it into the sauce and cook, over low heat, for about 10 minutes, stirring frequently to keep the sauce from adhering to the bottom of the saucepan. Beat in the lemon juice. Salt to taste (and pepper if desired). Finish by dropping a teaspoonful of butter on the surface of the sauce, if it is to stand for some time before being used.

Hollandaise Sauces

Standard Hollandaise Sauce (*page 16*)

Béarnaise Sauce (*page 12*)

Mayonnaise Sauces

Aïoli (*page 24*)

Basic Mayonnaise (*page 17*)

Rémoulade Sauce

This is a sauce quickly made by adding to 1 cup homemade mayonnaise, a few small pickles, chopped, a tablespoonful of capers, and a small quantity of anchovy paste, the amount of the latter apportioned according to taste — ½ to 1 teaspoon.

Oil and Vinegar Sauces

Basic French Dressing (*page 16*)

Oil and Vinegar Sauce (*especially for fish*)

Peel the lemon, removing all of the white part. Slice it very thin, and pour over it a dressing made as follows: Combine all ingredients. Chill in covered bowl. If to be used hot over hot fish, heat it briefly in a double boiler.

1 lemon
4 tablespoons olive oil
1 teaspoon vinegar
½ clove garlic, peeled and mashed
Salt and pepper
2 tablespoons parsley
Pinch of tarragon

Ravigote Sauce

Sieve the egg yolks. Stir in salt, pepper, mustard, and vinegar. Then add the olive oil, a little at a time, stirring briskly with a wooden spoon until a smooth, creamy sauce is produced. Stir in herbs and shallots. Chill the sauce before serving.

The yolks of 2 hard-boiled eggs
¼ teaspoon salt
¼ teaspoon ground peppercorns
½ teaspoon dry mustard
2 teaspoons vinegar
2 or 3 shallots, minced
6 tablespoons olive oil
1 tablespoon chopped chervil
1 tablespoon chopped parsley

Vinaigrette Sauce

This is ordinary oil-and-vinegar dressing dressed up. The base is 1 part vinegar (or lemon juice) to 4 parts oil, seasoned with a pinch of salt, ¼ teaspoon dry mustard (optional), and ground black peppercorns to taste. By the addition of 1 tablespoon of chopped mixed fresh herbs (parsley, chives, basil, or whatever herbs are at hand) it becomes *Sauce Vinaigrette*. Minced scallions (or shallots) or capers, or both, may be added.

Provençal Sauces

Cold Provençal Sauce (Sauce Provençale Froide)

2 cloves garlic
2 anchovy fillets
2 egg yolks
1 tablespoon cold water
Pinch of salt
¾ cup olive oil
Lemon juice

Pound the garlic very fine in a mortar with the anchovy fillets. Add the egg yolks, cold water and salt. Stir vigorously while incorporating the (generous) ¾ cup of olive oil. This sauce should be rather clear. Add a dash of lemon juice. Cold Provençal Sauce is used with grills, fish, or cold meat.

Hot Provençal Sauce I (Sauce Provençale Chaude)

3 tablespoons olive oil
1 tablespoon chopped onion
2 tomatoes, coarsely chopped (or
    ½ cup tomato purée)
1 tablespoon chopped parsley
2 cloves garlic, crushed
1 tablespoon flour, generous
¾ cup water
Salt and pepper
Bouquet garni (page 13)
"Walnut" of butter

Combine ingredients, except for butter, in a saucepan. Let boil for a moment over moderate heat, stirring until smooth. Then press through a sieve or use a food mill, and add the butter.

Hot Provençal Sauce II (Sauce Provençale Chaude)

Combine 2 egg yolks with 1 tablespoon of *Velouté* (see page 12), a shake of paprika, a small clove of garlic, pounded until liquid, and the juice of 2 lemons. Cook this in a double boiler until it thickens. Then remove it from the heat and add about 1 cup of olive oil, a little at a time, stirring constantly until sauce is of a velvety consistency.

Raïto

According to tradition, *Raïto* was originally Greek, imported by the Phocaeans to Massilia (Marseilles). It is a preparation also reminiscent of a traditional Sabbath Eve dish of the Jews and of the *"Adafina"* of the Portuguese Jews. It is, in any case, a sauce now seldom made except in Provence.

Brown the chopped onion with the flour in the oil. Blend in the wine and boiling water. Add the garlic, *bouquet garni,* tomato purée, and a little pepper. Let this cook until it is reduced by at least two-thirds. Put through a sieve and, before serving, add the capers and olives.

1 onion, chopped
2 tablespoons flour
2 tablespoons oil
2 cups red wine
2 cups boiling water
2 cloves garlic
Bouquet garni
1 generous tablespoon tomato purée
Pepper
1 tablespoon capers
¼ pound pitted olives

Rouille (*pages 20 and 69*)

Shellfish Sauces

Oil of Crab (or Lobster) Sauce
(*Sauce à l'Huile de Crabes ou de Langoustes*)

Pound the shells and claws of one or more lobsters or crabs which have been cooked in court bouillon (page 14). Pass these through a sieve and mix with enough olive oil to form a soft but not runny paste. This preparation may be used for stiffening a mayonnaise, rémoulade, ravigote, etc.

Oil of Crayfish (*also called Crawfish*)
(*Sauce à l'Huile d'Ecrevisses*)

Clean and cook the crabs in a court bouillon (page 14) to cover. Season with salt and pepper. When crayfish are cooked, remove the tails which can be used in another dish. Pulverize the rest and blend to a creamy consistency with oil. Heat the sauce slightly in a saucepan, stirring well.

½ pound small crabs
  per person
Court bouillon
Salt and pepper
Olive oil

Cream of Sea-Urchin Sauce
(*Sauce à la Crème d'Oursins*)

Remove the coral from one dozen cleaned sea urchins. Put through a sieve. Blend this purée with an equal quantity of Hollandaise Sauce (page 16) or Mayonnaise (page 17).

Tapenados

Tapenado may be served in the fashion of the Varois shepherds, spread on slices of brown bread. It also appears as an *hors d'oeuvre* at Le Prieuré restaurant at Villeneuve-les-Avignon.

Tapenado I

Crush ½ cup of stoned black olives with ¼ cup of freshened anchovies plus a good ¼ cup of capers (called *tapeno* in Provence). Season with 1 teaspoon (or more "to taste") lemon juice, 1 teaspoon dry mustard (optional), and a dash of pepper. Blend in just enough oil to make a sauce of rather firm consistency.

Tapenado II

This is the same as the preceding recipe with the addition of ½ teaspoon each of English (dry) mustard, thyme, and powdered bay leaf, and after the ingredients have been vigorously pounded, ¾ cup of cognac or local marc.

At Nyons, in the country of beautiful black olives, one adds 1 clove of garlic and ½ cup tuna fish.

Tomato Sauces

Tomato Sauce I (Sauce Tomate)

1 pound tomatoes
5 tablespoons oil
2 cloves garlic
Bouquet garni
Salt and pepper

Seed and quarter the well-ripened tomatoes (no need to peel them). Heat 3 tablespoons of oil in a small saucepan with 2 whole cloves of garlic. Toss in tomatoes along with a *bouquet garni,* salt and pepper. Simmer, covered. After about 12 minutes, uncover the saucepan and allow the sauce to reduce slightly. Then put it through a sieve or food mill. Turn this into a saucepan in which you have heated 2 tablespoons of oil. Simmer until reduced in quantity if you want a thick "*coulis.*"

Tomato Sauce II (Sauce Toulonnaise)

Lightly "yellow" minced onions in oil. Add wine, and peeled, seeded, chopped tomatoes. Season with salt and pepper plus garlic, parsley, a sprig of basil (in season), and a good pinch of saffron. Cook over low heat 25 to 30 minutes.

2 tablespoons minced onion
4 tablespoons olive oil
1 pound tomatoes
¾ cup dry white wine
Salt and pepper
2 cloves garlic, whole
¼ cup parsley, chopped
Sprig of fresh basil
Pinch of saffron

Truffle Sauces

Truffle Sauce (Sauce aux Truffes)

Clean and peel 12 large fresh truffles. Pound the peelings in a mortar with a little oil. Put through a sieve or food mill.

Slice the truffles and cook them in a saucepan in veal stock to cover, with 1 scraped carrot, the white part of a leek, 1 onion, 1 bay leaf, a sprig of thyme, and the pounded peelings. Moisten with ¾ cup of an old red wine. Let cook for a moment, and then serve the truffles on slices of toast, bathed in sauce. (Recipe from the collection of Armand Lunel.)

12 large truffles
1 carrot
1 leek
Veal stock
1 bay leaf
1 sprig of thyme
¾ cup red wine
6 slices of toast

Truffle Sauce à la Comtadine
(Sauce aux Truffes à la Comtadine)

Lightly fry slices of bread in oil, and set aside. Let onion "yellow" in 1 tablespoon of oil. Add to it the freshened anchovy. Moisten with the (reduced) red wine. Add bread crumbs, bouillon, and the cleaned sliced truffles, taking care not to allow the mixture to boil. To serve, cover the fried slices of bread with truffles and sauce. (Recipe of Madame Jouve de Carpentras.)

8 truffles*
1 tablespoon chopped onion
1 tablespoon olive oil
1 anchovy, freshened and mashed
1½ cup red wine, reduced to ¾ cup
¼ cup bread crumbs
Bouillon
2 slices of bread per person

* or 4 bottled truffles and the liquid they are packed in.

White Sauces

Béchamel Sauce (*page 12*)

Cream Sauce made with Oil (*Sauce Béchamel à l'Huile*)

Make a Béchamel Sauce (page 12) as usual but with olive oil instead of butter: the result will surprise you by its velvety smoothness.

Garlic Butter Sauce (*Sauce au Beurre à l'Ail*)

Pound 6 cloves of garlic in a mortar and put through a sieve. Mix this purée with 2 tablespoons butter. Blend until perfectly smooth.

At the moment of serving, add to the mixture ½ cup of Béchamel or *Velouté* (see page 12), or bouillon, stirring it with a wire whisk over quick heat without allowing it to boil. If a softer sauce is desired, add a bit of butter before removing from heat. Spoon sauce over cooked fish just before serving, or pass separately in a bowl.

Mornay Sauce

4 tablespoons butter
¼ onion, peeled and minced
4 tablespoons flour
½ teaspoon salt
1 cup hot, clear veal stock
1 cup hot milk
White pepper
Pinch of nutmeg
Pinch of cayenne
½ cup coarsely grated Swiss cheese
1 tablespoon finely grated Parmesan

Melt the butter and cook in it the minced onion. Don't allow the onion to brown. Stir in the flour to make a smooth paste. Combine the hot milk with the hot veal stock, and blend this into the *roux* (flour-onion-butter paste) a little at a time. Stir over low heat until a thick, smooth sauce is obtained. Then gradually beat in the mixed Parmesan and Swiss cheeses.

Saffron Sauce (see Béchamel Sauce)

Velouté Sauce (see Béchamel Sauce)

V
Soups

THE WORD "SOUP" was originally "sop" and meant a slice of bread served in or dipped into some kind of broth (example: *Aïgo-Boulido,* page 42), whereas "potage" was the contents of a pot of meat or fish boiled with vegetables. Today, however, soup is an omnibus word carrying on its ample back clear broths such as consommé, bouillons with or without their solid "makings," and thick soups such as the purées (thickened by the natural starch of vegetables), cream soups (made with béchamel), and *veloutés* enriched with cream and egg yolks.

Meat Soups

Pot-au-Feu Provençal

SERVES 6

1 pound plate beef
1 pound knuckle of veal
1 pound shoulder of mutton
1 calf's foot
3½ ounces lean bacon
1 marrow bone
Water to cover (about 1½ quarts)
1½ tablespoons salt (preferably sea salt*)
1 cup white wine
2 cloves garlic
1 onion, studded with cloves
2 medium white turnips, peeled
2 tomatoes
5 medium leeks, cleaned
12 small carrots, scraped
Bouquet garni
6 peppercorns
4 juniper berries
Toasted rounds of French or Italian bread
Olives and capers for garnish

Into an earthenware pot put the beef, veal knuckle, mutton, calf's foot, bacon, and marrow bone. Add water and sea salt. Start cooking over brisk heat, removing the scum as it rises to the surface. When the boiling starts, add the remaining ingredients except the toast and garnish. Lower heat and simmer for at least 3 hours, adding water, if necessary, to keep ingredients covered.

At serving time, skim off the fat. Remove the marrow bone, extract its marrow, and spread this on the toasted rounds of bread, which you then place in a soup tureen. Pour the bouillon over them through a fine mesh sieve.

Serve the meat surrounded by the vegetables and garnished with the olives and capers. Mandatory for this *bouilli provençal* is the accompaniment of warm Chick-pea Salad (page 190).

*Sea salt, both the fine grind and the coarse, is sold in most health food shops.

Quick Soup (Soupe Courte à l'Arlésienne)

SERVES 4

1 pound piece of boneless lamb or mutton (or 1 chop per person)
2 tablespoons olive oil
3½ ounces salt pork
2 tablespoons minced onion
1 whole clove garlic
1 quart water (or more)
Salt and pepper
½ cup rice
1 whole onion studded with cloves
1 carrot, sliced
Bouquet garni
Pinch of saffron

Slowly braise the meat, minced onion, and garlic in the oil. Moisten slightly, season to taste. Add the *bouquet garni*, cover and cook over low heat. When the meat is done, cover generously with hot water and bring to a boil. At this point add the rice and remaining ingredients. Let barely simmer, covered, for 30 minutes. Remove the mutton which you will serve with tomato sauce or some other Provençal sauce. Turn the soup, which should be very thick, into a hot serving dish.

Sausage Soup (Rate-Rate)

SERVES 2

This is an old Toulonnaise dish that is somewhat neglected nowadays, but that is very nice indeed. Made quickly, it has the double merit of providing both soup and meat courses at the same time.

Roast the little sausages in a 350° oven first pricking them to keep them from splitting. Brown the onion and tomato with them and, when everything is crackling in the fat rendered by the sausages, remove the sausages. Add to the pan juices the garlic, sage, salt, pepper, and enough water for your soup. Boil over high heat for several minutes. Then pour the bouillon over pieces of bread which have been strewed with grated cheese (in soup plates). Top with the sausages. (Recipe of Dr. Raoulx.)

10 little sausages
1 onion coarsely chopped
1 tomato, chopped (or
    ¼ cup tomato purée)
Water (about 9 cups)
1 clove garlic, peeled
Sprig of sage
Salt and pepper
1 slice of bread per person
Grated cheese

Seafood Soups

Conger Eel Soup (Soupe au Congre — also called "Soupe au Fielas")

SERVES 6

Fielas is the Provençal name for conger eel.

This dish is made the same way as Fish Soup (see page 40) except that conger eel is used instead of small fishes.

Cut the eel in small pieces which should be kept from disintegrating. Then proceed as for Fish Soup.

2½ pounds conger eel
6 or 8 small crabs (optional) from
    which the "feelers" have been
    removed
Seasonings (see Fish Soup)
1 slice of bread per person
Grated cheese

Crab Soup (Soupe aux Crabes)

SERVES 4

Clean the crabs thoroughly. In a large saucepan brown the onion, tomatoes (or tomato purée), and leeks in the oil. Add the crabs, turning them over in the mixture a few times. Add water to cover by one inch, the *bouquet garni,* garlic, saffron, salt and pepper. Cook over medium heat 15 to 20 minutes. Five minutes before the end of the cooking period, add the vermicelli.

2 dozen small* crabs (6 per person)
3 tablespoons olive oil
1 medium-size onion, minced
2 coarsely chopped tomatoes or
    ½ cup tomato purée
2 leeks, cleaned and minced
Water to cover
Bouquet garni
2 cloves garlic
Generous pinch of saffron
Salt and pepper
¼ cup vermicelli

* Not, of course, miniscule "oyster crabs."

Fish Soup (Soupe de Poisson)

2½ pounds fish
2 small crabs per person (optional but delicious)
¾ cup olive oil
1 leek (white part only) chopped
1 onion, chopped
2 cloves garlic, crushed
2 small tomatoes, chopped (or ½ cup tomato purée)
1 sprig each of fennel fern and savory
1 bay leaf
Salt and pepper
2 quarts water
1 large pinch saffron
2 cups spaghetti or large vermicelli*
Grated Gruyère cheese

Unlike the world-famous bouillabaisse, this fish soup is scarcely known at all outside Provence. It ranks high, however, in the hierarchy of Mediterranean dishes and many people consider it even superior to bouillabaisse. The delectable broth, full of suave and exciting fragrance is, in effect, a concentrate of all the enormous variety of little rockfishes whose gleaming colors enchant the eye. The bouquet of true fish soup is unique. We say "true" because there is also a counterfeit. That said, we give, herewith, the orthodox recipe for this incomparable soup.

One must buy very fresh fish for this soup, naturally. In the assortment available in fish markets one can (usually) find many species of rockfish: striped bass, groupers, eel. [This is our chance to make savory use of all those unfamiliar and low-priced fishes we customarily ignore. Many can be ordered in advance from merchants who don't stock them regularly or, in large coastal towns, from fishmongers in foreign sections.]

Pour the oil into a marmite or earthenware pot and brown in it the leek, the onion, garlic, tomatoes, fennel, savory, and bay leaf. Then add the fish and crabs. Let the whole mixture color, and then add the water. [To let something color means to cook it until it just *starts* to brown and not any longer.] Boil over medium high heat for about 15 minutes. Take out the crabs and the fish. Set crabs aside. Put the fish through a food mill, pressing well to extract all the essence. Discard bones, skin, and pressed-out meat of the fish. (Some Provençal families think it preferable to put the fish in a cloth and suspend it. The juice is allowed to flow into a bowl and the cloth is finally wrung out to extract all the flavorsome liquid.) What is produced is a luscious, smooth sauce which is then returned to the marmite with the crabs. Add more salt and pepper if needed — for this soup should be well seasoned — and the saffron. Bring to a boil, and toss in the spaghetti or vermicelli. When the pasta is cooked, serve the soup very hot with a bowl of grated Gruyère cheese on the table so that each person can help himself to it as he does to the (optional) crabs.

*Special pastas for this soup are sold in Provence but any of the smaller types found in supermarkets will do.

Mussel Soup (Soupe aux Moules) SERVES 4

Clean the mussels well (see Mussels, page 123), carefully removing the "beards." Heat the mussels, along with the *sliced* onion, garlic, and bay leaf in the two cups of water until they open. Then discard the shells, set mussels aside, and strain the liquor through a cloth. Reserve the strained liquor and the garlic.

In another saucepan, brown the *chopped* onion and the minced leek white in the oil. Add the tomato or tomato purée. Cook gently for a few minutes. Then pour in the reserved mussel liquor, adding water to make 4 cups of broth. Put back the cooked garlic (slightly mashed) and season with a pinch each of saffron and pepper. Bring the mixture to a boil. Toss in the rice or vermicelli. When these are cooked, return the mussel meats to the pot and heat them through before serving.

2 quarts mussels
2 cups water
1 small onion, sliced
3 cloves garlic, peeled
1 bay leaf
3 tablespoons olive oil
1 medium onion, chopped
White part of 1 leek, minced
1 tomato, chopped (or
   ¼ cup tomato purée)
Pepper and saffron (no salt)
⅓ cup rice or vermicelli

Sea Anemone Soup (Soupe d'Orties de Mer) SERVES 6

This succulent soup is one of the incomparable treasures of Provençal cuisine. It is all-too-often neglected or even forgotten completely. Let us give thanks to the good Tado, elderly fisherman of Porquerolles, who preserved this ancient recipe.

Wash the anemones carefully in several waters to rid them of every bit of sand. Cook the onions and garlic lightly in the oil. Add the anemones, saffron, and water and bring to a boil. Lower the heat and simmer for about 20 minutes. Put the soup through a food mill (or use a strainer) to obtain a rather thick bouillon. Return this to the soup pot, add the vermicelli, reheat, season to taste with salt and pepper, and cook about 10 minutes longer or until the pasta is soft but not mushy. Serve very hot with the grated cheese passed separately.

3 dozen sea anemones (Actinia*)
2 medium-size onions, chopped
4 whole cloves garlic
¼ cup olive oil
10 cups water
Salt and pepper
Pinch of saffron
3 tablespoons vermicelli
Grated Gruyère or Parmesan cheese

* Sea anemones are sold in fish markets in Italian sections of coastal towns in the United States.

Vegetable Soups

Basil Soup (Soupe au Pistou)

Basil soup, although it originated in Genoa, has for reasons obvious to anyone who reads this book, become thoroughly Provençal. And what a delicious thing it is! Unfortunately, it can be made only when fresh basil is available. The *pistou* (or *pesto,* in Italy) from which it gets its name can add authority and delight to any number of soups including spur-of-the-moment broth converted from refrigerator leftovers.

In proportions chosen at will, any or all of the vegetables in the following list are suitable for this soup: all types of fresh garden beans (fava, kidney, lima, string, wax, etc.), carrots, potatoes, tomatoes, zucchini. There should always be, however, at least one green vegetable plus potatoes and tomatoes.

The beans are shelled or the strings removed, the potatoes peeled and diced, the carrots scraped and cut in rounds, zucchini peeled and sliced, tomatoes skinned and chopped. All are put into a kettle with water to cover by 2 inches and seasoned with salt and pepper. The soup is then simmered for about 15 minutes, at which time 2 or 3 handfuls of large vermicelli are tossed in, the heat raised slightly, and the cooking continued for 10 to 15 minutes longer, until the pasta is cooked.

While the soup is cooking, prepare the "pommade" (the *pistou*).

Pound the basil leaves, garlic, and salt in a mortar until well crushed. Then add the cheese (in shavings rather than grated) and the olive oil, alternately, until the mixture has a creamy consistency. You should be able to *just* pour it. Before serving the soup, pour the *pistou* into the marmite and mix well. Or — the *pistou* may be passed separately in a bowl. In addition a bowl of grated cheese is usually served.

Pistou:
3 cloves garlic, peeled
Pinch of salt
1 cup (about) fresh basil leaves
¼ pound Gruyère or Edam cheese
2 or 3 tablespoons olive oil

Garlic Soup (*Aïgo-Boulido*)

This bouillon has always been very popular in Provence. It is a simple preparation and may be garnished in many ways. The ingredients are given *per person*.

Crush the garlic. Put it in a saucepan or soup pot with the water, salt and pepper, bay leaf, and herbs (if used). Boil rapidly for 15 minutes. Add the pasta (optional) and continue boiling until this is cooked. (The length of time depends, of course, upon the size pasta used.)

Aïgo-Boulido is served sprinkled with a little olive oil, and is either poured over the slices of bread or stirred, a little at a time, into beaten egg yolk, in which case, the pasta should be omitted. A double boiler is recommended to keep the broth and egg yolk warm while being combined.

This soup is one of the most ancient traditional dishes of Provence. The sage and garlic it contains are beneficial, hence two popular Provençal sayings: (1) *"L'aïgo-boulido sauvo la vido"* (Garlic soup saves life) and (2) *"Qu'a de sauvi dins soun jardin a pas besoun de médecin"* (He who has sage in his garden has no need of doctors).

1 clove garlic, peeled
1½ cups water
Salt and pepper
Piece of bay leaf
Olive oil
Sprig of sage
Sprig of thyme (optional) (or
  ½ teaspoon dried thyme and sage)
2 slices of bread
1 ounce vermicelli or
  1 egg yolk, beaten

Rhodanian Vegetable Soup (Potage Rhodanien)

SERVES 4

Cut the carrots, turnips, celery, and potato into small dice, and brown them quickly in the olive oil. When they are lightly cooked, add the water. Season with salt and pepper, and place over brisk heat. When the boiling point is reached, lower heat to medium and cook until the carrots are almost done (about 10 minutes). Then add the peas and garlic and cook 6 to 10 minutes longer or until the peas are "just done."

This soup is not strained. It is sprinkled with oil, ladled over the bread, which is placed in individual soup plates, and then sprinkled with the cheese.

2 carrots, scraped
2 small white turnips, scraped
1 medium-size potato, peeled
1 large stalk of celery, scraped
5 cups water
2 slices of bread per person
4 tablespoons olive oil
Salt and pepper
¼ cup (when shelled) peas
2 cloves garlic, peeled and crushed
Grated Gruyère cheese

Vermicelli Soup (Soupe Courte)

SERVES 4

Sauté the onions and tomatoes quickly in oil. When the onions are soft and yellow (don't brown them), add water, garlic (left whole), bay leaf, salt and pepper. Cook over moderate heat for 10 minutes. Then add the vermicelli and cook for about 8 minutes longer. Serve with a bowl of grated cheese.

1 medium-size onion, peeled
    and chopped
2 medium-size tomatoes, seeded
    and chopped
3 tablespoons olive oil
4 cups water
1 clove garlic, peeled
1 bay leaf
Salt and pepper
2 tablespoons vermicelli
Grated cheese

Potages

Fresh Bean Soup (Soupe Paysanne)

SERVES 4

Sauté the onion in the oil. Add the broth, beans, and squash. Cook over low heat until the vegetables are soft. Put through a *tamis* or food mill. Cook the vermicelli in water, separately, and add it to the soup. Season to taste with salt and pepper.

1 medium-size onion, peeled
    and minced
2 tablespoons olive oil
5 cups broth from any boiled meat
    (or liquor from cooked beans)
½ pound cooked wax or green beans
¼ pound peeled, diced squash
2 tablespoons vermicelli
Salt and pepper

Chick-pea Soup (Soupe de Pois Chiches)   SERVES 4

1½ cups chick-peas (dried or
  canned)
8 cups water
1 teaspoon salt
3 tablespoons olive oil
2 slices of bread per person, fried
  in oil
1 medium-size tomato, crushed
1 small onion, peeled and chopped
1 leek, minced
Salt and pepper

If dried chick-peas are used, soak them overnight. Canned chick-peas should be drained of their juice and washed under running cold water. In either case, drain well and then cover with water to a depth of 1 inch above the contents. Add 1 teaspoon salt, and simmer until the peas are soft. *Do not discard the cooking water.*

Sear the onion, leek, and tomatoes in the olive oil. When all is lightly cooked, pour over it the liquor from the cooked peas. Simmer for a few minutes, then add the peas, a dash of pepper, and additional salt if needed. Simmer the whole until all can be easily mashed or put through a food mill or blender. To serve, pour over slices of bread which have been fried in oil — or the bread may be omitted and cooked vermicelli substituted.

Onion and Tomato Soup (Potage Provençal)   SERVES 6

4 medium potatoes
Equal weight of tomatoes
Water to cover
Salt and pepper
4 medium onions, chopped
4 tablespoons olive oil
6 pieces of toast
Garlic

Peel potatoes and tomatoes. Put these into a soup pot with water to cover. Season with the salt and pepper and, after the ingredients come to a boil, cook over gentle heat for 2 hours.

Cook the onions in 3 tablespoons oil over low heat. Do not allow them to brown. They should be merely soft. Purée these in a food mill or a blender along with the cooked potatoes and tomatoes, and adjust seasoning to taste.

Pour the soup into a tureen and sprinkle with remaining 1 tablespoon olive oil. Put a slice of toast rubbed with a split clove of garlic into each plate and serve the soup over them. (Recipe from the collection of Gustave Pignot, president of the Club des Purs-Cent.)

Squash Soup (Soupe de Courge)   SERVES 4

1 pound squash (preferably one of
  the yellow squashes) peeled,
  seeded,* and chopped
1 tablespoon chopped onion
2 tablespoons butter or lard
Milk and water, half-and-half
Salt and pepper
2 tablespoons cooked rice

Lightly color the chopped onion in the butter or lard. Add the squash, and cook, over low heat, until soft. Put through a food mill to obtain a purée which you then dilute to the desired consistency with milk and water, half-and-half. Season to taste with salt and pepper. Return to heat and add the rice.

* Important: Make sure all fibers are removed before squash is chopped.

Tomato and Leek Soup
(Soupe à la Tomate)

SERVES 4

Quickly sear the leeks in the olive oil. Add the tomatoes. Season to taste with salt and pepper. Add the *bouquet garni* and the clove of garlic. When this begins to bubble, add water to cover and let simmer for 30 minutes. Put through a food mill or other purée device. Return to heat and add the rice or vermicelli. This tomato soup is delicious served cold (minus the rice or pasta), like chilled consommé or madrilène.

2 small leeks (white parts only)
3 tablespoons olive oil
2 pounds medium-size tomatoes, seeded and quartered
Salt and pepper
Bouquet garni
1 clove garlic, peeled
Water to cover (about 4 cups)
3 tablespoons vermicelli or rice, cooked

Tomato Summer Soup
(Potage Provençal d'Été)

SERVES 4

Color the sliced onions in oil. Add the tomatoes, garlic, *bouquet garni*, parsley, and water. Let this cook, over moderate heat, for about an hour. Put through a sieve or food mill. Then stir the cream of wheat or cream of barley carefully into this purée and continue cooking 15 minutes longer, adding a little more water if necessary. Add the salt and pepper during the second cooking. This soup is extremely refreshing. It will give you zest for life even when the thermometer says, "Wilt!"

2 large onions, sliced
2¼ pounds tomatoes, well ripened
2 tablespoons olive oil
1 clove garlic, peeled but left whole
Bouquet garni, plus sprig of parsley
4½ cups water
2 tablespoons cream of wheat (or cream of barley)
Salt and pepper

VI
*Hors D'Oeuvres
and Salads*

MANY DISHES that in English-speaking countries are usually considered vegetables or side dishes are called "salads" in France but served as hors d'oeuvres. To the thrifty, tempering hunger by starting off with the less expensive foods (exceptions: caviar, truffled pâté, etc., served on special occasions) has always been an appealing idea. In the United States, the custom, which has been spreading, is rumored to be something put over on husbands and children. Salad is "good for you." Husbands and children, having no natural enthusiasm about what is good for them, must be given it while the edge is still on the appetite. Calling it "hors d'oeuvres," however, makes it immediately more glamorous. And, besides, the term inspires the cook.

Anchovies

Anchoïade

SERVES 6

6 slices stale bread
6 large anchovies in brine
4 tablespoons olive oil
1 tablespoon lemon juice
Dash of pepper
1 clove garlic

Toast 3-inch squares of stale bread. Desalt the anchovies (page 12) and remove the bones and tails. Mash the fish with the back of a fork. [Important: don't use an electric blender for this]. When the anchovies are well crushed, blend them with a sauce composed of olive oil, a squeeze of lemon juice, a pinch of pepper, and a crushed clove of garlic. After having blended the puréed anchovies and the sauce, spread and tamp the mixture into the pieces of toast, using a morsel of untoasted bread as an instrument and pressing hard to encourage the toast to "drink" the paste flavor. Some people spread the purée on the bread and then grill the "tartines" under a flame.

Anchoïade de Croze

SERVES 6

12 anchovies in oil
12 anchovies in brine
12 almonds, pounded fine (or
    6 walnuts)
3 dried figs
2 cloves garlic
1 small onion
Lemon juice
2 tablespoons *fines herbes* (page 16)
2 sprigs fennel tops
1 small dried red pepper
3 (or more) tablespoons olive oil
1 tablespoon orange flower water*
Black olives for garnish
12 small brioches made without
    sugar†

This variation of the classic anchoïade was conceived by Count Austin de Croze, the celebrated gastronome. A "quintuple Provençal essence," he called it.

Mince the herbs, garlic, onion, and fennel very fine. Stem and chop the figs. Mix the two "hashes." Pound the hot pepper and nuts together in a mortar, and then the anchovies in oil. Freshen the brine-packed anchovies (page 12), bone them and add to the mixture with a dash of lemon juice, and then, little by little, the orange flower water. The perfume of the garlic will thus be considerably chastened.

Cut the little brioches in half, crosswise, and spread the upper halves with a thick layer of the paste. Brush the cut sides of the remaining halves with oil. Put your little brioches back together again and place them in a hot oven for 5 minutes. Arrange them on a platter and surround them with a darkly gleaming, velvet wreath of five black olives. Serve hot.

* Orange flower water is sold in specialty food stores and also may be ordered from Caswell-Massey Co., Ltd., Lexington Avenue at 48th St., New York, N.Y. 10017. It is lovely stuff and has many uses.
† Jewish egg loaf — called *Challah* — serves very well, cut in large cubes.

Anchovy Fritters (*Beignets d'Anchois*)

Freshen some anchovies (page 12). Cut them open and remove the backbones. Dry them well with a cloth. Plunge them in batter (page 12) and fry in very hot fat.

Celery with Anchovy Cream (Céleri aux Anchois)

Carefully clean 2 bunches of celery. Separate the stalks, and soak them in cold water for 1 hour. Remove the fibers. Wipe stalks dry with a clean cloth. Freshen 6 anchovies (page 12) and remove their bones. Sprinkle the anchovies with oil and a bit of vinegar, and mash them with the back of a fork until they are of a creamy consistency. The celery stalks are used to dip up the anchovy cream.

Parsley Anchovies (Anchois Persillade)

This is the best way to present plain anchovies. Desalt them (page 12) and remove the bones. Prepare fillets by arranging them crisscross in latticework piles in a large relish dish or oval platter. Sprinkle with chopped parsley, strew with capers, and moisten with oil and a splash of vinegar. Garnish with sliced hard-boiled eggs (optional).

Eggs with Capers (Oeufs Durs en Tapenado)

Shell one hard-boiled egg per person. Cut these in half lengthwise. Remove and mash the yolks and blend smoothly with Tapenado (page 32). Fill the egg whites with this mixture, making domed halves.

Eggs with Garlic (Oeufs à l'Ail)

[A simple, quick and delicious snack.]

Pound 10 cloves of garlic (cooked in water) with 2 anchovies (page 12) and ¼ cup capers (or 2 tablespoons bottled capers). Drain well and then mix with 4 tablespoons olive oil, a splash of vinegar, and a pinch of pepper. Put this sauce in the bottom of the plate in which slices of 6 hard-boiled eggs are to be served.

Fruit

Figs (Figues)

It is the custom of old Provençal families to include, in a platter of hors d'oeuvres, fresh figs, each on its own leaf. If you are in the country when the figs have just been gathered, you eat them still warm from the sun. Otherwise, they are chilled in the refrigerator or on ice to freshen them.

Melon

The custom of serving melon as an hors d'oeuvre is of fairly recent origin and certainly not restricted to Provence. There, however, only melons of the type for which the Department of Charente is famous are so served. The green rind melons are considered dessert fruit.

Olives

Like all Mediterranean people, the *Provençaux* are the great consumers of olives, both green and black. When the olive ripens, it turns black. It is then called *fachouiro* — that is to say, "become oily." Herewith some recipes for the treatment of olives "in the raw."

Black Olives (*Olives Fachouiro*)

First, prick the olives all over. Strew generously with salt. Leave them to steep, pouring off, daily, the liquid that they yield. As soon as they have lost their bitterness, put them into a stoneware or earthenware pot, sprinkle them with ground peppercorns, moisten them with good oil, strew with bay leaves and sprays of thyme. Let stand in a cool place for several days to "season" before serving.

Crushed Olives (*Olives Cachado*)

This is an hors d'oeuvre that is very common in Provence, but it takes a bit of getting used to in order to appreciate the little tang of bitterness of olives crushed with their pits.

The method of preparation is very simple. The olives are tapped smartly with a hammer or cleaver to open them slightly without mashing, then steeped in cold water for a week (water changed daily), and then in brine (1 part salt to 8 parts water) for a week and flavored as in the preceding recipe.

Green Olives (*Olives à la Pichoulino*)

These olives are set to marinate in a preparation consisting of wood ashes combined with water (the mixture should be just lightly moist).

They are stirred once a day. When the pits can be removed easily from the flesh, the olives are washed several times in fresh water. They are preserved in salted water (2¼ pounds of salt to 8½ quarts of water), and flavored with bay leaves, sprigs of fennel, an orange rind, and whole coriander seeds.

Stuffed Olives (Olives Farcies)

Freshen some anchovies (page 12), remove the bones, and cut the flesh into small narrow fillets (each anchovy should make 4 fillets). Roll each fillet very snugly around 2 capers, and poke it into a stoned green olive.

Pastries

Little Provençal Pastries
(Petits Pâtés à la Provençale)

Prepare a rich pastry dough (pâte brisée, page 19). Roll it out thin and cut out with a glass or cup, making an equal number of rounds. Put aside half of these "discs" and garnish the remaining ones with the anchovies pounded with the garlic, parsley, and a little olive oil, mixed with the meat and bound with one of the egg yolks. Cover each garnished disc with another pastry disc. Press the edges firmly together (dampening the rim of the lower crust helps), and brush with the other egg yolk. Place on a buttered pan or cookie sheet and bake in a hot oven (425° to 450°) for 20 minutes.

1 pound (scant) rich pastry dough
4 anchovies
1 clove garlic
2 teaspoons parsley
½ pound cooked ham, minced
¼ pound cooked veal, minced
Olive oil
2 egg yolks, beaten separately

Little Tuna or Anchovy Pastries
(Petits Pâtés au Thon ou aux Anchois)   SERVES 4

Pound together the tuna and bread crumbs in a mortar. Add the butter. Bind with the egg yolk. When this flavorsome forcemeat is well blended, spread on pastry rounds and bake as in the preceding recipe. (The tuna may be replaced with pounded anchovies. And the pastries may be made with puff paste which is lighter.)

10 ounces tinned tuna fish in oil
½ cup bread crumbs, soaked in
   water and pressed out
1 egg yolk
8 rounds of very rich pastry dough
"Walnut" of butter, softened

Pissaladièra

1 pound onions, minced
6 anchovies
¾ pound bread dough (for French or Italian bread)
¼ cup black olives
2 tablespoons olive oil

Here is one of the most savory of Niçoise specialties. In Nice and in several other coastal towns of Provence, it is sold in the marketplace or the bakeries. However, it is a very easy thing to make at home.

Start by cooking the onions in oil without letting them brown. Use very low heat and stir frequently until the onions have the consistency of a purée.

Set the dough to rise in a warm place, free from drafts, until it has doubled in bulk. Then cut down and roll it out to ¼-inch thickness (or a trifle thinner). Fit this into a well-oiled pie plate. Prick the dough all over with the sharp tines of a fork and spread it with the purée of onions. Top with anchovies (or, alternatively, blend mashed anchovies with the onion purée before spreading). Sprinkle with olive oil. Strew with black olives and bake for 1 hour at 350° to 375°.

Quiche Provençale

Pastry dough
3 medium onions
3 tablespoons oil
4 cloves garlic
2 tomatoes
Bouquet garni
Salt and pepper
2 eggs
1 cup cream

Line an 8-inch flan ring set on a baking sheet with unsweetened tart pastry (Continental pie crust, page 19).

Prepare a filling as follows: Combine in a little oil the onions, finely chopped, 4 whole garlic cloves, peeled, 2 tomatoes, peeled, seeded, chopped (excess juice pressed out), a *bouquet garni* composed of a sprig each of parsley and thyme and a bay leaf tied together with a kitchen thread, and salt and pepper to taste. Sauté for about 30 minutes. Discard the *bouquet garni* and let the vegetables cool a little. Beat 2 eggs with 1 cup cream and combine the mixture with the vegetables. Pour the filling into the pastry-lined flan ring and bake the quiche in a moderately hot oven (375°) for 30 to 35 minutes, or until the custard is set and a knife inserted near the center comes out clean. Serve warm or hot. (Recipe created by Eugène Bonfillon, Chef de Cuisine of La Réserve, Beaulieu-sur-Mer.)

Peppers

Broiled Peppers (*Poivrons Grillés*)

Use 4 large red or green bell peppers. Cut them in half and remove the seeds. Soak in oil for half an hour, then grill them. Slice them in strips or rings and sprinkle with oil to which a dash of vinegar has been added. The peppers may be sauced, instead, with a Tapenado (page 32). This hors d'oeuvre may be eaten hot or cold.

Pepper Salad I (*Poivrons en Salade*)

Little, young, tender green peppers make an excellent hors d'oeuvre. Open them and take out the seeds. Cut them into narrow strips. Sprinkle with salt, oil, and vinegar (1 part vinegar to 4 of oil). These prepared peppers are also delicious combined with peeled tomatoes in a salad.

Pepper Salad II
(*Poivrons en Salade Châteaurenard*)

Prepare peppers as in the preceding recipe but add to them: little new onions (scallions); quartered, hard-boiled eggs; and a handful of chopped parsley . . . all bathed in olive oil. This dish sharpens the appetite with a flourish.

Peppers à la Toulonnaise

SERVES 4

Put the peppers into a hot oven and remove them as soon as little brown or black patches begin to appear on the skin. Wash them in cold water, rubbing off the skin. Cut peppers in half and remove the seeds. Then cut the flesh lengthwise into narrow strips. Arrange these in a relish dish or other suitable serving dish. Top with the anchovies. Sprinkle generously with the oil and a little vinegar. Let marinate in the refrigerator for several hours. Serve very cold.

4 to 8 green bell peppers
    (depending on size)
3-ounce tin of anchovy fillets
1 teaspoon vinegar
⅓ cup olive oil

Seafood

Canapés of Brandade de Morue

This very simple and satisfying hors d'oeuvre or first course is made by toasting large slices of bread, spreading them thickly with *Brandade de Morue* (page 96) which is then sprinkled with grated Gruyère cheese and grilled until lightly browned.

Fish Salad (Salade Antiboise)

1 pound pollack or conger eel, sliced
2 cups boiled, peeled, diced potatoes
1 cup boiled, peeled beets, diced
2 tablespoons lemon juice or vinegar
Salt and pepper
2 tablespoons capers
2 anchovy fillets, chopped
1 or 2 gherkins
6 tablespoons olive oil

This is an unusual and piquant dish.

If you have leftover fish that has been poached in a court bouillon (page 14), use this. Otherwise, poach the fish slices, remembering that they must be cooked gently and not too long so that they will stay firm and whole. When cooked, cut into small squares. Drain well.

Mix the vegetables, anchovies, gherkins, and capers. Season with salt and pepper. Combine and add the olive oil and the lemon juice or vinegar. Pour the sauce over the fish squares, turning the mixture over with great care to coat well without mashing the fish.

Mussels with Saffron (Salade de Moules au Safran)

1 pound tiny new potatoes
2 quarts mussels (opened over low heat without water)
1 cup mayonnaise made with lemon instead of vinegar
Pinch of saffron

Boil the little potatoes. Drain and peel them and allow them to cool. Slice them thin. Heat the mussels in a shallow pan of hot water just until they open. Remove and discard the shells. Drain meat well.

Add a pinch of saffron to the mayonnaise. Combine potatoes, mussels and mayonnaise, mixing carefully so as to crush the ingredients as little as possible.

Tomatoes

Summer Salad (Tomates en Salade)

This is the classic summer hors d'oeuvre. It is always based on tomatoes but is subject to infinite variation. The tomatoes, which should be ripe and rather firm, are sliced or quartered and the seeds removed with the point of a knife. Typical additions are anchovies, tuna, green peppers, sliced cucumbers, cooked rice, and black olives, proportioned according to taste and whim [or what's on hand]. It is sprinkled with chopped parsley or with basil and parsley, half-and-half, a little salt, and olive oil.

Tomato and Anchovy Salad (Salade Niçoise)

Traditionally, this salad, which is a delicious summer hors d'oeuvre, is arranged on a round or oval platter, rather than in a salad bowl.

Cut very firm tomatoes in slices, and remove the seeds. Salt lightly and lay them on a platter. Arrange some freshened anchovy fillets (page 12) over them in a crisscross pattern. Strew with little lozenges of green pepper and sliced black olives. Sprinkle with olive oil and vinegar. Pepper lightly. The salad may be garnished with leaves of fresh basil and slices of hard-boiled eggs.*

* Salade Niçoise oftener than not also includes morsels of tinned tuna fish — preferably the kind packed in olive oil.

Tomato with Codfish "Mayonnaise" (Morue d'Été)

SERVES 4

Cut the tomatoes in half. Salt cut surfaces (lightly) and turn face down to drain. Then garnish the halves with the codfish and vegetables and cover with mayonnaise or Rémoulade (page 29). Sprinkle with a few drops of lemon juice and top each half with a few capers.

1 pound tomatoes
Pinch of salt
¾ pound poached fresh codfish
2 sweet peppers cut in strips
1 cucumber, peeled and diced
1 cup mayonnaise or rémoulade
1 tablespoon lemon juice
2 tablespoons capers

Tomatoes and Potatoes with Capers (Salade Provençale à la Tapenado)

SERVES 4

Slice 1 pound tomatoes. Seed them, and then salt the slices and set them aside to drain. Pour off and discard the liquid thus obtained. Boil ½ pound little new potatoes, then peel and cut them in rounds. Chop a handful of parsley or fresh fennel tops with a clove of garlic. Mix all this with ¼ cup Tapenado (page 32).

Other Hors D'Oeuvres

Artichokes and Beans (Salade Aixoise)

This salad, proportioned according to individual taste, consists of quartered young artichokes, green string beans, quartered cold boiled potatoes, seeded quartered tomatoes, strips of raw green pepper, freshened anchovy fillets, black olives, capers, parsley, tarragon, oil, vinegar, salt and pepper.

Bathed Bread (Pan Bagnat)

Bread
Tomatoes
Onion rings
Oil
Freshened anchovies
Green (bell) peppers

Prototype of an hors d'oeuvre of Nice which is eaten not only at the beginning of a meal but also for breakfast, lunch, and on a picnic.

Use, preferably, a round loaf but, lacking that, a "short" long one. Split it in half, through the middle. Saturate cut side of both halves with olive oil, and salt them lightly. Garnish one half with freshened anchovies, slices of fine, ripe tomatoes, onion rings, and (optional) strips of skinned green peppers. Put the other half loaf over this and press together firmly. [That's all there is to it . . . and it's delicious!]

Young Beans with Salt (Fèves à la Croque-au-Sel)

It is an ancient Provençal custom, when the first, very tender lima beans are in season, to serve them raw, right in their pods, as hors d'oeuvres. Each person shells his own and eats them, dipped in salt.

Chicken Liver Canapés (Canapés Rivarol)

4 small pickles (gherkins)
4 teaspoons chopped parsley
4 cloves garlic
4 slices decrusted bread, toasted
Juice of 1 lemon
Salt and pepper
4 chicken livers
2 tablespoons butter

Toast slices of decrusted bread.

Finely mince small pickles, chopped parsley, and 4 small, peeled cloves of garlic. Pound together in a mortar, and blend with the juice of a medium-size lemon, salt and pepper.

Meanwhile, cook chicken livers in butter. Mash these and combine them with the garlic-herb-lemon mixture and spread the slices of toast with it.

Chicken Liver Pâté (Terraieto aux Senteurs de Provence)

½ pound pork liver, skinned
½ pound chicken livers
Sprig of thyme (or ¼ teaspoon dried)
3 juniper berries
Salt and pepper
4 tablespoons cognac
4 tablespoons white wine
1 bay leaf
¼ teaspoon allspice
½ pound fresh pork fat*

Marinate pork and chicken livers for 24 hours in the wine and cognac seasoned with thyme, bay leaf, juniper berries, salt, pepper, and allspice.

Separately, melt the pork fat. Drain the marinade from the livers and sauté them in this fat. Then pound them in a mortar or put them through a *tamis* or food mill. Work this forcemeat vigorously until it becomes a soft, velvety purée. Let it chill and then fill little pottery jars with it, sealing the surface with a thin layer of the melted fat. (Recipe created by M. G. Landry-Panuel, Chef de Cuisine of the restaurant La Rascasse at Marseille, and Provençal agent for the Chaîne des Rôtisseurs.)

*Or salt "fatback" which has been simmered for 10 minutes in water, and drained well.

Eggplant Caviar (Caviar d'Aubergines)   SERVES 6

Cut the eggplants in half, lengthwise, and broil them, skin side up. Remove skin and chop the flesh very fine to make a purée which you season with salt, pepper, onion, olive oil, and parsley. Blend in lemon juice or vinegar to taste. This "caviar" can be used as a dip or spread on slices of lightly toasted bread.

2 medium-size eggplants
1 medium-size onion, chopped
Salt and pepper
3 tablespoons olive oil
1 tablespoon minced parsley
Dash of vinegar or lemon juice

Mushrooms in Oil (Champignons à l'Huile)

Clean the mushrooms by blanching them in boiling water for 2 to 3 minutes. Drain.

Separately, make a court bouillon in proportions of 1 part vinegar to 3 parts water, seasoned with garlic, salt, peppercorns, and a strong *bouquet garni*. Let this cook for about an hour, then strain. Add more seasoning if needed. Immerse the mushrooms in the court bouillon and boil over medium heat for 10 minutes. Cool them in the liquor. When well cooked, they should be drained and dried very well. Put them into a bowl with the bay leaf, thyme, a few grains of freshly ground pepper. Pour in olive oil to cover completely. Set in a cool place to season. Wait at least a month before eating them. (Recipe of Mme. Léon Verane, Auberge du Lapin Blanc at Solliès-Pont.)

12 large mushrooms, round and firm
Court bouillon (to cover by 2 inches)
Bouquet garni
1 bay leaf
Olive oil
1 teaspoon thyme
½ teaspoon freshly ground peppercorns
1 teaspoon salt

Monaco Onions (Oignons à la Monégasque)

Combine ingredients in a saucepan. Bring to a boil. Lower heat and simmer for 1 hour. Serve very cold. (Recipe of P. Bouillard.)

¾ pound small peeled onions of equal size
1½ cup water
½ cup vinegar
1 tablespoon olive oil
5 tablespoons powdered sugar
3 tablespoons tomato purée
Several sprigs of celery
Freshly ground pepper
Salt

VII. *Pastas*

Gnocchi

CONTRARY TO what is generally supposed, the origin of this dish is not Italian but *Provençal-Niçois*. Even the name "gnocchi" is derived from the Niçois dialect's "inhoc," which is pronounced "EE-YOCK."

Gnocchi

Put the milk in a saucepan with the butter, salt, pepper, and a pinch of nutmeg. Working fast, and using a wooden spoon, stir in the flour and beat briskly. Place over very low heat and continue to stir

2½ cups milk
½ cup butter (generous)
Salt and pepper
Nutmeg
1½ cups flour (scant)
5 eggs
Béchamel Sauce
Grated cheese
Water with 1 tablespoon olive oil

vigorously until the moisture evaporates and the dough has become rather dry. As soon as it no longer clings to the saucepan, take it away from the heat and beat in, one at a time, 5 whole eggs, working them in continuously with the spoon. Then add 2 tablespoons grated cheese.

Bring to a boil 3 or 4 quarts of well-salted water and drop into it bits of the paste the size of almonds. This can be done either with a pastry tube or simply by flipping bits off the end of a spoon with one finger. Cook a small quantity at a time for 4 to 5 minutes. Remove with a slotted spoon. Drain well, and then transfer to a fireproof dish. Moisten with thin Béchamel Sauce (page 12) and sprinkle with grated cheese. Set the dish in the oven for 10 to 15 minutes to glaze.

Potato Gnocchi (*Gnocchi aux Pommes de Terre*)

2½ pounds potatoes
3½ tablespoons butter
¾ cup flour
½ cup grated cheese
Salt and pepper
Pinch of nutmeg

Boil potatoes in their jackets. Peel and mash them while they are still hot and then beat in the butter. When this is well blended, add the flour, working it in, a little at a time, with a wooden spoon. Add grated cheese, salt, pepper, and a pinch of freshly-grated nutmeg. When all is well blended, proceed as in the preceding recipe.

Ravioli (*Railloles*)

3 cups flour (scant)
9 egg yolks
Salt and pepper
½ cup water
2 cups minced cooked beef, veal, or
   ham
1 medium onion, peeled, minced,
   and fried until clear
1 tablespoon olive oil
½ cup cooked, chopped spinach
Boiling water
1 tablespoon olive oil

We think of ravioli as an Italian dish. And so, indeed, it is. But, actually, its long-forgotten origin was the ancient "ralhôla" (*railloles* in French) which was made — and still is — in the hilly Provence of the east and in Nice.

Prepare a light noodle dough with the flour, 5 of the egg yolks, 1 teaspoon salt (no pepper), and ½ cup tepid water. Let this rest for about half an hour.

The filling may be made from leftover meat, from beef stew or roast veal, or from cooked (or raw) ham, or a mixture of these. Chop the meat fine. Combine with a minced onion cooked in olive oil until soft. Season with salt and pepper. Add spinach and the remaining 4 egg yolks.

Roll out the dough. Then, with a small spoon, spread one-half of it with little heaps of filling the size of walnuts, placed 2 inches apart. Cover with the remaining half of the dough which you moisten slightly with a brush dipped in water. Press between the humps with a finger or with the back of a ruler so that the dough above and below the little lumps of filling sticks together firmly. Then cut between them with a wooden pastry wheel to make little cushions (as many as there are filled squares).

Drop these ravioli into boiling, salted water to which you have added 1 teaspoon of olive oil. Cook gently, covered, for 15 minutes after the water returns to a boil. Drain them and then dip them in cool water. Drain again.

Put the *railloles* is an ovenware dish. Moisten with the juices from a roast or a stew. Sprinkle with grated cheese and lightly glaze under a broiler. (Tomato sauce may be substituted for the meat juices or gravy.)

Spaghetti

Spaghetti Mentonnaise

SERVES 6

Chop the onions fine. Add green pepper cut in thin strips, and the tomatoes cut in small pieces. Cook all these over medium heat in the olive oil. Moisten with the bouillon (or white wine and water). Season with salt and pepper plus a pinch of powdered thyme or rosemary, powdered fennel, fresh basil. Add little black olives. Cook the spaghetti as directed on the package. (Don't overcook.) Drain it well, and then blend this sauce into it. Serve strewn with grated cheese.

½ pound spaghetti
2 medium-size onions, peeled (or ¾ cup peeled shallots)
1 seeded green pepper
3 medium-size peeled, seeded, tomatoes
3 tablespoons olive oil
2 or 3 leaves fresh basil
½ cup bouillon or white wine and water (half-and-half)
Salt and pepper
Pinch of dried thyme, rosemary, or fennel
½ cup (generous) little black olives, stoned
Grated cheese

Spaghetti à la Monégasque

Color 3 peeled whole cloves of garlic in 2 tablespoons olive oil. Then add and cook in this same oil 3 medium-size, peeled, seeded tomatoes cut in slices.

Separately, dissolve 2 or 3 desalted anchovies in 1 tablespoon oil in a small saucepan. Add to them the capers, stoned olives (black or green), tarragon or basil. Combine the two mixtures and turn them into a pot of cooked, drained, hot spaghetti. Let simmer for 3 minutes and then serve at once. Grated cheese should be served separately and sprinkled on individual servings.

Spaghetti
3 tablespoons olive oil
3 cloves garlic, peeled
3 tomatoes, peeled, seeded, and sliced
2 freshened anchovy fillets (page 12)
1 tablespoon capers
¼ cup stoned olives
3 sprigs fresh tarragon or basil (or 1 teaspoon dried)
Grated cheese

VIII. *Bouillabaisses*

BOUILLABAISSE is an inspired creation in which white fish and rockfish, bathed in oil, seasoned with garlic, onions, tomatoes, and herbs, and covered with water, are subjected to a veritable tempest of boiling. Vegetables, herbs, and fishes marry their essences to produce a magic synthesis — the golden bouillon that, powdered with saffron, is at once genial and lusty, velvety and appetizing, reflecting all the dreams and sorcery of the Mediterranean. Bouillon of the sun, savory and substantial, it evokes all the splendor of those shores and the gaiety of their dazzling skies.

Bouillabaisse! It should, in truth, have been made mandatory to inscribe this world-famous word on the first page of this book. For it plays the leading role, ranks first in the entire gamut of Provençal dishes. "Bouillabaisse, this golden soup," writes Curnonsky, the prince of French gastronomes, "this incomparable golden soup which embodies and concentrates all the aromas of our shores and which permeates, like an ecstasy, the stomachs of astonished gastronomes. Bouillabaisse is one of those classic dishes whose glory has encircled the world, and the miracle consists of this: there are as many bouillabaisses as there are good chefs or *cordons bleus*. Each brings to his own version his special touch. But all must have rockfish from the sea, and always freshly caught." To say that there is no specific recipe for preparing bouillabaisse is nonsense. The truth is that there are many variants to be found all up and down the coast, each claiming to be the sole authentic version. There are those who add mussels and those who never do. There are the *Toulonnais* who add potatoes, and the *Marseillais* who repudiate these with horror, claiming that they rob the fish of its soft and velvety quality. There are some who prepare, ahead of time, a court bouillon of some common fish and use this, puréed, as a base for their bouillabaisse. Others cook the ingredients in oil; the whimsical add a glass of white wine, nay, even cognac or absinthe. Nothing of this sort is necessary. All that is required is to remember the three essential factors: (1) the freshness of the fish; (2) the proportions of the ingredients; and (3) the method of cooking. Let us note, also, that lobster is not indispensable though it makes the bouillabaisse richer, but several crabs and shrimps are desirable and even necessary.

Here, then, is the recipe for this matchless dish.

Bouillabaisse

The quantities indicated below are for 8 to 10 persons. For a bouillabaisse to be good, a great variety of fish is required, and for this reason it is more rewarding to make the dish for a goodly number of congenial table companions.

Needed are at least 5½ pounds seafood, including a selection of rockfish — hogfish, sea robin, porgy, or scup — and a selection of goosefish, conger eel, whiting, tinker mackerel, crabs, and shrimps, and, optionally, a few spiny lobsters, cut in half lengthwise. [Mediterranean fish that cannot be found in the United States include *rascasse, saintpierre, rouquier, chapon, pageot, saran, murene,* and *girelle.* There are, however, many fish available that may be substituted. For example: sea bass, flounder, grunt, haddock, perch, weakfish, scrod, red snapper and gray snapper, and sea trout.]

Vegetables and seasonings should include 1 or 2 onions, minced, the white part of 1 leek, coarsely cut up, 4 garlic cloves, crushed, 3 or 4 tomatoes, peeled, seeded, and coarsely chopped, a small piece of fennel, a bay leaf, a strip of orange rind, a stalk of thyme (wild thyme, if available) or, lacking thyme, savory, 3 or 4 pinches of powdered saffron, salt and pepper, and a scant ½ cup of olive oil.

Put all the vegetables and seasonings into a soup kettle. Clean the fish and add the firmer varieties, such as hogfish, eel, shrimps, crabs, and lobsters. Shake the soup pot with a slow circular motion to impregnate the fish well. Pour over the fish a generous 3 quarts water and set the pot over high heat. A tempestuous fire is essential for the broth and the oil to blend properly at a brisk boil. Without it, the "union" will not be complete, and your bouillabaisse will not be perfect.

Boil the bouillabaisse rapidly for 5 or 6 minutes and add the delicate fish. Continue boiling it for 6 to 8 minutes longer and add more seasoning, if necessary. Bouillabaisse should be highly flavored.

Have ready some slices of stale French bread about ½ inch thick, allowing 4 or 5 slices per person. Put these slices in deep individual soup plates. Remove the fish carefully from the soup pot and arrange it on 1 or 2 platters. Pour enough of the broth over the bread to moisten it. The fish is served separately.

Remarks:

Bouillabaisse may not be kept waiting but is waited for. It must, therefore, be served as soon as it is ready.

Bouillabaisse is not a soup. To serve a soup plate full of bouillon in which pieces of bread float is a blunder. When properly cooked, there should be only enough of the unctuous broth to moisten the bread generously. A similar mistake is to toast the bread. At most it should be dried in the oven a couple of seconds.

If you care to add potatoes in the mode of Toulon, put quartered ones in the pot at the same time the firmer species of fish are added, or with the delicate fish if the potatoes are sliced. The latter presentation is preferable. Serve the potatoes on the same platter as the fish. The beautiful "saffroned" tint of the potatoes adds something extra to the harmonious presentation.

As we said above, some cooks make a court bouillon with whole little fish and the heads of large ones (except for the *rascasse,* which must always come to table with its head on). The fish and broth are put through a strainer or food mill and used in place of the boiling water for the bouillabaisse. With this method, the flavor of the broth is intensified while only the handsomer fish are sent to the table.

If mussels are included, they should be left in their shells and served along with the fish.

The fish is sometimes served with *Rouille* (page 20), the special, highly seasoned sauce that, in Provence, sustains so many devotees.

Aïgo-Sau

2¼ pounds white fish
1 onion, minced
2 seeded, chopped tomatoes
3 potatoes (about)
2 or 3 cloves garlic
Bouquet garni, see directions
Salt and pepper
Slices of bread

Put 2¼ pounds eviscerated and cleaned white fish, cut in pieces, into a soup pot. Add 1 onion, minced, 2 tomatoes, seeded and coarsely chopped, several waxy potatoes, peeled and quartered, 2 or 3 garlic cloves, and a *bouquet garni* composed of 1 bay leaf and a sprig each of fennel, thyme, celery, and parsley. Season the mixture with salt and pepper and sprinkle it with oil. Mix well and add water to cover. Set the pot over high heat, bring the mixture rapidly to a boil, and boil it until the potatoes are tender. Serve the bouillon on slices of bread, and the fish and potatoes on a separate platter.

The fish may, alternatively, be served with *Rouille* (page 20).

La Bourride
(*a subtle form of Bouillabaisse*) SERVES 8 to 10

4½ pounds white fish
1¼ cups boiling water
1½ cups dry white wine
1 leek, cleaned and minced
1 medium onion, peeled and chopped
1 carrot, scraped and chopped
2 slices fresh fennel
2 bay leaves
Strip of orange peel
Sprig of thyme
Salt and pepper
½ cup (or more) of *aïoli* (page 24)
1 egg yolk per person
8 to 10 slices stale bread

This dish belongs in the top rank of Provençal specialties. The origin is of deepest antiquity. Indeed, it is said that the Phocaeans already knew and rejoiced in *bourride* when they first landed, two thousand years ago, on the shore of the bay of Marseille. That so remarkable a dish could be so little known (except in private households) is a mystery.

A *bourride* is made with white fish (not whitefish) *only*. Mullet, ocean perch, and pollack are all suitable. The most sumptuous *bourride* is made with ocean perch alone.

This recipe makes 8 to 10 servings.

Cut the fish into serving portions. Make a court bouillon (page 14) with the water, white wine, leek, onion, carrot, fennel, bay leaves, orange peel, thyme, salt and pepper. Immerse the fish in this, bring it to a boil, and cook at a rolling boil for 12 minutes. Then remove the fish and strain the bouillon.

Separately, you will have made an *aïoli*. Reserve 2 tablespoons per person of this and put the rest of it into a casserole along with 1 egg yolk per person.

Now comes the crucial moment! Place the casserole (or saucepan) just off the heat. Pour into it the liquor from the fish pot, a little at a time, stirring continuously with a wooden spoon until you have produced a perfect blending. This operation completed, place the casserole over gentle heat and continue to stir with the wooden spoon until a smooth "cream" results. *Above all,* be on guard to prevent the sauce from boiling. Unless you are, the mixture may curdle beyond all remedy.

Place the slices of stale bread in the serving plates and pour the "cream" over these. Arrange the fish on a platter, and offer the reserved *aïoli* [or, even more Provençal, a bowl of *Rouille* (page 20)] in a sauceboat to accompany it.

Codfish Bouillabaisse (Bouillabaisse de Morue)

Codfish bouillabaisse, obviously, is not the equal of a bouillabaisse made of fresh fish, but it is a less expensive dish and has a large following. Then, too, it can be made far from the shores of the Mediterranean.

In a soup kettle brown lightly in oil 1 large onion and the white part of 1 leek, both minced. Add 1 large tomato, coarsely chopped and also lightly browned. Add 1½ quarts water, a *bouquet garni* composed of 1 sprig each of thyme and fennel, a bay leaf, and a bit of orange rind, 2 garlic cloves, crushed, a good pinch of saffron, and a little pepper. Set the pot over high heat, bring the mixture rapidly to a boil, and add 2¼ pounds potatoes, peeled and sliced. Boil the mixture until the potatoes are half cooked and add about 2½ pounds freshened salt cod, cut into pieces. Taste the bouillon and add salt if needed. Cook the mixture until the fish is tender.

Pour the bouillon over slices of bread placed in deep soup plates. (The bread may be covered with grated cheese or rubbed with garlic.) Arrange the codfish on a platter with the potatoes around it, and sprinkle with chopped parsley.

1 large onion
1 leek white
1 large tomato
1½ quarts boiling water
Bouquet garni, see directions
2¼ pounds potatoes
2½ pounds freshened salt cod

Bouillabaisse with Eggs
(Also called "One-eyed Bouillabaisse")

In a small saucepan or flameproof casserole brown lightly in olive oil 2 leeks and 1 onion, both minced. Add 2 tomatoes, seeded and chopped, a *bouquet garni,* a frond of fennel fern, a bit of orange rind, 6 or 7 potatoes (preferably yellow and waxy), cut into slices, and several pinches of saffron. Pour in enough water to cover amply. Set the pan over high heat and bring the mixture rapidly to a boil, as with all bouillabaisses. Boil the mixture until the potatoes are just about tender. Poach 1 egg

2 leeks, 1 onion, 2 tomatoes
Bouquet garni
Fennel fern, orange rind, saffron
6 or 7 potatoes
1 egg per person
Slices of stale bread
Chopped parsley

per person in the bouillon. Season to taste. Pour the broth over slices of stale bread in a deep platter. Arrange the potatoes, sprinkled with chopped parsley, and the eggs on another platter, and serve.

Bouillabaisse of Little Peas

1 onion
2 or 3 potatoes
3 cups shelled little peas
Bouquet garni
2 or 3 cloves garlic
Spray of fennel
Salt and pepper
1 egg per person
Sliced bread

This is an ancient Provençal way of dressing up little green peas — one of the multiple forms of bouillabaisse. Why not restore it to its former place of honor?

Sauté 1 onion, chopped, in oil without letting it color too much. Add several potatoes, cut into thickish slices, and cook them for a moment without letting them brown. Pour 1 quart boiling water over the mixture and add 3 cups shelled little peas. Season the mixture with a *bouquet garni*, 2 or 3 garlic cloves, a spray of fennel, and salt and pepper. Boil the mixture, covered, over high heat until the peas and potatoes are tender.

Poach 1 egg per person in the broth. Lay a slice of bread in each soup plate, top it with a poached egg, and ladle some of the soup over it.

Revesset (*a minor form of Bouillabaisse*)

Revesset I. Select fish such as fresh sardines, *bogues* (known also as *boöps!*), *sauclés,* or the like.

In a soup pot cook equal quantities of spinach and chard with a few sorrel leaves until they are almost tender. Season the greens with salt and pepper and add a quantity of fish equal to the vegetables. Cook the mixture for about 15 minutes longer. Prepare slices of bread and lay them in soup plates. Pour the bouillon and greens over the bread and serve the fish separately.

Revesset II. Clean 2 pounds fresh sardines **[Americans at home who want to make a *revesset* will have to make do with fresh herring.]** or fresh anchovies, leaving on the heads which improve the flavor of the bouillon. Mix them with some bread crumbs, 1 onion, chopped, 1 garlic clove chopped with 2 tablespoons chopped parsley, 2 or 3 tomatoes, cut into pieces, salt and pepper, and oil. Cover the mixture with water, bring it rapidly to a boil, and boil it briskly for 10 minutes or so. Serve over slices of bread, as in *Revesset I.*

Sardine Bouillabaisse

This is a "poor man's bouillabaisse," certainly, but one that has been very popular in the Toulon region. Needless to say, it calls for fine, very fresh (not tinned) sardines, such as those known in Provence as "dawn sardines" (*sardines d'aube*).

Follow the recipe for Codfish Bouillabaisse, substituting for the codfish 2¼ pounds fresh sardines, scaled and cleaned, and boil them for only 5 or 6 minutes.

Spinach Bouillabaisse (*Bouillabaisse d'Épinards or Épinards à la Marseillaise*)

Here is an original dish that is in the authentic tradition of Marseille cuisine.

Wash 2½ pounds spinach and blanch it in boiling salted water. Drain the spinach and chop it. In a soup pot brown 1 large onion, chopped, in hot olive oil. Add the spinach, turning it over several times in the hot oil. Add 6 or 7 waxy potatoes, peeled and cut into slices, and cover the contents of the pot with 1 quart boiling water. Season the mixture with 2 garlic cloves, peeled, a sprig of fennel, and salt and pepper. Cover the pot and cook the bouillabaisse over low heat until the potatoes are tender. Poach 1 egg per person in the bouillon.

Prepare slices of bread as for bouillabaisse and have each diner place 2 or 3 on his plate. Serve the bouillabaisse from the pot with a ladle, placing a poached egg on a slice of bread in each plate.

2½ pounds spinach
1 large onion
Olive oil
6 or 7 potatoes
1 quart boiling water
2 garlic cloves
Sprig of fennel
Salt and pepper
1 egg per person
Slices of bread

Rouille (*see also page 20*)

Mix together 2 or 3 garlic cloves, peeled, 1 or 2 hot red peppers, fresh or dried, ½ cup soft fresh bread crumbs that have been soaked in water and pressed out, and 3 to 4 tablespoons olive oil. Crush the mixture with a pestle until it has a creamy consistency. Add 2 or 3 spoonfuls of broth from a bouillabaisse or an *aïgo-sau* and serve with the fish. But, *attention!* This sauce is very potent and doesn't suit all palates.

A variation of *rouille* omits the bread crumbs and, after the garlic and red pepper have been well pounded in a mortar, adds 1 egg yolk and about 1 cup olive oil, drop by drop, to make a sort of mayonnaise. This method produces a *rouille* of less vigor.

2 or 3 garlic cloves
1 or 2 hot red peppers
½ cup soft bread crumbs
Olive oil
Broth from bouillabaisse

IX
Eggs

6 chilled, hard-boiled eggs
2 tablespoons bread crumbs, soaked
in milk and pressed out
1 tablespoon minced anchovy fillets
(or 1 teaspoon anchovy paste)
1 tablespoon minced parsley
½ clove garlic, minced
Salt and pepper
Olive oil
Dry bread crumbs

Baked

La Berlingueto

SERVES 4

Preheat oven to 350°. Shell the eggs and halve them lengthwise. Remove and sieve the yolks. Mix yolks with the bread crumbs, anchovies, garlic, and parsley. Season, being prudent with the salt because of the anchovies. Garnish each half egg white with this filling. Use what is left over to make a bed in the bottom of a flat, well-oiled, heatproof dish, and arrange the stuffed eggs on it. Strew sparingly with dry bread crumbs and sprinkle with olive oil. Bake until thoroughly heated and delicately brown. (Recipe from the collection of l'Armana Prouvençau.)

Baked Eggs with Mushrooms
(Oeufs aux Champignons à la Manosquine)

SERVES 4

8 large mushrooms of uniform size
1 small clove garlic, peeled
1 small onion, peeled
1 scant tablespoon parsley
1 scant tablespoon fresh tarragon
¼ cup dried bread crumbs
1 hard-boiled egg, sieved
4 tablespoons (scant) pork fat
Anchovy butter
8 fresh raw eggs
Salt and paprika
Grated cheese
Tomato sauce

Clean the mushrooms. Remove the stems and mince them fine along with the garlic, onion, parsley, and tarragon. Carefully stir in the bread crumbs, the thoroughly minced or sieved hard-boiled egg, and the pork fat.

Season the mushroom caps with salt and paprika and fill each one with the "hash." Arrange on an oiled, oven-proof platter. Top each cap with a blob of anchovy butter. Bake at 280° to 325° for about 20 minutes, basting frequently with the juices yielded.

Remove platter from oven. Carefully break a fresh egg over each cap. Salt it, dust with a little grated cheese and return the platter to the oven to bake until the eggs are set but still soft. Serve with hot tomato sauce.

Provençal Baked Eggs
(Oeufs Cocotte Provençale)

SERVES 4

8 eggs
2 tablespoons oil
Salt and pepper
1 tablespoon parsley, chopped
½ clove garlic, minced
1 tablespoon minced fresh basil
   (optional)
4 ripe tomatoes, chopped

Combine all ingredients except the eggs. Simmer them 15 to 20 minutes (until the juice from the tomatoes has evaporated). Half-fill pottery ramekins or custard cups with this fondue. Crack an egg carefully into each cup. Place the cups in a steamer or in a deep skillet. Pour in hot water to half the height of the cups. Cover tightly and cook over moderate heat (or in a 350° oven). The steam will poach the eggs. Salt lightly before serving.

Baked Eggs with Tomatoes
(Oeufs sur le Plat aux Tomates)

1 tomato per person
Olive oil
2 eggs per person
Salt and pepper
Minced garlic
Chopped parsley

Cut the tomatoes in half. Seed them carefully without breaking them. Season with salt, pepper, parsley, and a bit of garlic, and fry them lightly (cut-side down only) in the oil. Then slide them, including the oil in the skillet, onto an oven-proof dish fried-side up. Break an egg over each tomato half. Bake at 400° and you will have the best *"oeufs sur le plat"* in the world (but don't salt the eggs until the moment of serving).

Eggs Fried à la Gavote (Oeufs Frits à la Gavote)

[This is a *real* ham-and-egg sandwich. No bread!]

Grill 2 thin slices of ham for each egg. Oil a skillet and put half the ham slices into it. Break an egg on each slice and cover with a second slice of ham. Do not salt. Fry in butter or oil over low heat until the eggs are set, turning the "sandwich" once.

It should be noted that in *some* of the omelet recipes which follow, the quantities listed are to serve 4 to 6 persons, in others only 2 persons. This is because the flat, unturned omelet is, in effect, smooth, dense scrambled eggs and, therefore, a larger *"omelette"* can be made in one operation. The true French omelet, soft, delicately browned and buttery, is best when made, one at a time, with a great deal of butter, *and never more than 3 eggs* (to serve 2 persons).

The temperature of the fat into which the omelet mixture is poured is vital to the success of the finished product. It should be hot throughout the cooking. Because it can be *seen* heating, butter is a little easier to manage than oil. The moment it *starts* to seethe and turn brown is the moment to turn the eggs into it. They should be stirred fast for a moment, then continuously lifted to allow the uncooked liquid to run to the bottom. When almost set, the egg mass is rolled over on itself and tilted onto a hot platter.

An almost limitless variety of "filled" omelets can be made simply by spreading ¼ cup to ½ cup of cooked or raw filling over the surface of the 3-egg turned omelet just before rolling it up. Among the additions most popular in Provence are: *Brandade de Morue* (page 96); chopped, cooked mussels; fried diced potatoes; *Ratatouille* (page 193); fried sea anemones; chopped, seasoned spinach; highly seasoned tomatoes or thick tomato sauce; truffles; fried whitebait; and a mixture of fresh tuna, tomato purée, and mashed anchovies.

Omelette à l'Aixoise

1 medium-size potato, cooked
2 medium-size tomatoes
2 teaspoons olive oil
2 tablespoons butter
6 eggs, beaten
½ teaspoon salt
¼ teaspoon pepper
Pinch of minced chervil

Skin and seed tomatoes, and sauté in olive oil, then combine with peeled and diced potato. Season the beaten eggs with salt, pepper and chervil and fold them into the vegetable mixture. Heat the butter in a skillet and proceed as for any well-cooked omelet. It should be cooked through but not dry.

Artichoke Omelet (Omelette aux Artichauts)   SERVES 2

3 very tender young artichokes
3 eggs
2 tablespoons oil
Salt and pepper

This is the most typically Provençal of omelets; an exquisite dish. Well-cooked, "round," not moist and not folded, it may be served hot or cold.

Remove the outer leaves of the young artichokes. **[If the artichokes are very young, the chokes need not be removed.]** Snip off the tips of all the other leaves. Cut artichokes lengthwise in six pieces each. Brown these for a minute or so in 1 tablespoon oil. Beat the eggs, season with salt and pepper, and add the artichokes. Heat the other tablespoonful of oil and cook the omelet in this over medium-high heat.

Artichoke and Tomato Omelet (Omelette à la Nicarde)

This is a variation of the above recipe using half as many artichokes (quartered instead of sliced) and an equal quantity of peeled, seeded, crushed tomatoes.

Fisherman's Omelet (Omelette Pêcheur)   SERVES 4

½ pound fish fillets*
2½ pounds mussels
Court bouillon to cover
¼ pound mushrooms, sliced
¼ cup white wine
3 tablespoons olive oil
Lemon juice
1 cup medium thick béchamel sauce
6 eggs
1 tablespoon parsley and garlic minced together
Salt and pepper

Poach the fish in a court bouillon (page 14), greatly reduced so that the flavor is pronounced. There should be enough to cover the fish fillets in a pan just large enough to hold them. Remove the fish and discard skin (if any) but reserve the liquor. Steam the mussels open in a little water. Discard shells and chop the mussels coarsely if they are large. Strain and reserve the liquor. Sauté the mushrooms in 1 tablespoon oil, over medium heat. Finish with white wine and a dash of lemon juice.

Make a Béchamel Sauce (page 12), using for the liquid the broth and juices from the court bouillon, mussels, and mushrooms. Cut the cooked fish fillets into small pieces and fold these with the mushrooms

* *Daurade* is the traditional fish but bream, carp, porgies, red snapper, or sea bass are all suitable.

and mussels into the béchamel. Season with salt and pepper.

Beat the eggs with the minced parsley and garlic. Heat the remaining oil and make a flat, moist omelet. Cover this with the hot fish mixture. Roll up the omelet and serve promptly on a hot, hot platter. (Recipe created by Jean Bernhard, proprietor and chef of the Restaurant aux Mets de Provence at Toulon.)

Harvester (Onion) Omelet
(Omelette Moissonnière)

SERVES 4 TO 6

The name of this savory and sustaining omelet derives from its popularity at harvest time when Provençal people like to carry it in their lunch boxes to the fields, vineyards, and orchards. It is, of course, eaten cold.

Remove the outside skin of the onions and, with the point of a paring knife, make a little cross in the center of each one and insert a clove. Put these onions to soak for half a day in the water flavored with the vinegar. When ready to prepare the omelet, bring the onions to a boil in the water and cook 10 minutes. Drain well. Cut up the onions (removing the cloves) and sauté them lightly in 1 tablespoon olive oil (adding more if necessary to prevent scorching). Season the beaten eggs with salt and pepper. Add the remaining oil to the skillet and when this has been made hot, pour the eggs over the onions, stir over medium heat for a minute or so, and then proceed as for the conventional, plump, well-cooked (but not folded) omelet.

4 medium-size onions
4 cloves (1 per onion)
Water to cover
1 tablespoon vinegar
8 eggs, beaten
Salt and pepper
3 tablespoons olive oil

Poached or Boiled

Eggs with Anchovies (Oeufs aux Anchois)   SERVES 2

Put the tomato sauce in hot oil. When it is just bubbling, break the eggs into it, turn heat to medium and spoon the sauce over the eggs until they are set. Top with the anchovy fillets.

1 cup highly seasoned tomato
   sauce, preferably homemade
4 tablespoons olive oil
4 eggs
4 anchovy fillets

Poached Eggs Mireille
(Oeufs Pochés Mireille)

SERVES 4

Mix the boiled rice with just enough saffron sauce to color and flavor it. The saffron flavor should not dominate. Fill the pastry shells three-

1½ cups boiled rice
4 pastry shells
4 bread slices fried in oil
4 poached eggs
1 cup thick tomato sauce (page 32)
1 cup saffron sauce (See Béchamel Sauce, page 12)

quarters full of this rice and set them, alternately with the fried bread slices, on a hot platter. Lay a hot poached egg on each slice of bread and cover with saffron sauce. Spoon the tomato sauce over the rice in the pastry shells. Both sauces must be kept hot until the moment of serving.

Eggs Mollets (in the following recipe) may be substituted for poached eggs and some people consider them preferable.

Eggs Mollets (Oeufs Mollets)

These are a form of soft-boiled egg. The eggs should be at room temperature. They are put, very carefully, using a slotted spoon, into enough boiling water to completely cover them. The heat is then lowered and the eggs are cooked at hardly more than a simmer for 6 to 7 minutes, then lifted out (again with a slotted spoon) and placed in cold water. Shell them immediately. A light tap makes it possible to remove the shells without breaking the whites. To reheat, place in hot salted water for a few minutes. Don't let the water boil.

Scrambled

As with an omelet, eggs and egg mixtures to be scrambled must be lifted as they cook, allowing the uncooked portion to flow underneath. Scrambled eggs, however, should be removed from the heat before they are quite set because the warmth of the pan will complete the cooking, and a *"brouillade"* should stay soft.

Although the *Provencaux* favor the use of olive oil more than any other fat for most purposes, they concede the affinity of butter and eggs and sometimes, as in the recipe immediately following, even incorporate bits of cold butter in the batter.

Scrambled Eggs and Truffles (Brouillade aux Truffes)

SERVES 2

Since the only truffles most people are likely to come across in the United States are the bottled or canned variety and cost upwards of $1.25 per truffle (small size at that), this recipe has chiefly academic interest. However, anyone lucky enough to come across the big, flat, very dark mushrooms sometimes seen in Italian vegetable markets, can construct something very fine by way of facsimile.

Beat the eggs as for an omelet. Season with salt and pepper and then incorporate 1 tablespoon of cold butter cut in small pieces. Cut the truffles into discs (or chop them coarsely). Fold them into the beaten eggs. Melt the remaining tablespoon of butter, and when it is hot, turn the mixture into it and cook over low heat, stirring constantly, until it is almost set. Serve on a heated platter.

3 eggs
¼ pound truffles
Salt and pepper
2 tablespoons cold butter

Soufflé

Soufflé de Brandade

SERVES 3 OR 4

Add 4 beaten egg yolks to 2 cups of hot *Brandade de Morue* (page 96). Beat the 4 egg whites to a "snow" and fold these gently into the mixture. Butter a soufflé dish (or individual ramekins) and bake in a 350° oven for about 30 minutes, or until a silver knife thrust into the center of the dish comes out dry.

Stuffed Eggs

Eggs Stuffed with Anchovies (*Oeufs Farcis aux Anchois*)

SERVES 3 OR 4

Crush the tomatoes and cook them in the oil along with the onion and anchovies. Season with pepper and bay leaf. When the tomatoes are cooked, add the yolks of the eggs, mashed. Blend well. Garnish the egg whites with this mixture, reserving a little of it. This reserve, with the addition of the white wine, constitutes a little sauce which is poured over the eggs after they are arranged on a flame-proof platter. Put under the broiler for a moment to glaze.

2 medium-size tomatoes, peeled and seeded
1 tablespoon olive oil
1 small onion, chopped fine
3 tablespoons minced, freshened anchovies
1 tablespoon white wine
Pepper (but no salt!)
Bay leaf (small)
6 hard-boiled eggs, halved lengthwise

Lenten Stuffed Eggs
(*Oeufs Farcis au Maigre*)

SERVES 4

Mash together the egg yolks, anchovies, capers, and parsley. Season lightly to taste. Blend in the Béchamel Sauce (page 12), a tablespoonful at a time (because egg yolks differ in size, a full half-cup of sauce may not be needed — the mixture should be soft and smooth but not at all runny). Fill the egg whites with this farce, pressing pairs together to form whole eggs. Spread the remaining egg mixture in a shallow, heatproof baking dish. Place the stuffed egg whites on this bed, sprinkle them with bread crumbs, and dot each one with butter. Bake 10 minutes in a 350° oven.

6 hard-boiled eggs
3 tablespoons freshened, cleaned, boned, minced anchovies
1 tablespoon capers
3 sprigs of parsley, minced
Pepper and (very little) salt
½ cup (about) béchamel sauce, rather thick (1 tablespoon butter, 1 tablespoon flour, ½ cup milk)
Butter
Bread crumbs

X
Fish

MEDITERRANEAN FISH are different from those that swim in other waters. Even species classified under the same name — mackerel, sole, and tuna, for instance — have only a family resemblance, like wines from French grapes grown in California and in France. Happily, there are many excellent understudies for the major roles in Provençal fish dishes. And olive oil loves fish. Once these two blessings are recognized, gastronomes may be encouraged to take more enthusiastic advantage of the many available, usually inexpensive, less-known fishes in British and American markets. A dozen or more such "unknowns," commonly snubbed in favor of familiar varieties, may go into, for example, the rich purées that are the bases of many an opulent Provençal dish, such as *Bourride* (page 66). It is on just such tricks of knowledgeable preparation that a reputation for setting a distinguished table may rest.

The recipes that follow (after some directions that apply to fish in general) had, unavoidably, to be listed alphabetically by their French titles rather than English ones, as in the rest of the book. This is because, in most instances, any of several American fish are suitable, although, in each case, the first fish listed is the one usually considered the best substitute. A glance at the index will, in many cases, yield other interesting possibilities. Bass, for example, is the accepted proxy for *daurade,* but bream, grouper, porgy, and snapper will also do.

Something ought to be said right here about the term "bass," a designation that confuses practically everyone. There are so many kinds of bass (so-called) from both salt water and fresh: black bass, striped bass, little-mouth bass, sea bass, perch, etc. Even bar. The word itself is misleading, being a corruption of *bærs,* the Anglo-Saxon word for perch. Bass *is* perch. And the barsedized perch has dozens of cousins, including some with other names. Indeed, any of the spiny-finned, deep-bodied, edible sparoids can take over for *baudroie, daurade, loup, mulet,* or *rouget.* Striped bass is, of course, plentiful on the east coast of the United States, and the spunky black bass in lakes and streams. California's white sea bass differs in taste from either, but is a beautiful counterpart.

Broiling

An Ancient Broiling Technique for Non-fatty Fish

Because certain fish (*pageot,* that specialty of the Midi, particularly) tend to dry out when broiled, a special method of treatment for them was developed long ago by the Provençaux. Non-Mediterraneans, although they can't buy *pageot,* will find the method suited to many a dry-type fish they *can* buy (cod, haddock, or halibut, for example).

The recommended procedure is this: A few hours before fish is to be broiled it is immersed in a vessel containing just enough salted olive oil to cover (proportions, 1 teaspoon salt to 1 cup olive oil). It is exposed to strong sunlight for 3 to 4 hours, then drained and broiled.

Broiling is an essentially Provençal method of cooking fish and, indeed, is the treatment best suited to many of the Mediterranean fish. It improves the flavor of their delicate flesh and is a particularly good way to prepare any of the perch family (bass, bream, carp, mullet, porgies, scup, snapper, sea perch, sheepshead, etc.). The ideal procedure is as follows: Make several slanting incisions on each side of the scaled, eviscerated fish, and roll fish in olive oil. Place a frond of fresh fennel in each incision. Make a good bed of wood embers (or preheat electric grill or gas broiler). Place the fish on a rack over the embers (or under the broiler) and, during the cooking, baste with a branch of thyme soaked in oil, returning the thyme to the bowl of oil after each basting. If fresh thyme is not available, olive oil, generously seasoned with dried thyme, may be used. Turn the fish once during the cooking. The length of time is determined by the size and weight of the fish. Serve with mayonnaise or a *Rémoulade* Sauce (page 29). Some people think it enough just to sprinkle the fish with oil on the serving platter.

Mullet and saltwater perch may be flamed with fennel at the table. Light a branch of dry fennel and "present" it for several instants to the grilled fish. *Rouget,* however, is not flamed but, instead, after broiling, is served well sprinkled with olive oil. Connoisseurs set aside the liver when the fish is cleaned, cook it lightly, and mix it with the oil to make a sauce right on their plates.

Fresh sardines (young herring) may also be broiled (whole). They emerge crisp and delicious, but they should not be flamed.

It is important to remember that large fishes demand *moderate* broiling heat because they need longer cooking. For small fishes the fire may be brisk.

Sautéing

Poisson Meunière (Fish Meunière)

We hesitated to include this recipe under the heading of *cuisine provençale* because, often, butter is its dominant ingredient. However, after experiment, we are happy to state that, not only can it be given a Midi accent by the use of half olive oil and half butter, but that this has the advantage of preventing the butter from darkening.

The fish, having been cleaned and eviscerated, is rolled in flour and bedded down in a pot or pan where butter (the size of half an egg) sings with an equal amount of oil (about 2 or 3 tablespoons of each, depending, naturally, upon the size of the fish to be cooked). The fish is sautéed over gentle heat, an equal amount of time on each side. It is salted, peppered, and plattered forth sauced with the lovely juices from the pan and dressed in a thin coat of minced parsley trimmed with thin lemon slices.

For Cooked Fish

Poupeton de Poissons (Fish Mousse) SERVES 4

2½ cups cooked fish
½ cup (about) cream
½ cup bread crumbs
Milk
3 eggs
3 medium size mushrooms
½ teaspoon salt
¼ teaspoon pepper
3 medium size tomatoes
Olive oil
3 tablespoons grated cheese
Sautéed tomatoes

This recipe provides a fine way of using leftover fish such as bouillabaisse or *bourride*.

Pound the leftover fish in a mortar with enough cream to make a thick paste. Add the bread crumbs, briefly soaked in milk and then pressed out. When all is well blended, beat in, one at a time, 3 egg yolks and the grated cheese. Then fold in the egg whites, beaten to a "snow," the mushrooms, salt and pepper.

Pour the mixture into an oiled mold. Place the mold in a bowl of hot water, and bake about 20 to 25 minutes at 350°F. Serve promptly, surrounded by the tomatoes, thickly sliced and sautéed in oil. (Recipe of Dr. R. Boissier.)

Alose (Shad)

Alose à l'Avignonnaise
(Shad à l'Avignonnaise) SERVES 4

A 3-pound shad
4 tablespoons olive oil
Salt and pepper
½ lemon, sliced
⅓ cup cognac
½ pound sorrel, washed (or substitute spinach)

Cut the shad into slices about 2 inches thick. Put these into a baking dish with the oil, salt and pepper, lemon slices, and cognac. (It is the alcohol which, during the cooking, softens the bones of the shad). Add the sorrel or spinach. Cover the casserole tightly, and cook over low heat for 2 hours. At the end of the first hour, add a few tablespoons of water to the pot if necessary, but there should be very little moisture. Cover again snugly.

Eel is a food fish regrettably neglected in most American kitchens — and for no better reason, usually, than a dislike for its snaky looks. Yet the flesh, fresh or smoked, is delicious and should have a much larger and more appreciative public.

Provence has several types of eel from rivers, lakes, and the sea. In the United States, only the saltwater conger eel is known to most fishmongers, and even that must usually be spoken for in advance. However, any of the following recipes are adaptable to the conger. Also, if enough customers ask for eel, eel will be supplied. But — and this is *very* important — eel is a fish that must be fresh, beyond the slightest question. (In France it is always kept alive until the moment of purchase — except, of course, when smoked.) The flavor and texture are further improved if, when skinned, most of the layer of fat between skin and flesh is removed.

Anguille à la Broche (Eel on a Spit)   SERVES 4

Cut the eel into 2-inch (or slightly smaller) slices and set it to marinate for 24 hours in a glass or earthenware dish in the oil, with lemon juice, salt, pepper, thyme, and bay leaf.

To cook, thread the pieces alternately with the lemon slices on a spit or, lacking a spit, on small skewers. Broil, using medium flame. Baste with the marinade, turning the spit or skewers to grill on all sides.

A 1½-pound eel, skinned
4 tablespoons olive oil
1 tablespoon lemon juice
Salt and pepper
2 sprigs of thyme
1 bay leaf
1 lemon, sliced

Anguilles des Mariniers du Rhône (Rhône Bargemen's Eels)   SERVES 4

Cut fresh, skinned eel in pieces and roll these in seasoned flour. Meanwhile, chop and lightly brown the onion and the peeled, seeded tomatoes in the olive oil. Add the pieces of eel and when well-colored, add the red wine. Let cook 5 or 6 minutes over moderate heat. Then add the capers and the peeled, crushed cloves of garlic. Season highly with salt and pepper, and cook another minute or so before serving.

4 pounds eel, skinned
Seasoned flour
1 onion
2 tomatoes
3 tablespoons olive oil
¾ cup red wine
¼ cup (or more) capers
2 cloves garlic
Salt and pepper

Catigot d'Anguilles à la Gardiane
(A Ragout of Eels)

1 or 2 small eels per person
4 tablespoons olive oil
12 cloves garlic
   (peeled and crushed)
1 bay leaf
Sprig of thyme (or ¼ ounce dried)
Snip of hot pepper pod
Piece of orange peel
Salt
½ cup red wine

In an earthenware pot large enough to accommodate the number of eels to be cooked, combine the oil, garlic, bay leaf, thyme, orange peel, and pepper pod.

Skin the eels, cut them in pieces about 2 or 3 inches long, and salt them slightly. Put them into a saucepan, sprinkle the wine over them and add water to just cover. Simmer for 20 to 30 minutes, according to the thickness of the pieces of eel. Serve on hot plates.

Congre Braisé Provençale
(Braised Conger Eel)   SERVES 5 OR 6

4 tablespoons olive oil
2 carrots, peeled and minced
2 medium-size onions, peeled and
   minced
Piece of fresh fennel
Salt and pepper
Sprinkle of nutmeg
½ cup good white wine
Piece of eel (2 to 3 pounds), skinned

Pour the oil into an earthenware cooking pot and let it get hot. Add the vegetables and seasonings, and lay the piece of eel on this bed. Pour the wine over all and cook, covered, over very low heat for 45 minutes. Before serving, dust with a mixture of fine bread crumbs and minced parsley.

Terrine d'Anguille à la Martégale
(Baked Eels Martégale)   SERVES 8

5 pounds eel, skinned
White part of 3 medium size leeks,
   minced
4 cloves garlic, peeled and minced
½ cup parsley, chopped
Salt and pepper
2 bay leaves
1 cup stoned, black olives
1½ cup dry white wine
3 tablespoons olive oil
Bread crumbs

This is the dish traditionally served in Martigues for the "Big Supper" of Christmas Eve. It is an excellent recipe and deserves to be cherished and used.

Cover the bottom of a shallow ovenware dish with minced leeks to make a thick bed. Strew this with the parsley and garlic (mixed). Season with salt and pepper, add bay leaves and olives. Moisten with the wine and then bed down the eel on this fragrant couch. Powder her ["her" because connoisseurs say female eels are superior . . . and profess to be able to distinguish them from males] with bread crumbs and sprinkle her with oil. Bake for 1 to 1½ hours, depending on the thickness of the eel.

Baudroie de la Mère Figon
(*Bass or Hake Mère Figon*) SERVES 4–6

Fry the slices of fish in the oil (or oil and butter) over high heat. When well-colored, remove fish from skillet. In the oil left in the pan, cook the onion and tomato or tomato purée. Add the pounded anchovies and flour. Stir in the wine and water a little at a time to make a smooth sauce. Replace the fish slices. Season with salt and pepper to taste. Re-heat, and serve garnished with the olives and capers, and sprinkled with the mixed garlic and parsley.

2½ pounds bass or other substitute, sliced
3 tablespoons olive oil (or butter and oil, half-and-half)
1 medium-size onion, chopped
1 large tomato chopped (or 4 tablespoons tomato purée)
2 teaspoons flour
2 freshened, pounded anchovies
¼ cup white wine and water, half-and-half
¼ cup (or more) stoned black olives
2 to 3 tablespoons capers
Salt and pepper to taste
Garlic and parsley, minced

Baudroie à la Provençale
(*Bass or other Rockfish à la Provençale*) SERVES 4–6

Slice the fish into serving portions and brown them in 2 tablespoons of the oil. Cook the mussels in the water with bay leaf, thyme, salt and pepper until they open (about 5 minutes). Discard shells and strain the liquor through a very fine sieve. Reduce liquor, if necessary, until there is about three-quarters of a cup of it. Combine this with the white wine and pour over the fish in a baking pan. Add more salt and pepper if needed and bake the fish at low heat, turning the slices to cook them through.

Meanwhile, cook the minced onion in 1 tablespoon of oil over medium heat until soft. Then moisten it with some of the liquid from the baking pan. Cut the bread in slices slightly larger than the slices of fish. Rub with garlic and fry them in oil. Arrange the fish on the bread, surround it with the mussels and cover the whole with the tomato sauce.

The amount of sauce, however, is a matter of personal preference. Some like the fish generously covered, others prefer only a light glaze with the fish showing through.

2½ pounds bass or substitute
2 quarts mussels (in their shells)
1½ cups water
1 bay leaf
Sprig of thyme (or ¼ teaspoon dried)
Salt and pepper
½ cup oil (about)
¾ cup white wine
1 onion, minced
1 clove garlic, peeled
8 slices of bread
2 cups (more or less) thick tomato sauce

Filets de Baudroie Raimu (Rockfish Raimu) SERVES 4

2 cups Fish Soup (page 40) strained

2 pounds fillets of bass or other rockfish

1 pint mussels or winkles, steamed open (page 123)

8 slices of bread, lightly fried in oil

3 tablespoons *Aïoli* (page 24)

1 tablespoon *Rouille* (page 20)

Lemon juice

Chopped parsley

This excellent dish was created by chef G. L. Panuel in honor of the great actor, Raimu, to whom it has been dedicated. It is elaborate, and is best made when the larder already has *aïoli* and fish soup at hand, but it is well worth the effort of making.

Poach the fish fillets in the strained fish soup along with the mussels or winkles. When the fillets are cooked through, transfer them carefully to the slices of fried bread, reserving mussels. Reduce the liquor in which the fish was cooked until there is about one cupful. Then, away from the heat, blend in the *aïoli* and the *rouille*. Cover the fillets with this sauce and garland the platter with the mussels and winkles. Sprinkle with lemon juice, shower lightly with parsley . . . and rejoice!

Daurade

This wonderfully gaudy Mediterranean fish, noted for the delicacy of its flesh, has no exact counterpart in American and English waters. Even in France, a number of other attractively tinted fish are frequently substituted, sold under a name that sounds the same but is written "dorade." However, sea bream serves very well and so do grouper, pollack, porgy, snapper, etc. Any recipe given in these pages for mullet is also suitable for daurade and its substitutes.

Daurade Farcie (Sea Bream, Sea Bass, or Equivalent Stuffed with Mussels)

A whole, cleaned, 3-pound fish

1 quart mussels

2 cups white wine

1 small onion (sliced)

1 clove garlic

½ teaspoon dried thyme, 1 bay leaf

1 onion (chopped)

1 tomato (chopped) or ¼ cup tomato purée

¼ cup olive oil

Salt and pepper

¼ cup chopped parsley

1 hard-boiled egg, minced

1 tablespoon butter

1 tablespoon flour

1 egg yolk, slightly beaten

Open the mussels by steaming them in a saucepan over medium heat with the wine, onion *slices,* garlic, and the herbs (mixed). Remove the shells. Strain, reserving the cooking liquor.

Cook the *chopped* onion and the tomato or tomato purée in the olive oil. Season with salt and pepper. Add the parsley and minced egg. Stir in the mussels. Make an incision in the stomach of the cleaned fish, and stuff the cavity with the mixture. Sew up (or skewer) the opening. Sprinkle the fish with oil, and bake it on an ovenware platter at 350°, basting frequently with small quantities of oil and wine.

To the strained liquor from the cooked mussels, add the butter and flour, blended together into a paste. Stir this for several minutes over low heat to eliminate the raw taste of the flour, then beat in the raw egg yolk. Stir (again over low heat) to cook the egg. Check for seasoning. Serve the fish blanketed with this sauce.

Daurade à la Niçoise
(Baked Stuffed Porgy or equivalent) SERVES 4

Brown the fish well on both sides in hot oil and then transfer to a baking dish. Season with salt and pepper. Sprinkle with oil. Cover with thick, seeded slices of tomatoes. Bake at 400° for 10 or more minutes, depending upon the thickness of the fish. Baste with oil 2 or 3 times during the cooking. Several minutes before taking it from the oven, strew it with the anchovies wrapped around olives.

A 2-pound whole fish
Olive oil
Salt and pepper
3 large tomatoes
Anchovies
Stoned black olives

Daurade à la Provençale
(Bass, Bream, Mullet, etc. à la Provençale) SERVES 4

Roll the fish in flour seasoned with salt and pepper. Fry in oil over medium heat until cooked through. Remove from pan and keep warm. Meanwhile, lightly brown the minced onion in the oil left in the pan. Stir in flour and continue stirring over low heat until a golden *roux* is produced. Then add the water, wine, garlic, tomato, and *bouquet garni*. Cook this gently until the sauce is somewhat reduced. Remove the *bouquet garni* and mask the fish in the sauce. Serve on hot plates.

A 2-pound bass (or equivalent)
Salt and pepper
Olive oil
1 tablespoon flour
1 medium-size onion, minced
½ cup water
Scant ½ cup dry white wine
1 small clove garlic
1 fat tomato, seeded and chopped
   (or ¼ cup tomato purée)
Bouquet garni

Daurade à la Toulonnaise

Make a bed of sliced tomatoes and onion rings in an ovenware platter and, allowing about ½ pound of fish per person, lay the fish on top of it. Season with salt and pepper plus one or two sprigs of fennel fern. Moisten generously with white wine and cover with chopped shallots, garlic, and parsley, mixed together. Bake at 350° (allow about 7 minutes per pound) and serve surrounded by cooked, shelled mussels.

Loup

Loup au Bleu des Martigues
(Bass or Catfish of Martigues)

SERVES 4

½ medium-size onion, sliced
2 peeled, crushed cloves garlic
2 freshened anchovies, boned and mashed
2½-pound catfish or bass
Salt (stingy) and pepper
Scant ½ cup white wine
Scant ½ cup bouillon or water
1 tablespoon flour
1 tablespoon olive oil
"Walnut" (about 1 tablespoon) butter
Lemon juice

In an oiled baking pan, toss together the sliced onion, garlic, and anchovies. Place the bass or catfish on this bed. Season, going light on salt because of the anchovies. Moisten with white wine and bouillon (or water), half-and-half (about ¾ cup in all) and bake in a moderate (325° to 350°) oven for about 25 minutes.

Separately, lightly brown the flour, blending into it the olive oil. When the fish is cooked, pour the juices from the pan into the brown *roux* and whip briskly with a wire whisk. Let this cook for a minute or two over low heat, stirring continually. Then enrich the sauce with a "walnut" of butter. Stir in a few drops of lemon juice and, at the moment of serving, either blanket the fish in the sauce or serve it separately.

Loup Farci (Stuffed Bass or Catfish)

Follow recipe for *Daurade Farcie* on page 88.

Loup Farci, Grillé et Flambé à la Farigoulette
(Bass or other Rockfish with Wild Thyme
Stuffing, Grilled and Flamed)

This is quite a dish!

Choose a fine bass or other rockfish, eviscerated and cleaned. After having salted and peppered it, garnish the interior with a mixture of tarragon-flavored mustard, tomato purée, several thin slices of onions and tomatoes, and finish by stuffing a bouquet of wild thyme into the cavity.

Make two, slightly diagonal incisions, lengthwise, on each side of the fish from head to tail, cutting clear through to the bone. Bathe these, as you did the insides, with tarragon mustard. Salt and pepper the skin, then slide thin slices of onions and fresh tomatoes into the slits.

Put the fish, thus prepared, on an oiled baking pan and sprinkle, generously, with more olive oil. Ideally, the fish is grilled over wood embers for several minutes on each side but "indoor cooks" will have to make do with gas or electric broilers. In any case, when the fish is brown outside and half cooked (about 4 minutes on each side), pour over it the sauce left in the bottom of the pan, and finish the cooking in a 325° oven, basting frequently with the juices the fish yields up.

Transfer the fish, carefully, to a metal platter, moisten with the juices and surmount it with a bouquet of wild thyme, previously dried and heated in the oven. Light this and carry the platter, flaming, to the table with (if the fish is large) an apple in its mouth [a surprise for any fish!].

Loup de Roche aux Herbes à la Façon du Maître (Rock Bass or Catfish in the Style of the Master) SERVES 6

This recipe, conceived by Georges Caracci, Fish Chef of the Palais de la Méditerranée at Nice, won First Prize at the Auguste Escoffier Culinary Conference in 1953. It is reproduced here, just as it was written, chiefly for the reader's interest in the length to which an imaginative chef will go to impress competitors and astonish his public. It is a fine dish, of course. But, for fear of discouraging some other valiant cook, we have not headed the recipe with the list of ingredients. Let that hardy soul make his own marketing list!

Choose a handsome local bass, catfish, or other rockfish (about 3 pounds). Season its insides with salt and freshly ground pepper. Stuff it with herbs (chervil and tarragon), plus celery and fennel cut into thin straws, minced onions and shallots. Fill the head with sprigs of rosemary, thyme, and bay leaf. Immerse the fish, very carefully, for a few seconds, in a deep pan of boiling water. The skin may then be easily sponged off with a cloth.

Generously butter a cooking pan of suitable dimensions and place the fish in it, covered with blanched lettuce leaves, and well-moistened with a sauce which is made as follows:

Gently simmer, in 1 pound of butter, the flesh of a few inexpensive local fish, along with some mushrooms, garlic, and vinegar. Finish with a bit of garlic and about 1 cup of champagne. Add peppercorns. Simmer several minutes. Put the sauce through a food mill and pour it over the fish.

Bake the sauced fish for about 20 minutes, basting often. Transfer it to a hot platter. Reduce the remaining sauce somewhat. Top the fish with unsalted butter. Add more salt and pepper if needed, and then blanket the fish completely with the sauce which should be dense. Garnish with several fine slices of truffle.

The fish should be accompanied by Antiboise Sauce which is a Béarnaise Sauce (page 12), lightly fortified with crushed, fresh tomatoes and finely chopped onions cooked in butter with a "point" of garlic, *fines herbes,* and a pinch of basil. Serve very hot with little steamed potatoes.

Maquereaux (Mackerel)

Maquereaux à la Crème d'Anchois (Mackerel with Anchovy Butter)

Simple and very Provençal is this treatment for mackerel: Bake a split and boned (optional) mackerel, flesh side up, in a generously oiled dish for 15 to 20 minutes at 350° and, while it is still very hot, spread it with anchovy butter (page 14).

Maquereaux à la Martégale

Select small "tinker" mackerel for this dish — 1 or 2 per person, depending on size. Clean and flour them, season with salt and pepper, and cook over moderate heat in hot olive oil until they are nicely browned all over. Remove from pan and keep them hot.

Add 2 tablespoons (or more) olive oil to the pan and 2 or 3 peeled, whole cloves of garlic. When the garlic starts to brown, add a bay leaf and cook over high heat for one minute. Sprinkle the cooked fish with lemon juice and spoon the garlic over it.

Slices of pollack or whiting may be prepared the same way.

Maquereaux au Fenouil (Mackerel with Fennel)

Dried fennel stalks are specified for this dish. These are difficult to obtain outside of Provence. But when fresh fennel is in season, a very agreeable dish of mackerel may be prepared by making a bed of fennel cut into "straws" in a lavishly oiled skillet. This is covered and cooked for a few minutes. Tinker mackerel, 1 or 2 per person, are then laid on top, salted and peppered and sluiced with water. Cover and cook over low heat for 15 to 20 minutes. Separately beat the yolks of 2 eggs with a pinch of powdered fennel. Add a large "walnut" of butter, salt and pepper, and cook in a double boiler, stirring constantly, until mixture is thickened and smooth. Cover the mackerel with this sauce.

Melet (Whitebait)

Friture de Melet
(French-fried Whitebait)

1 POUND SERVES 4 OR 5

Whitebait, known as *blanchailles* throughout most of France, travels under a number of aliases in Provence: *melet, nonats* (or *nounats*), and *poutina.* By whichever name, it is the young, "small fry" of eels, herrings, sprats, and (probably) related fishes. *Poutina,* however, is netted so young that some of the little fishes aren't quite out of their eggs yet, and this roe is cooked along with the whitebait as in the famous "Whitebait and Oyster Crabs" of the old Ritz-Carlton Hotel in New York. The whitebait are often prepared the same way; that is to say, they are spread on a clean cloth, doused with lemon juice or vinegar, rolled in flour, and deep fried. In Provence, the fat is, of course, olive oil. They are then salted and served in their golden crisp beauty with lemon juice or lemon wedges.

They may also be sautéed in shallow fat in which a little minced onion has been lightly cooked. Browned in this flavored oil, then salted and peppered, they are delicious.

Whitebait fritters are much the same thing. The little fish are dipped, a ladleful at a time, in fritter batter, and fried in deep hot (370°) oil.

Merlan (Whiting)

Merlan à la Marseillaise

SERVES 4

Heat the mussels with the water until the shells open and can be removed and discarded. Strain the cooking liquor through a very fine sieve or muslin cloth to remove the sand. Reserve the strained liquor and (of course) the mussels.

Arrange the small whiting or whiting slices in a skillet with the *bouquet garni,* onion, and carrot. Season with salt and pepper. Pour the mussel liquor over the fish in the skillet. Cover, and set over quick heat. As soon as the fish (which should be carefully turned once) is cooked through, remove it from the pan. Reduce the bouillon if necessary. There should be about 1 cup. Remove pan from heat and blend in the 2 egg yolks. Add a few drops of lemon juice. Reheat the sauce at low temperature. Add the mussels and pour over the fish.

2¼ pounds mussels
1 cup water
4 small whiting or slices of larger whiting, allowing ½ pound per person
Bouquet garni
1 onion, peeled and minced
1 carrot, peeled and minced
Salt and pepper
2 egg yolks, beaten
Lemon juice

Merlan à la Provençale

For this dish it is best to use large whiting and have it filleted. Allow, roughly, ½ pound of fillets and 1 medium-size tomato per person. Peel, seed, and chop the tomatoes, and cook them for a few minutes in olive oil with salt, pepper, and a minced clove of garlic. Carpet a shallow baking dish with a layer of tomatoes. Arrange the fish over the tomatoes and cover with another layer of tomatoes. Sprinkle with bread crumbs and a few drops of olive oil. Bake 15 to 20 minutes at 350°. Garnish with parsley. Mackerel may be prepared the same way.

Merlan à la Toulonnaise

Roll slices of whiting — 1 per person — in flour. Fry them in oil. Drain on absorbent paper and keep hot.

Prepare a thick tomato sauce (page 32) without salt.

Open 1 pound of mussels in ½ cup of water over medium heat. Remove from shells as soon as they are open. Strain 1 cup of the cooking broth through fine muslin or a double layer of cheesecloth and add it, with the shelled mussels, to the tomato sauce. Simmer until the sauce is somewhat reduced in quantity.

Arrange the slices of fried fish on a hot platter and blanket them in the tomato-mussel sauce.

Merlan en Raïto

Flour, fry, and drain the fish as in the above recipe and then simmer it for a few minutes in *Raïto* sauce (page 31) and serve very hot.

Merlan Frit aux Tomates
(Fried Whiting with Tomatoes)

Cut large whiting into slices of equal thickness (1 slice per person). Flour these and brown them in oil. Separately, fry 2 thick slices of seeded tomatoes per person. Serve the fish surrounded by tomato slices and the whole strewed with mixed chopped parsley and garlic.

Salt cod (*morue*), because it travels well, keeps well, and is available all year, is an immensely popular food in Provence and, indeed, in Spain, Portugal, and other parts of the world. It is sadly neglected in the United States, except for certain sections of New England. But the *Provençaux* convert it into dozens of dishes full of character, the most famous among these being, of course, *brandade de morue,* almost as representative of the cuisine as the better-known bouillabaisse.

Salt cod in the United States is usually sold, already filleted, and packed in 1-pound packages or little wooden boxes, and readers are strongly advised to use this type for all recipes, rather than stockfish. Stockfish is the dried salt cod one sees, split, flattened, and stiff as a board, hanging around in food stores of foreign sections. It must be soaked for days in many changes of water before anything can be done with it, and that with unpredictable results. (See also page 20.)

Salt cod must almost always be "freshened" before it can be used. Standard procedure is to soak it in cold water to cover, overnight or longer. It is then drained, covered again with cold water and gently poached — preferably in a *non-metal* cooking vessel — until the flesh flakes easily. After this it is ready to be put to its many delectable uses.

Morue à la Mode de Besagne
(Salt Cod as Prepared in Besagne) SERVES 3 TO 4

Cut the fish in bite-size pieces. Poach these in water to cover, drain, and set aside. Color the onion in the olive oil and add to it the tomatoes, coarsely chopped, or tomato purée, parsley, garlic, bay leaf, salt and pepper. Cover and simmer these ingredients for about 20 minutes. Then add the potatoes and enough additional hot water to completely immerse them. Continue cooking, over low heat. As soon as the potatoes are done, spread the mixture over the poached cod, and simmer for 5 minutes longer, adding the olives and the pinch of saffron.

1 pound freshened salt cod fillets
1 tablespoon olive oil
2 tablespoons chopped onion
2 tomatoes, peeled and seeded (or ½ cup tomato purée)
1 peeled, crushed clove garlic
1 tablespoon chopped parsley
Tiny pinch of salt
Pinch of pepper
1 bay leaf
4 medium-size peeled potatoes
½ cup stoned black olives
Pinch of saffron

Beignets de Morue à la Pernoise
(Garlicky Codfish Fritters à la Pernoise) SERVES 4 TO 6

2 cups Brandade de Morue (see below)
1 cup freshly mashed, unseasoned, potatoes
3 or 4 eggs, beaten as for an omelet
Flour
Oil

Blend the *brandade*, mashed potatoes, and eggs together. Place this mixture on a floured board or tabletop, and make balls of it the size of an egg. Flatten these and fry them in oil. Note, however, that these "fritters" should *not* be deep-fried. You need just enough oil in the pan so that, as soon as one side has taken a nice color, the fritter can be turned and browned on the other side without swimming.

Brandade de Morue

2 pounds freshened salt cod fillets, blanched (page 20)
4 cups olive oil
1¼ cups milk
1 clove garlic, peeled
White pepper
Lemon juice
Fried bread (or patty shells)
(Optional) truffles

According to the Larousse etymological dictionary, the word *brandade* is borrowed from the modern Provençal word meaning "something stirred." The dish is also known in Provence as *gangasse* from another word, *gangasser,* which also means "to stir." Some iconoclasts recommend the use of an electric blender for this mandatory stirring, but purists tolerate no such tampering with traditional procedure. Furthermore, they insist the results are not all the same. With or without mechanical aids, here is a *brandade* for 6 persons.

Bring both the olive oil and the milk to room temperature and keep them tepid throughout the entire process of "mounting" your *brandade.*

Pound the garlic in a mortar. Add the blanched codfish and pound both to a soft paste. At this point, start incorporating the olive oil a scant teaspoonful at a time, alternating with drops of warm milk, but without ever ceasing to stir rapidly; the *brandade* gains in fine texture through rapid stirring. If it becomes too thick, add more warm oil and milk. Complete the seasoning by adding a few drops of lemon juice (to taste) and fine white pepper. A *brandade* should have the consistency of mashed potatoes (which it looks like). It is served warm, *not hot,* surrounded by slices of bread fried in oil, or — and this is a fine way to serve it — in a *vol-au-vent* crust or individual patty shells (preferably homemade). For a richer dish, one or two sliced or chopped truffles are scattered over the surface of the *brandade.*

Morue en Brochettes
(Salt Cod Broiled on Skewers)

Cut freshened (see page 20) cod fillets into cubes 1¼ inches in diameter. Thread these on skewers alternately with cherry tomatoes. Roll the loaded skewers in olive oil and then in bread crumbs, and place them under the broiler or on a grill over a good bed of embers (preferably of vine shoots). Broil and serve at once.

Morue en Capilotade
(Salt Cod Casserole with Capers)   SERVES 4 OR 5

The term *capilotade* comes to France from Italy by way of Spain . . . but, wherever it turns up, it means "with capers."

Cut the cod fillets in pieces and fry them in 2 tablespoons oil. Arrange them in an ovenware dish. Meanwhile, prepare a sauce as follows: Color the chopped onion in the remaining oil. Add the vinegar, and let the liquid reduce over moderate heat. Then stir in the flour and, using a wire whip, beat in the bouillon or water. Add the capers and *bouquet garni*. Simmer for 25 to 30 minutes. Season with pepper *only* (no salt). Pour this sauce over the pieces of fried cod, completely blanketing them. Simmer over very low heat (or bake in a 250° oven) for 30 minutes longer — but watch to make sure it never boils.

1 pound freshened cod fillets (page 20)
3 tablespoons olive oil
¾ cup vinegar
2 tablespoons chopped onion
4 tablespoons flour
3 cups (about) hot water or bouillon
2 tablespoons capers
Bouquet garni
Pepper

Le "Chopin" de Morue Victor Petit   SERVES 5 OR 6

The origin of the term "chopin" is obscure. One thing is certain: it has no connection with the pianist and composer. One clue the translator finds is in the verb *chopiner,* which means "to drink long," and this the diner would certainly do. The dish was named in honor of a brilliant journalist of Toulon — "a knowledgeable gastronome." He must also sometimes have been a thirsty one. One meaning of *chopin* is "a windfall" or "piece of good luck . . . also an amorous conquest. But *chopiner* is to tipple.

Cut the freshened cod in pieces and steam them for about 30 or 40 minutes.

While the codfish is yielding up its juices, boil the potatoes and onions. This done, and the codfish cooked, crumble the fish into a salad bowl. Then peel and quarter the potatoes and toss them into the salad bowl along with the onions, cut in small pieces. Finally, gently mix

1 pound freshened cod fillets (page 20)
4 medium-size potatoes in their jackets
2 peeled onions
Olive oil
Lemon juice
Pinch of salt (or none)

together the contents of the bowl, moisten with oil and lemon juice, salting stingily, if at all. "I dare claim," Victor Petit commented, "that this humble treat is worthy of consideration by the most exacting gourmets."

Morue aux Épinards
(Salt Cod Baked with Spinach)

SERVES 6

1 pound freshened salt cod
   fillets (page 20)
1 tablespoon chopped onion
1 pound (about) fresh spinach
1 large clove garlic, minced
2 tablespoons olive oil
1 tablespoon flour
1 cup hot milk
½ teaspoon pepper
Salt (perhaps)
½ teaspoon dry mustard
½ cup bread crumbs

Cut the freshened cod in pieces and poach them. Cook, drain, and chop the spinach. Brown the chopped onion in 1 tablespoon oil along with the minced garlic. Combine the spinach, onion, and flour. Add the milk and blend well. Season with pepper and mustard plus (cautiously) a little salt. Cook over low heat for 5 or 6 minutes.

Spread half the spinach mixture in the bottom of a baking dish. Cover with the codfish and top with the rest of the spinach. Strew the bread crumbs over the top, sprinkle with the remaining oil (more oil may be added if crumbs seem dry), and set the dish in a hot oven to brown.

Morue à la Marseillaise

SERVES 6

1 pound freshened salt cod fillets
3 onions, peeled and chopped
2 large tomatoes, peeled, seeded and
   chopped (or ½ cup tomato purée)
3 tablespoons olive oil
4 peeled, quartered potatoes
¾ cup white wine
½ cup hot water
Pepper to taste
¼ pound mushrooms, sliced, (or
   2 tablespoons dried mushrooms
   briefly soaked in water and drained)
¼ cup desalted green olives

Sauté the onions lightly in the olive oil. Add the tomatoes or tomato purée and stir over low heat for a few minutes.

Cut the cod fillets in small pieces and add them, along with the potatoes, to the onion-tomato mixture. Stir over medium heat for 3 or 4 minutes. Add wine and hot water. Season with pepper. Bring contents of saucepan to a boil then lower the heat and cook gently until the potatoes are almost done. Add the mushrooms. Simmer until these are cooked through. Serve, garnished with the olives (whole, halved, or sliced).

Morue à la "Matrasso"

This is an ancient Provençal recipe for salt cod and, although the origin of the name is obscure, it must surely derive from *matras* — a round-bottomed glass flask with a long neck. For here is a meal that is guaranteed to start a terrible drought.

Grill the salt cod over a wood fire, without having previously freshened it, and then eat it, just as it is, moistened only with a little vinegar, and accompanied by several cloves of garlic and some potatoes baked in the hot ashes. [And reach for the flagon!]

Morue à la Niçoise
SERVES 4

Civilized man has learned the delight inherent in certain food contrasts: apple pie and cheddar; apricots and sour cream; curry and Bombay "duck"; sausage and pancakes. Salt cod and sweet potatoes are another such, new to the Anglo-Saxon palate, but a happy surprise.

Cut the freshened cod in bite-size pieces. Dip these in batter and sauté them in hot olive oil. Drain well.

In a little of the oil from the pan, color the onion, garlic, and tomato or tomato purée. Dredge with flour and moisten with water. Peel and quarter the sweet potatoes and submerge them completely in the sauce (adding more water if necessary). Season with pepper (omitting salt). Add the *bouquet garni* and olives. Cover and cook over gentle heat. When the potatoes are almost done, add the pieces of fried codfish, being careful not to break them. Continue cooking for a few minutes longer. Arrange on a hot platter with the potatoes.

¾ pound freshened salt cod fillets
Frying batter (page 12)
Olive oil
1 onion, peeled and chopped
1 peeled, crushed clove garlic
1 large tomato, peeled, seeded, and coarsely chopped (or ¼ cup tomato purée)
Flour
A little water
2 medium-size sweet potatoes
Pepper
Bouquet garni
¼ cup stoned black olives

Ragoût de Morue (Salt Cod Stew)
SERVES 4

In English, unfortunately, the word "stew" evokes no irresistible picture. By contrast, in France, the synonym *ragoût* has such connotations of lusciousness that *ragoûter* is a verb meaning "to restore the appetite." Of something untempting, the French say, *"Ce mets-là n'est guère ragoûtant."* (That dish isn't very appetizing.) Maybe when a stew is called a *ragoût,* it turns out better.

Simmer the onion and tomato (or tomato purée) in a saucepan with oil until they are well cooked. Add the potatoes plus water to just cover. Season with the *bouquet garni* and the garlic. Cover, and cook over gentle heat for 10 to 12 minutes.

Meanwhile, cut the freshened cod in squares, dredge these with flour, and fry them in oil in a separate pan.

As soon as the potatoes are cooked, add the fried fish, and sauté all together for a few minutes. Before serving, sprinkle with chopped parsley and scatter tiny black olives over the platterful.

¾ pound freshened, poached salt cod fillets
1 peeled, chopped onion
1 peeled, chopped tomato (or ¼ cup tomato purée)
Olive oil
3 peeled, quartered potatoes
Water to cover
Bouquet garni
1 whole clove garlic
Flour
Chopped parsley
½ cup tiny black olives

Morue à la Saint-Tropez

SERVES 4

¾ pound freshened salt cod fillets
¼ cup dried mushrooms
4 tablespoons olive oil
1 peeled, chopped onion
2 peeled, seeded, chopped tomatoes
3 peeled, sliced potatoes
1 cup white wine
1 cup hot water
Pepper and (*careful!*) salt
Pinch of saffron
Green olives

Another ragout for the appetite.

Set the dried mushrooms to soften in water to cover.

Cook the onion and tomatoes in 2 tablespoons of the oil over moderate heat until the onion is soft. Cut the cod fillets in pieces and simmer these in the onion-tomato mixture until fish is partly cooked. Separately, brown the potatoes rapidly in the remaining oil and add them to the fish. Moisten with the wine and simmer until liquid in pan is reduced by about half. Then add the hot water. Season with pepper and (cautiously) salt. Raise the heat slightly and mix in the mushrooms (drained) and the olives. Stir in the pinch of saffron and cook until the potato slices are just done.

Morue du Toréador

SERVES 4

2 red bell peppers, sliced
5 tablespoons olive oil
2 chopped tomatoes
1 pound leaf spinach
    (not chopped)
¾ pound freshened salt
    cod fillets
2 unpeeled cloves garlic
1 cup Mornay Sauce
Fried onion rings

Sauté the sliced peppers in 2 tablespoons olive oil, and cook the tomatoes separately in 1 tablespoon oil. Blanch the spinach by dropping it into a large potful of rapidly boiling water. Boil 3 minutes. Drain well, pressing out all the excess liquid.

Poach the cod. When it is soft, drain, dry, and separate it into squares which you sauté with 2 garlic cloves in the remaining 2 tablespoons of oil.

Arrange the fish on an ovenware platter with the peppers, spinach, and tomatoes around it, alternating the colors, and finish with a thin layer of tomatoes and peppers, mixed. Cover lightly with Mornay Sauce (page 34). Put the dish under the broiler for a few minutes to glaze, and serve, surrounded by fried onion rings.

Mulet (Mullet)

Mullet — gray, red, or striped — are all good choices for *mulet* recipes. But so is bass. In fact, *Larousse Gastronomique* clearly states, ". . . all recipes for bass are suitable for gray mullet."

Mulet à la Ligure

SERVES 3 OR 4

Rinse the cleaned fish and dry well. Season with salt, freshly ground pepper, and mustard. Sprinkle generously with oil, and broil. When cooked on both sides, set the fish aside on a platter to keep warm.

Dissolve the meat extract in the white wine. Chop and combine the mushrooms, onion, and (optional) truffle. Mix with the bread crumbs. Coat the fish with this mixture. Sprinkle with a little more wine if the crumbed surfaces look too dry. Dot with butter and bake 10 minutes in a 375° oven. Serve very hot.

1 4-pound bass or mullet (or four small ones)
Salt and pepper
Mustard
Olive oil
1 teaspoon meat extract (see page 18)
4 medium-size mushrooms
1 small onion, peeled
(Optional) 1 truffle
4 tablespoons soft bread crumbs
Butter
½ cup white wine (plus)

Mulet à la Martégale

ALLOW ½ POUND PER PERSON

A very simple way to treat mullet or bass is to lay the fish, seasoned with salt and pepper, on a bed of tomato slices and onion rings, in an ovenproof dish. Moisten liberally with oil and top the fish with a layer of overlapping thin slices of lemon. Bake the fish, thus prepared, in a medium (350°) oven. The juices should be allowed to reduce considerably. If they are still too abundant by the time the fish is nicely cooked, remove the fish and keep it warm. Raise the heat and simmer the *cuisson* (pan juices) until they are boiled down to about half the original volume.

Mulet au Vin Blanc

SERVES 6

Remove the black skin of the interior surfaces of a cleaned, 4-pound mullet or bass. Salt and pepper the cavity and line it with a garnish composed of the fennel, bay leaf, parsley, and (optional) garlic.

Pour the oil into a heatproof platter. Add the lightly fried onion. Place the fish on this "couch," and sprinkle with the dry white wine. Powder with fine bread crumbs, cover with buttered paper (butter-side down, of course), and bake at 350° for about 25 minutes, basting frequently with the juices from the pan, adding wine and water, mixed half-and-half, if more basting liquor is needed.

4-pound mullet or bass
Salt and pepper
Spray of fennel, bay leaf
Small bouquet of parsley
(Optional) 1 clove garlic
3 tablespoons olive oil
1 sliced, fried onion
¾ cup dry white wine
Fine bread crumbs
Butter
Wine and water, half-and-half

Rougets

According to *Larousse Gastronomique, rouget* is a name given to several species of fish which have little in common except their color. Escoffier refers readers to red mullet. Waverley Root, however, in his *Food of France* (that most comprehensive and informative book) is skeptical about this definition and thinks *rouget* is "a sort of *grondin*." But he and we agree that *rouget* in Provence (especially in Toulon) is a delicious thing. In the absence of true *rouget* (whoever he is), bass or red mullet may be substituted in all of the following recipes.

Rougets Clarisse

1 fish (about ½ pound) per person
Salt and pepper
Olive oil
Powdered rosemary
Powdered thyme
Fresh parsley
Lemon juice
2 or 3 truffles
Meat extract

Prick the fish lightly all over with the tines of a fork. Season with salt and pepper. Sprinkle with olive oil and then with powdered rosemary and thyme. Stuff the interiors with sprigs of parsley. Sprinkle the fish liberally with lemon juice and set them aside to marinate for 30 minutes or so in this aromatic bath. Then broil them, basting frequently with the marinade.

Separately, melt 2 or 3 tablespoons meat extract in 3 or 4 tablespoons olive oil. Season with salt and pepper. Heat the truffles in this just long enough to warm them. Cover the fish with this sauce. Bake 5 or 6 minutes in a 350° oven. Serve, garnished with chopped parsley. (Recipe of Auguste Escoffier.)

Rougets au Fenouil sous la Cendre
(Bass or Mullet with Fennel Baked in Hot Ashes)

Bass
Bread crumbs
1 slice fennel
Butter
Olive oil
Salt and pepper

Allow one fish (¼ pound to ½ pound each) per person. Garnish their interiors, using the livers mashed with a combination of bread crumbs (soaked in water and pressed out), minced fennel, and butter, creamed to a paste with olive oil — proportioned approximately as follows: 1 part livers to 1 part soaked crumbs, half as much fennel, one-quarter as much oil creamed with the same amount of butter as oil. Stuff and tie up fish.

Season the fish with salt and pepper. Wrap each one first with a piece of oiled white paper which has been sprinkled with minced fennel, then with 2 pieces of *un*-oiled paper. Seal with a flour-and-water paste.

Place the wrapped fish on a thick bed of hot ashes. Cover with another thick layer of very hot ashes over which are placed several glowing coals. Cook thus for 20 minutes. To serve, lift away the (by then, charred) outer layers of paper and serve the fish, just as they are, in the sheets of oiled paper. (Recipe of Prosper Montagne.)

Rougets aux Feuilles de Vigne

For this dish, allow 2 rock mullet (or bass) weighing about ¼ pound each for every person to be served. Clean the fish but do not remove the livers. Make diagonal incisions along their backbones. Season with salt and pepper and oil the fish copiously. Wrap in vine leaves which have been plunged in boiling water for a minute or two to make them supple.

Arrange the fish on a long, handsome, heatproof dish. Sprinkle with oil. Bake 15 to 20 minutes at 375°. Serve in the baking dish. (Recipe of Auguste Escoffier.)

Rougets au Gratin à la Salonaise   SERVES 4

1 3-pound bass or mullet
1 small onion, minced
5 tablespoons butter, creamed
1 cup coarsely chopped fennel
2 cups water
1 cup milk
2 tablespoons flour
Salt and pepper

We are indebted for this recipe to one of the foremost epicures in Provence. Note that it has the great merit of respecting the classic method of cooking *rouget*, which is to broil it and then to finish it with a highly accented Provençal sauce. A perfect dish which demonstrates how cooks can be inventive while still observing classic procedures.

Choose medium-size mullet or bass, scaled and eviscerated. Carefully remove and reserve the livers. Fill the interior of each fish with minced onion and 3 tablespoons butter. Oil and broil under (or over) medium heat.

Cook the fennel in the water. Let this reduce; after removing the fennel, there should be only 1 cup of fennel "infusion." Mix this liquor with the milk. Melt the remaining butter, blend in the flour. Combine with the fennel-milk mixture.

Meanwhile, spread the livers on aluminum foil or well-oiled parchment paper and bake them 10 minutes at 350° or until they can be crumbled into the sauce which is then seasoned to taste with salt and pepper.

Spread the fish on an ovenware dish. Cover with the sauce which should be abundant. Heat in a 350° oven for about 10 minutes or until bubbling and palely golden. (Recipe of Louis Giniès, well-known writer in Aix-en-Provence.)

Rougets des Îles d'Or

SERVES 4

1 2½-pound bass or rock mullet
1 medium-size onion
1 small clove garlic
3 sprigs parsley
½ cup stoned, small black olives
½ teaspoon thyme
Lemon slices
Thin slices seeded tomatoes
2 small anchovy fillets, freshened
½ teaspoon saffron
2 tablespoons white wine
Butter, olive oil
Salt and pepper

Scale the bass (or mullet), but don't eviscerate it. Place it in a heatproof, earthenware dish on a bed of onion, garlic, and parsley chopped together, with the black olives and a pinch of thyme.

Top the fish with lemon and tomato slices, anchovy fillets, saffron, and wine. Dot with butter. Moisten with olive oil. Season with salt and pepper, and bake 10 to 15 minutes in a 350° oven, basting from time to time with the juices in the baking dish. When the fish is cooked, not much juice should be left, and what there is should be rich. If need be, add a bit more butter and blend it well with the sauce just before serving. (Recipe conceived by Jean Bernhard, proprietor and Chef of the restaurant Aux Mets de Provence in Toulon.)

Rougets Marines à la Niçoise

SERVES 4

4 small mullet or bass
Salt
2 cups white vinegar
1 onion
1 carrot
4 shallots, peeled and minced
1 tablespoon whole peppercorns
Bouquet garni
1 stalk of celery, chopped
3 or 4 cloves
Sprig of parsley
Olive oil

This preparation, typical of Nice, makes an excellent *hors d'oeuvre* or cold entrée.

Wash, drain the mullet or bass and place side-by-side on a platter. Cover with a light blanket of salt, and leave them for 3 hours.

Meanwhile, prepare a marinade with the vinegar, onion, carrot, shallots, *bouquet garni,* celery, cloves, parsley, and peppercorns. Boil this mixture for half an hour.

Rinse and dry the fish and then broil them. Place in a terrine and cover with the marinade. After 48 hours of maceration, drain off the marinade, return the fish to the terrine and cover with good olive oil. Set in a cool place. Three days later, your fish will be at their peak of perfection but will "keep" for several days longer under refrigeration. (Recipe of Paul Bouillard.)

Note: Sardines, small sea bream, and tinker mackerel are all equally suitable for this treatment.

Rougets à la Marseillaise

1 small fish per person
Olive oil
Salt and pepper
3 or 4 tomatoes
1 medium-size onion, minced
3 sprigs parsley
1 clove garlic
½ cup white wine

Do not eviscerate the fish. Start by browning them in oil in a skillet. Season with salt and pepper.

Peel and seed the tomatoes and chop them coarsely. Add onion, parsley, and garlic, all minced. Blend in white wine and pour all this over the sautéed fish. Bring to a boil, cover, and finish cooking in a 350° oven (about 10 minutes). The sauce should have reduced by half.

This dish is equally good served cold.

Rougets en Oursinado (Bass in Sea Urchin Cream)

Scale but do not eviscerate the fish, allowing ½ pound per person. Let them marinate for 2 or 3 hours in oil to cover, seasoned with salt and pepper. Put several stalks of fennel on the grill. Place the fish on these and broil them (or, if the broiling is to be done *under* the heat, place the fennel *over* the fish).

Pour Cream of Sea Urchin Sauce (page 31) over the broiled *rougets* on a serving platter.

Note: In Provence, the red scales of the *rougets* are sometimes pounded in a mortar with enough olive oil to make a thinnish sauce which is trickled over the surface of the dish, by way of decoration, just at the moment of serving.

Rougets en Papillottes "Baumanière" (Bass Baked in Oiled Paper)

Allowing one half-pound fish per person, lay them on sheets of paper abundantly glossed with olive oil. The paper should be large enough to enclose the fish. On one side of each fish place a bay leaf, and, on the other a thin slice of lightly smoked pork loin (smoked pork chop will serve). Wrap them individually, closing the ends of the packages by twisting the paper [like birthday party "crackers" — the kind that have paper hats inside]. Set them in a 350° oven in a deep, generously oiled ovenware dish. The fish, thus packaged, should be turned over from time to time during the cooking which should be completed in about 20 minutes. They should go to the table still *"en papillotte"* and should not be opened until they are served so that the full fragrance may be retained.

Serve with rice simmered in a fumet (page 16) of mussels, or cooked in broth and mixed, at the last moment, with a few mussels.

Present, at the same time, a hollandaise sauce made with melted butter in which a few anchovy fillets have been marinated. (Recipe of R. Thuillier, Hôtellerie de Beaumanière, Les Baux-de-Provence.)

Rougets au Safran (Bass with Saffron)

Per person:
1 ¼-pound bass or mullet
2 teaspoons olive oil
½ small tomato
Salt and pepper
⅓ clove garlic, crushed
Sprig of thyme
Small piece of bay leaf
¼ teaspoon coriander
Pinch of saffron
2 or 3 tablespoons white wine

Rather small fish are used for this dish. Wipe them dry with a clean cloth or paper towel, but don't eviscerate them. Place in a shallow baking dish, sprinkle with oil, and surround them with peeled, seeded, roughly chopped tomatoes seasoned with salt, pepper, crushed garlic, fresh thyme, bay leaf, coriander and — most important — a pinch or two of saffron. Moisten with white wine and bake for about 8 minutes in a 350° oven, counting the time from the moment the juices in the pan begin to bubble. Garnish with lemon slices. This dish is often eaten hot but is better still when served cold.

Saint-Pierre

Saint-Pierre, commonly known as *jean-dorée,* is a fish of the John Dory *(Zeidae)* family, a popular ingredient of bouillabaisse, and not found in American waters. The wall-eyed pike is, however, an excellent substitute, and if that is unavailable, fresh water perch will do very well in its place.

Saint-Pierre au Gratin   A 4½-POUND FISH SERVES 6

The fish should be split open, eviscerated and cleaned, salted and peppered. A stalk or two of fresh fennel should be placed in the cavity and the fish then laid down on a couch of peeled, thinly-sliced potatoes (about 2 cups) in an oiled baking dish. All this is then encircled with tomato halves, skinned, seeded, and seasoned with salt and pepper, and sloshed with olive oil. A scatter of thyme and bread crumbs finishes the preparation and the fish is then baked at 325° until it is cooked through and the crumbs are golden. Garnish with tiny black olives.

Saint-Pierre des Pêcheurs (Fishermen's Pike)

For this dish which is similar to the preceding, the fish is baked on a bed of thinly-sliced, peeled onions and potatoes, lightly sprinkled with olive oil and good white wine. It should be basted frequently during the cooking, and removed from the oven as soon as the fish flakes easily.

Sardines

The true sardine is a European, the young of the pilchard. In America, the little fellow who comes in a tin, neatly bedded down with his siblings under a blanket of oil, is, technically, not a true sardine at all but only a distant relative, and is seldom sold straight from the sea in his natural state. Happily, olive oil is second nature to him as it is to his overseas cousin, and in all the following recipes for sardines, fresh herring are suitable as substitute.

Beignets de Sardines (Fresh Herring Fritters)

Very small fresh herrings (2 or 3 per person) with the heads and bones removed but the skin left on, are used for these luscious fritters. They are tricky to handle but worth all the effort. The prepared fish are salted and peppered, then dipped in a light batter (page 12) and fried in deep olive oil at 370° for 3 to 5 minutes. The fish should be cooked in the hot oil, a few at a time, and removed and drained on paper before they get too dark because they will look browner when removed than they did while frying.

The herring dipped in the same batter may also be sautéed in shallower oil in a skillet.

Sardines à la Cacane

Dry the herring well and set them aside. Into a large saucepan put the oil, tomatoes, garlic, herbs, salt and pepper. Cook for a few minutes, then stir in the wine. Place the herring in the saucepan and add enough *boiling* water to just cover them. Let cook briskly for 15 minutes. Lift the herring carefully from the pot, lay them in a deep, ovenproof platter, and set aside in a warm place. Strain the saucepan juices, reserving the garlic. Bring the fish liquor to a boil once more and stir in 2 tablespoons flour mixed to a thin paste with a little of the liquor. Finally, thicken this sauce with the egg yolks beaten with the olive oil. Pour the sauce over the sardines in their warm platter and sprinkle with the reserved, cooked garlic, minced together with an equal quantity of crisp parsley.

4 tablespoons olive oil
2 tomatoes, peeled, seeded, minced
24 whole cloves garlic, peeled
Sprig of thyme
2 bay leaves
Salt and pepper
¾ cup white wine, simmered down to ½ cup
2½ pounds fresh herring, cleaned and (optional) decapitated
2 tablespoons flour
4 egg yolks
2 whole cloves
1 tablespoon olive oil
Parsley

Sardines à la Capucine
(Capucine Herring Casserole)

SERVES 6

1 pound filleted herring
Olive oil
2 cups peeled, seeded, coarsely-
    chopped tomatoes
1 cup very thinly sliced onions
1 small head of lettuce
¾ cup equal amounts of garlic and
    parsley minced together
Salt and pepper
Bread crumbs
Thin lemon slices

This is a very ancient Provençal recipe, associated particularly with Toulon. It is a fine thing to restore the dish to a place of honor for it is easy to prepare and delicious, especially in summer.

Oil an ovenproof dish abundantly and fill it with layers of tomatoes, onions, and lettuce leaves, each lightly strewed with the garlic and parsley mixture, salt and pepper. The top layer should be tomatoes. Place the herring on this bed. Arrange a few slices of lemon over them. Powder with bread crumbs. Sprinkle with olive oil and bake at 325° for about an hour.

Sardines Farcies aux Épinards
(Herring Stuffed with Spinach)

SERVES 4

6 small herrings per person
2 pounds spinach
1 small minced onion
4 tablespoons olive oil
Salt and pepper
Nutmeg
Bread crumbs

Clean and decapitate some fine, very small herring (about 6 to a person). Slit open the stomachs and remove the backbones and tails. Spread them out on a cloth, open side up.

Wash, cook, drain, and chop spinach as usual (2 pounds should be enough for 4 persons). Sauté it for a few minutes in 3 tablespoons olive oil in which a small, minced onion has been lightly colored. Season to taste with salt, pepper, and a pinch of ground nutmeg. Stir over medium heat to blend.

Arrange the spinach in the bottom of an ovenware platter, reserving 1 tablespoon for each fish. Put a spoonful in each fish which you then roll up, starting with the large end and rolling toward the tail. Tie or skewer to hold in shape. Then push the fish into the dish of spinach with their little tails in the air. Powder with bread crumbs and sprinkle with oil. Bake 4 to 6 minutes in a 350° oven. Serve in the baking dish.

Sardines Farcies aux Herbes
(Herring Stuffed with Herbs)

Prepare the herring as for Herring Stuffed with Spinach (above).

The stuffing may have a base of spinach, chard, or salad greens or a combination of one or two of these, previously blanched, drained, and chopped fine. Add a chopped clove of garlic and, for each two cups of chopped greens, 3 tablespoons bread crumbs soaked in milk and pressed out, and 1 well-beaten egg, salt and pepper. Spread a layer of this stuffing on each herring, and finish cooking as in the preceding recipe.

Sardines à la Victor Gelu

Stuff herring as for one of the preceding dishes. Then poach them in simmering water. Drain and chill. To serve, arrange the fish on a platter and cover with a mayonnaise lightly tinted with tomato sauce and flavored with minced tarragon or fresh basil. Decorate the platter with fillets of anchovies, capers, thinly sliced gherkins, quartered tomatoes, and hard-boiled eggs. (Recipe from the collection of Marcel Provence.)

Sardines Grillées (Broiled Herring)

Herring may, of course, be broiled just like any other fish. In Provence, however, the fishermen prefer to bypass the grill and, instead, toss the fish directly onto hot coals. *Watch it!* Let your gaze wander and you may come up with a piece of carbon, but if you're attentive, the result of this method of broiling can be surprising and delicious.

Sardines Fraîches Marinées (Marinated Fresh Herring)

For this dish it is best to have the herring filleted at the market. It can be made in either a skillet or an ovenware platter. In either case the fillets are arranged in layers with onion rings or slices of lemon (sometimes a few of each) between the layers. They are seasoned with salt and white pepper, and then white wine (enough to just cover the fish) is added, and they are then baked at 300°. When the fillets are cooked through, they must be thoroughly drained. They may be either reheated or served cold, sprinkled with oil and lemon juice. (Recipe of Dr. P. Comte.)

Sardines Panées Calendal (Breaded Herring)

1 or 2 herrings per person
Salt and pepper
1 egg
1 tablespoon olive oil
Flour
Bread crumbs
Lemon slices
4 tablespoons oil
4 tablespoons butter
1 tablespoon capers
1 hard-boiled egg, mashed
2 anchovy fillets, mashed

Allow 1 or 2 herrings per person, depending on size. Remove the heads. Split, bone, and season the fish with salt and pepper. Beat an egg with 1 tablespoon olive oil. Roll the fish in flour, then dip them in the egg mixture and then roll them in very fine bread crumbs. Bake at 350°, basting with olive oil, or fry in oil in a skillet, turning them once. To serve, dress each fish with a quarter slice of peeled lemon. Pour over them a sauce made of half olive oil and half butter, flavored with the capers, egg, and anchovy fillets. Serve very hot.

Sole

Sole is considered one of the finest of food fishes, possibly *the* finest. Probably more elaborate recipes have been developed for using it than for any other fish that ever came out of the sea, but, like the true sardine, real sole is European and must be flown in for American tables. However, many American flatfishes are, if less delicate, nevertheless satisfying substitutes and just as cooperative with the cook. Among these are flounder, dabs, lemon sole.

Recipes for famous sole dishes (*Sole Bonne Femme, Sole Florentine, Sole Véronique,* etc.) are to be found in almost any good, comprehensive cookbook. Listed here, therefore, are only three suggested treatments, all simple, all typically Provençal.

Sole Calendal

SERVES 6

6 fillets of flounder or other flatfish
Court bouillon for poaching
3 tablespoons butter
2 tablespoons flour
Salt and pepper
1 cup (scant) red wine
Grated cheese

Poach the fillets in a well-herbed court bouillon (see page 14). Be careful not to overcook them. Lift the cooked fish from the cooking liquor and arrange it on a baking platter. Melt 2 tablespoons of the butter. Blend in the flour and cook, stirring continuously over low heat for a few minutes to color the flour, then blend in the red wine, a little at a time. Salt and pepper to taste. Remove from heat and add the remaining tablespoon of butter. Turn this sauce over the poached sole. Powder with grated cheese, and set the pan under the broiler for a moment or two to glaze, watching attentively to make sure no burned patches mar the beauty of this simple dish.

Sole à la Provençale (Sole with Eggplant) SERVES 3

Fry the fillets of sole or flounder in olive oil. Season with salt and pepper. Place each (small) fillet on a slice of fried eggplant and spoon a tablespoonful of tomato sauce over each one. Top with 1 tablespoon browned butter and serve sprinkled with minced *fines herbes*. (Recipe of M. Silvestre, Buffet de la Gare d'Avignon.)

6 fillets of sole
¼ cup (or more) olive oil
Salt and pepper
6 slices fried eggplant
½ cup tomato sauce
¼ pound butter
Fines herbes (page 16)

Sole à la Saint-Henry

This is the simplest and most Provençal treatment of all. The fish is cleaned and the head removed but it is not filleted. It is sprinkled generously with oil and broiled (carefully watched to anticipate overcooking or burning it), and it is served covered with a purée of sea urchins (see Cream of Sea Urchin Sauce, page 31).

Stockfish (Dried Codfish)

Stockfish is codfish (and sometimes hake) dried, and, until treated, stiff as linoleum. Before it can be used it must be soaked for 3 or 4 days in several changes of water, then cut in pieces. Dried fish of this type can be found, usually hanging from strings, in European market sections of large American cities. American dried salt cod sold in small wooden boxes can be substituted and is really much more satisfactory, requiring only a few hours (not days) of soaking. Directions are given on the box.

Stocaficada SERVES 6

Soak the stockfish as indicated above.

Cook the onion and leek in 2 tablespoons of the olive oil over medium heat for 2 or 3 minutes (do not brown). Then add garlic, pepper, and the *bouquet garni*. Put in the other tablespoon of oil and the pieces of fish and cook over gentle heat for another few minutes, turning the fish once or twice. Add the tomatoes or tomato purée which should be cooked for 5 or 6 minutes in olive oil to modify the sharp flavor, and diluted with water. Add water to cover contents of pan. Simmer for at least 1½ hours. Then add the sweet potatoes, peeled, and cut in thick slices, and the olives. When the potatoes are done (about 10 or 12 minutes), serve the *stocaficada* very hot.

1 pound stockfish (see above)
3 tablespoons olive oil
1 large onion, minced
1 leek, minced (white part only)
2 whole cloves garlic, peeled and crushed
Bouquet garni
Pepper
4 tomatoes, peeled, seeded, and chopped (or 1 cup tomato purée)
1 pound sweet potatoes, peeled
¼ pound small black olives, pitted

Under one or another name, *stocaficada* is known and loved in many countries, particularly among Spanish-speaking people. For many others, it will be a new experience in taste discrimination, for the contrasts of flavors that combine to make stocaficada are as inspired as the partnerships of pears and *Camembert*, English mustard with roast beef.

Stockfish à la Provençale

1 pound salt codfish (not shredded)
1 onion, minced
1 leek (white part only), minced
3 tablespoons olive oil
2 tomatoes, coarsely chopped
2 cloves garlic, peeled and crushed
Bouquet garni
2 sprigs of parsley
Dash of cayenne pepper
Dash of paprika
1 cup white wine
1 cup water
Salt (*careful!*) and pepper

Soak the fish as indicated in the above recipe, and cut it in pieces. Cook onion and leek in oil (also as in above recipe), and add tomatoes and garlic. So far, the procedure is the same as for *stocaficada*. But now, let all simmer until the juice from the tomatoes has completely evaporated before adding the pieces of stockfish. Season to taste (being very stingy with salt if, indeed, it is needed at all). Add *bouquet garni,* parsley, cayenne, and paprika. Moisten with white wine and water. Cook over low heat 35 to 40 minutes, by which time the moisture will have almost completed evaporated, leaving a thick but abundant sauce. Arrange the stockfish on a hot platter and serve the sauce separately.

Thon (Tuna Fish)

Mediterranean tuna fish is very much smaller than the Florida (*Neothunnus allisoni*) and the Pacific Coast (*Thunnus saliens*) species. Also, it is most often cooked in slices, fresh rather than tinned. Good as tinned tuna is, we hope that soon more people will discover the rewards of the fresh kind — because fresh tuna fish *can* be ordered in American fish markets and more could be made available if people asked for it.

Thon en Chartreuse   SERVES 6

This dish has, obviously, no relationship to either the entrées prepared in a mold of that name or the liqueur. It may or may not have originated in Chartres. It is, in any case, simply tuna baked in a typical Provençal sauce . . . and very good, too.

Clean the fresh tuna by laying it in a shallow pan and soaking it for 1 hour in water to cover with vinegar added. Drain. Remove all the skin, and cook the fish slice in 2 tablespoons olive oil without allowing it to brown. Meanwhile, color the onions in the other 2 tablespoons of olive oil. Add the tomatoes (or tomato purée), the white wine, *bouquet garni,* parsley, bay leaf, garlic, salt and pepper. Stir over medium heat until they are well blended and the vegetables well cooked. Spread half of this mixture in a baking dish. Lay the slices of tuna on this bed and cover with the rest of the sauce plus the liquid left in the pan in which the fish was cooked. Top with 2 or 3 slices of lemon, and bake for about 20 minutes at 350°.

1½-pound slice of fresh tuna fish
Water and 1 tablespoon vinegar
4 tablespoons olive oil
4 peeled, minced onions
4 peeled, seeded, sliced tomatoes
　(or 1 cup tomato purée)
1 cup dry, white wine
Bouquet garni plus parsley and a
　bay leaf
2 peeled, crushed cloves garlic
Salt and pepper
Lemon slices

Thon des Îles d'Or
SERVES 6

Marinate the slice of tuna in the oil seasoned with the lemon juice, anchovies, salt, pepper, and nutmeg.

Drain this marinade into a skillet and in it brown the onions and garlic. Add the tomatoes and place the slice of tuna on this bed. Cover, and simmer for about 20 minutes. Remove fish and keep it warm. Pour the wine and bouillon into the skillet. Cook the vegetable-broth-wine mixture uncovered over low heat until the sauce is well reduced. This may take an hour. Stir to prevent vegetables from adhering to the pan. Return tuna slice to skillet and cook about 5 minutes over moderate heat. When the fish is hot, transfer it to a hot platter and spoon sauce over it.

1½-pound slice of fresh tuna fish
6 tablespoons olive oil
Dash of lemon juice
2 crushed (tinned) anchovies
Salt and pepper
Pinch of nutmeg
2 peeled, chopped onions
3 peeled, chopped cloves of garlic
3 seeded, chopped tomatoes
½ cup white wine
½ cup bouillon or water
2 tablespoons capers
Garlic and parsley chopped
　together

Thon Frit à la Marseillaise
(Deep-Fried Tuna Fish)

Fresh tuna fish may be deep-fried with excellent results if it is sliced ¾ inch thick and then cut into "fingers" ¾ inch wide (in other words, as wide as they are deep), marinated for an hour in water with a dash of vinegar, and drained well. The fingers should then be carefully dried with a clean cloth or paper towel, rolled in flour, and dropped a few at a time into hot (370°) oil. Remove with a slotted spoon and drain on paper. Salt while still hot and serve on a platter, garnished with deep-fried parsley (page 18).

Truites (Trout)

Truites Vauclusiennes (Vauclusian Trout)

Allow 1 brook trout per person. [Any fresh water trout may be substituted (such as Rainbow), but frozen trout are not suitable for this treatment; they are too dry.]

Put a bay leaf in the interior of each fish. Paint their outsides with olive oil, and wrap them in thin slices of smoked bacon. Place the fish over a dozen branches of rosemary and broil them on this bed, about 3 minutes on each side. Serve sprinkled with lemon juice.

XI. *Shellfish and Others*

THIS CHAPTER includes all sorts of burrowers, crawlers, creepers, jumpers, and undulators — such as clams, crabs, lobsters, mussels, sea urchins, squid — even frogs and snails.

Clams (Palourdes, Clovisses, Praires)

In Provence, most mollusks are usually eaten raw with a few drops of vinegar or lemon juice. However, the mussel recipes given in this chapter are, with the exception of the mussel pilaf, suitable also for clams and cockles.

Crabs

Crabs Fishermen's Style
(*Crabes à la Mode des Pêcheurs*)

Because even large crabs contain a rather small quantity of edible meat, it is wise to allow at least two robust crabs per person, preferably, they say, one male and one female. **[The romantic French!]** Simmer the crabs in a highly seasoned court bouillon (page 14) for at least 30 minutes. Remove and discard the dark substances in the interiors of both crabs, being careful to reserve the coral (eggs) of the female. With the point of a knife, lift the flesh free of the shells, cut it into bite-size pieces and serve it in the shells.

The crab is eaten with a sauce considered by some to be the finest sauce ever devised for shellfish, hot or cold, made as follows: pound the coral in a mortar with a peeled, sliced clove of garlic, 2 egg yolks, ½ teaspoon dry mustard, a dash each of vinegar and lemon juice, salt and pepper to taste, and enough olive oil to dilute to the consistency of heavy cream.

Crabs and Rice
(*Pilau de Riz aux Crabes*)   SERVES 6

12 crabs
Olive oil
Water
Bouquet garni
1 onion, minced
1 tomato, peeled and chopped, or
    ½ cup tomato purée
Salt and pepper
Pinch of saffron (generous)
⅔ cup raw, washed, rice
Grated cheese

This is a variation of Pilaf with Mussels (page 126) and may even be made with a combination of crabs and mussels.

Remove the claws and crack the shells of the crabs with a sharp blow. Cook quickly in hot olive oil on both sides. Then add water to cover, and the *bouquet garni*. Simmer for about 20 minutes. Remove the crabs and strain the cooking liquor.

Cook the minced onion over medium heat in 1 tablespoon olive oil until soft but not brown. Add the tomato or tomato purée and simmer for a few minutes. Season with salt and pepper and a pinch of saffron. Add the strained liquor and enough water to make 2 cups of liquid. Bring to a boil. Add the rice. Lower heat and cook until all the moisture has been absorbed. Several minutes before serving, return the crabs to the pot to reheat.

To serve, pile the rice in a dome on a hot platter, sprinkle with grated cheese, and arrange the crabs around the base of the dome.

Crayfish

Crayfish (called "crawfish" in the United States) is not very plentiful in American markets except in a few regions. Lobsters (the smallest the law allows to be taken) or, in a crisis, very large shrimps, may be substituted.

Crayfish à la Provençale
(Écrevisses à la Provençale)
SERVES 6

Fry the onion in the oil. Add the crayfish, and cook over medium heat just long enough to turn the shells pink. Warm the cognac in a separate pan. Ignite it, and ladle it over the pan of crayfish. Let the flame burn out, then moisten crayfish with the white wine. Add the *bouquet garni* and tomato purée. Season generously with salt, pepper, and the pinch of cayenne. Let all this simmer for 6 minutes longer. Serve, sprinkled with the "hash" of garlic and parsley.

3 dozen crayfish
3 tablespoons olive oil
1 peeled, chopped onion
½ cup (or more) cognac
1 cup (generous) white wine
Bouquet garni
½ cup tomato purée
Salt and pepper
A pinch of cayenne pepper
Garlic and parsley chopped together

Stuffed Crayfish Petrarch
(Coquille d'Écrevisses Pétrarque)
SERVES 6

Cook the crayfish in court bouillon to cover for (not more than) 6 minutes. Let them cool enough to handle. Then very carefully separate the meat from the shells, keeping 12 of the best shells intact. Crumble the flesh rather fine.

Cut the ham in very small pieces and cook it for a few minutes in 5 tablespoons of the butter. Stir in the flour and then, gradually, the milk. Bring to a boil, stirring continuously. Remove from heat and season with salt, pepper, and freshly grated nutmeg. Stir in the crumbled crayfish meat and blend well. Let the mixture become lukewarm, then beat in the egg yolks. Fill the 12 shells with the mixture. [Small ramekins may be used in place of the shells.] Sprinkle with crumbs, dot with the remaining butter. Arrange the shells on a flat, shallow pan or cookie sheet, crown each with a truffle (optional), and slide under the broiler or into a very hot oven to brown lightly.

2½ pounds live crayfish
Highly-seasoned court bouillon (page 14)
6 ounces raw ham*
7 tablespoons butter
6 tablespoons flour
Salt and pepper
Grated nutmeg
2 egg yolks
Fresh bread crumbs
4½ cups milk
Truffles (optional)

* Use dry-cured ham (such as Smithfield) or prosciutto. Never use tenderized or the so-called "ready-to-eat" type.

Frogs' Legs

Frogs' Legs Provençale (Grenouilles Provençale)

Unless the frogs' legs are unusually large, allow 3 pairs per person. They can (and should be) bought already skinned. Soak them in cold water for 3 hours, changing the water twice. Drain, and thoroughly dry. Roll them in flour seasoned with salt, pepper, and finely minced garlic. Fry them in olive oil over medium heat, turning to brown thoroughly. Drain on absorbent paper and serve with a small amount (about 2 tablespoons per serving) of Tomato Sauce I (page 32).

Lobster (Langouste)

The five lobster recipes that follow all specify *langouste*, a spiny lobster which, in the United States, is found only on the West Coast. But the more widely known East Coast lobsters — particularly those from Maine's chilly waters — are every bit as good *provided they are small* — never heavier than one pound. Lobsters of the minimum legal limit (6 inches long) are the best of all . . . for any purpose.

Langouste à l'Américaine   SERVES 8

Américaine? Armoricaine? American? Everybody has a theory about which spelling is right and where it came from. Some say the origin was a misspelling of *Américaine.* On the other hand the lobsters from Amorique in Brittany have long been famous. But broiled live lobster is as American as corn on the cob. As for us, we say the term is *Américaine* and that it means "American," although it isn't . . . quite.

In any case, even though the origin of this dish wasn't Mediterranean, it has acquired the "droit de cité" in Provence. For, what about the tomato, the very basis of the sauce? This, alone, should be reason enough for including here a recipe for a dish that enjoys as much favor on that coast as Bouillabaisse, *Aïoli, Pieds et*

Paquets, and other Provençal specialities. Here, then, is the recipe for the lobster featured by the celebrated Provençal chef, Foucou:

For 8 persons, 4 lobsters averaging just under 1 pound each should suffice. The proportions of the other ingredients may be increased or decreased according to the number to be served.

Split the lobsters lengthwise. Remove and mash the coral and intestines. Reserve these to use as a thickening agent. Season the lobsters with salt and freshly ground black pepper. Cook in very hot oil (meat-side down first) until the shells turn red. Then chop together the tomatoes (peeled and seeded), onion, shallots, and carrot. Add the paprika. Stir these vegetables into the pot containing the lobsters and simmer for a few minutes. Then pour in the white wine, Madeira, and cognac, meat extract, and gravy. Add the *bouquet garni.* Simmer 4 to 5 minutes. Then remove the lobster halves and continue cooking the sauce over moderate heat until it is reduced by half. This will take about 15 minutes. Put the sauce through a fine-mesh sieve and return it to the cook pot. Put the lobsters back in the pot and let them simmer in the sauce 8 to 10 minutes longer.

At serving time, arrange the lobsters on a platter, flesh-side up. Bind the sauce with the reserved mashed intestines and coral, the butter and the flour. Stir over low heat. Spoon the sauce over the lobsters or, if preferred, serve it separately in a sauceboat.

"You will note," adds M. Foucou, "that, contrary to the general practice, I do not flame the lobsters with cognac. This procedure, to my mind, does nothing to improve the dish. On the contrary, there is risk, in flaming, of altering the dish and giving it a disagreeable bitterness."

4 lobsters
Salt and pepper
½ cup olive oil
4 medium-size tomatoes
1 medium-size onion, peeled
1 or 2 shallots, peeled
1 carrot, scraped
½ teaspoon paprika
3 cups dry white wine
½ cup Madeira and ¼ cup cognac, mixed
3½ tablespoons beef extract
Bouquet garni
3½ tablespoons butter
1 tablespoon flour

Curry of Lobster (*Langouste au Curry*)

This is the same as *Langouste à l'Américaine* except that, during the cooking, 1 tablespoon of curry powder or (preferably) curry paste* is stirred in, and the sauce is bound with fresh cream. The *Provençaux* sometimes serve it accompanied by Creole Rice but, for most people, so lively a flavor as Curry of Lobster demands a bland partner such as a simple pilaf or just plain, boiled rice.

* Curry paste may be ordered from: Trinacria Importing Co., 415 Third Ave., New York, N.Y.

Lobsters in Oil (*Langouste à l'Huile*)

Allow one small lobster per person. Drop them into boiling water deep enough to cover them by 2 inches, and cook them exactly 18 minutes (no longer) at a rolling boil. Cut them in half lengthwise, and extract and mash the livers and coral. Blend these with enough oil to make a smooth, creamy paste. Season to taste with salt and pepper. Spread the cut side of each lobster with this sauce. Delicious, hot or cold!

Lobster and Little Peas
(*Langoustes aux Petits Pois*)

SERVES 4

3 tablespoons olive oil
1 peeled, chopped onion
2 peeled, seeded, chopped tomatoes
4 small lobsters, cut in half, lengthwise
1 cup white wine
2½ cups water
Bouquet garni
2 cloves garlic, peeled and crushed
Salt and pepper
Generous pinch of saffron
2 cups shelled, tiny peas
French or Italian bread, sliced

Sauté the onion and cook the tomatoes over brisk heat in the oil. Place the lobsters on this bed and, as soon as they are heated through, pour the wine and water over them and add the *bouquet garni,* garlic, salt, pepper, saffron, and the peas. Cover, and cook over medium heat 8 minutes (from the time the liquid in the pot comes to a boil). Place the slices of bread in individual plates, pour the sauce and the little peas over them, and serve the lobster separately.

Cold Provençal Lobster
(*Langoustes à la Provençale*)

SERVES 6 (ALLOW 1 LOBSTER FOR 2 PERSONS)

3 small female lobsters
1 cup plus 2 tablespoons olive oil
1 small onion, peeled and minced
1 small tomato, peeled and chopped
Salt and pepper
Sprig of fresh fennel (or 1 tablespoon fennel seeds)
½ cup white wine
1 egg yolk
Lemon juice

Remove the lobsters from the shells, retaining the coral and the brown matter. Cut the meat into bite-size pieces. Cook the coral in 2 tablespoons olive oil along with the onion and tomato. Remove coral and add the lobster meat to the oil. Sauté quickly. Pour in the white wine and cook, covered, over moderate heat for about 20 minutes.

Meanwhile, pound the coral and the brown matter in a mortar. Then beat in the egg yolk and, on this base, "mount" a mayonnaise by beating in the remaining (1 cup) olive oil, a little at a time. Season to taste with salt, pepper, and lemon juice. When lobster is cooked, transfer to a hot serving dish. Mix the mayonnaise with the sauce from the lobsters. Serve very hot.

Broiled Lobster (*Langoustes Grillées*)

This is simply lobster (in France, spiny lobster) grilled over the embers of burning rosemary branches or vine shoots on a grill brushed with olive oil. The lobsters are cooked for about 25 to 30 minutes, depending on size — long enough for the meat to be cooked all the way through. When the shells reach the crackling point (without being really burned) they can be easily detached.

Serve the broiled lobsters with *vinaigrette* sauce (page 30) made, of course, with olive oil, and supplemented by the pounded coral and intestines of the lobsters.

Mussels (Moules)

Why people who eat oysters and relish clams in many guises look with dubiety upon the mussel is one of the unsolved mysteries among food prejudices. For mussels are among the richest of seafoods: hearty, full of iodine and other beneficial substances, satisfying, and inexpensive. A good dish of mussels revives flagging spirits, brightens the eye, and enraptures the informed palate. What's more, Atlantic Coast mussels are smaller and more delicate in texture than their Mediterranean cousins, and are often to be had for the taking, needing only to be pried loose from rocks along the shore. There are three rules, though, that every mussel-gatherer must obey: (1) Make certain that the waters are free from any suspicion of contamination. (2) Take mussels only from rocks that are submerged daily by the tides. (3) Discard any that are not tightly closed before they are cooked.

Pretreatment of Mussels for all recipes

Scrub the shells *thoroughly* with a stiff brush and cold water. Carefully cut off the "beards." Soak in cold water for 2 hours. Drain and wash again. Put the mussels in a kettle containing ½ cup white wine (or water, but wine is better). Cover and bring to a boil and cook for about 6 minutes, removing the mussels as fast as their shells open. (Some are more tenacious than others.) Strain the liquor in the kettle through a fine sieve to use as broth (or in cooking).

Mussels Broiled on Skewers
(Brochettes de Moules)
SERVES 4

Use 2 quarts of fine fat mussels for this dish. Pretreat as above, then discard the shells and thread the meat on skewers alternately with small squares of fresh pork fat (preferably from along the chine). **[In summer, if there are rosemary plants in the garden, substitute these fragrant stalks for the metal skewers.]** Put the filled skewers on a broiler grid over hot wood or charcoal embers. Remove when pork fat is cooked and crisp on the edges. Serve surrounded by broiled tomatoes.

The brochettes may also, of course, be broiled in a gas or electric oven, and bacon squares may be used if no fresh pork fat is available, but in neither case will the result be wholly authentic.

Deep-fried Mussels Brochette (*Brochettes de Moules Balaguier*)

These are prepared exactly as in the above recipe except that instead of broiling the skewered mussels and pork squares (or bacon), they are breaded and dropped into oil in a frying kettle (370°).

Mussels à la Martégale

SERVES 4

2 quarts mussels
2 cloves garlic, chopped
1 tablespoon olive oil
¼ cup soft bread crumbs
¼ cup tomato purée
Chopped fresh parsley and fresh basil

Open the mussels as usual but leave them over heat long enough to be well cooked. Remove one shell from each.

Lightly brown the chopped garlic cloves in the olive oil. Don't let them get dark. Add the bread crumbs and tomato purée, and toss in the mussels. Cook, covered, over medium heat for 2 or 3 minutes. Serve hot, sprinkled with the parsley and basil.

Mussels Stuffed with Spinach (*Moules Farcies aux Épinards*)

2 quarts large mussels
1 pound spinach or 1 package frozen
Salt and pepper
Pinch of ground nutmeg
3 tablespoons olive oil
White part of 1 leek
1 small onion
Fine, dry bread crumbs

Open mussels over high heat in ½ cup water but leave them in their shells.

Cook the spinach, fresh or frozen. Chop very fine and season with salt, pepper, and a pinch of ground nutmeg. In 2 tablespoons olive oil, sauté the leek, minced, and a small onion, peeled and finely chopped. Combine with the seasoned spinach. Stir until well blended together.

Garnish the mussels in their shells with this stuffing, and tie upper and lower shells with thread to keep them joined. Lay them side by side in a shallow ovenware casserole. Fill the spaces between the mussels with the rest of the spinach. Sprinkle with fine, dry bread crumbs, and then with oil, and set in a hot (400°) oven for about 10 minutes to brown, watching carefully to make sure the crumbs are not scorched.

Mussels Stuffed with Mushrooms
(Moules Farcies au Gratin)

Open well-scrubbed, large mussels over high heat, with the white wine seasoned with pepper, bay leaf, fennel, and thyme. Remove the mussels from the kettle. Discard one shell of each mollusk, leaving the mussel sitting on the other. Set the filled shells on a heatproof platter or other "cook-serve" dish.

In 3 tablespoons oil, quickly sauté the onion and mushrooms. Then add the soaked, pressed-out bread crumbs, the tomatoes (or tomato purée), and chopped parsley. Season with pepper and nutmeg. When this filling is nicely colored, garnish each mussel shell with it, being sure that the mussel itself is completely covered. Sprinkle each filled shell with dry crumbs and then with a few drops of the remaining tablespoon of oil which should be heated to the boiling point. Set the platter in a hot oven to be *gratinéed*. When the mussels are golden, take the platter from the oven. Sprinkle with the lemon juice.

2 quarts large mussels
½ cup white wine
Pepper (NO salt)
Bay leaf
Slice of fennel or ½ teaspoon fennel seeds
Pinch of thyme
4 tablespoons olive oil
Small onion, chopped
15 small mushrooms, chopped fine
½ cup soft bread crumbs, soaked in milk and pressed out
2 tomatoes, peeled, seeded and chopped or ½ cup tomato purée
¼ cup chopped parsley
Grated nutmeg
Dry, fine bread crumbs
Juice of 1 lemon

Fisherman's Mussels (Moules à la Pêcheur)   SERVES 4

Combine and chop the vegetables and herbs. Soak the bread crumbs in milk and press out milk. Stir crumbs into vegetable mixture. Season with salt, pepper, and a few drops of lemon juice. Blend the softened butter with the egg yolk, then gently combine the two mixtures.

Open the mussels in ½ cup water over the medium heat. Remove the top shell of each and, with the stuffing, blanket the mussels left in the lower shells. Place these garnished mussels on large slices of French bread on an ovenware platter. Bake about 8 minutes in a 350° oven. Serve with lemon slices.

2 quarts mussels, well cleaned (page 123)
1 clove garlic
5 shallots
3 sprigs parsley
1 sprig fresh tarragon
2 sprigs fresh thyme
1 cup bread crumbs
Milk
Salt and pepper
½ cup softened butter
Lemon juice
1 egg yolk
Sliced French bread
Lemon slices

Pilaf (Rice) with Mussels
(Pilau de Riz aux Moules)

SERVES 4 OR 5

2¼ quarts mussels
1 cup water, boiling
1 large onion
1 large tomato
2 tablespoons olive oil
¾ cup raw rice
Bouquet garni
Pepper and saffron
Grated cheese

Wash and trim mussels (page 123), and cook them in the boiling water until they open. Strain and save the water (now flavored) in which the mollusks were cooked. There should be 1½ cups. If there is more, boil it down; if less, add water.

Meanwhile, peel and fry the onion and tomato, both chopped, in 2 tablespoons olive oil. Wash the rice and turn it over in the vegetables to color. Then moisten, a little at a time, over medium heat, with the reserved liquor from the mussels. Add the *bouquet garni,* pepper, and a touch of saffron (add no salt without testing because mussel broth can be *very* salty). Turn the rice over gently with a fork. Add more liquor from time to time if the rice at the bottom of the pot begins to stick. When the rice is *just done,* fold in the mussels (taken from their shells). Pile in a cone shape on a hot platter and serve covered with grated cheese.

Mussel Soufflé (Soufflé aux Moules)

SERVES 6

3 pounds mussels, scrubbed and
  bearded
½ cup white wine
White pepper
Lemon juice
2½ tablespoons butter, melted
½ cup flour
4 eggs, separated
Salt (use warily, if at all)

Open the mussels as usual in a skillet containing the white wine, a pinch of pepper, and the lemon juice. When they open, remove and discard the shells. Set the meat aside. Strain the broth through a very fine sieve or several layers of cheesecloth, and reserve it.

Stir the melted butter and flour to a smooth *roux* and mix this with a scant half cup of the reserved broth.

Pound half the mussels in a mortar and rub them to a paste with the egg yolks. Add salt (?) and pepper to taste. Cool to lukewarm. Then beat the egg whites to a firm snow and fold them into the cooled paste. Add the remaining mussels. Turn the mixture into a greased soufflé dish (or any straight-sided baking dish). Set the dish on the middle rack of an oven that has been preheated to 400°. Reduce heat at once to 375°. Bake 30 to 35 minutes or until a silver knife dipped into the center of the dish comes out clean and dry. [Ovens differ, temperamentally, and some cooks have the best results with soufflés baked at 325° throughout the cooking time which then usually runs a little longer: 40 to 42 minutes. This method tends to produce a texture at once delicate and self-sustaining.]

Saffron Mussels (*Moules au Safran*)

SERVES 6

Steam the mussels in seasoned hot water to open. Then remove one shell from each. Strain and reserve the liquor. Color onion in olive oil. Add a large, peeled, chopped tomato (or scant ½ cup tomato purée) and a peeled, crushed clove of garlic in 2 tablespoons olive oil. Moisten with the white wine and then let all this cook down until the moisture has almost completely evaporated. Then stir in ½ cup of the mussel liquor. Season with pepper, a very small pinch of paprika and two of saffron. Fold in the minced parsley. This dish may be eaten hot or cold.

3 pounds mussels
½ cup water
1 onion, peeled and chopped
1 large tomato, or a scant ½ cup
   tomato purée
1 clove garlic
3 tablespoons olive oil
½ cup white wine
Pepper, pinch of paprika
½ teaspoon saffron
½ cup minced parsley

Mussels "*Tante Gracieuse*"

2½ CUPS MUSSELS SERVES 3–4

Open the mussels as usual. Discard the shells. Strain and reserve the liquor.

Separately, make a mayonnaise with 1 egg, 1 teaspoon paprika, 1 teaspoon celery seeds, a whisper of curry powder, and 1 cup olive oil. Do NOT SALT. When mayonnaise is very firm, add a scant teaspoonful of vinegar and 1 tablespoon tomato paste. Then fold in 1 egg white, beaten to a snow. Thin slightly with (about) 1 tablespoon of the mussel liquor. Turn this sauce into a salad bowl with the mussels and blend well. Serve cold.

Walsdorff-Victoria* Mussels

SERVES 4–5

In a saucepan, combine the onion, herbs, peppercorns, and wine. Let them bubble for 5 minutes. Then put in the well-cleaned mussels, cover tightly, and cook for 10 minutes. Remove the empty shell of each mussel and set the occupied halves on a heatproof platter.

Separately, make a "snail butter" as follows: pound ingredients in a mortar.

Using the tip of a knife, cover each mussel on its half shell with the snail butter, allowing about 1 teaspoonful per mussel. When all have been garnished, set the platter in a preheated (350°) oven for 5 to 6 minutes or until the mussels are heated through and the butter has melted — *but no longer!*

Note: Any unused portion of the snail butter can be refrigerated or even frozen (very snugly wrapped to prevent the garlic odor from affecting other stored foods), later to glorify a simple hot

2½ pounds fat mussels
1 medium-size onion, peeled and
   minced
2 teaspoons peppercorns
2 sprigs each of parsley and thyme
½ cup white wine

Snail Butter
  2 cloves garlic, peeled
  2 shallots, peeled
  2 tablespoons parsley, chopped
  Salt and pepper
  A pinch of cayenne
  1¼ tablespoons butter
  1 tablespoon (scant) fresh tarragon

* The Walsdorff-Victoria is a hotel in Cannes.

loaf of French bread or, joined with the mashed yolks, to stuff hard-boiled eggs, or to add a fillip to an uninspiring boiled potato.

Sea Urchins (Oursins)

Although sea urchins are available in the Italian fish markets of the United States, they are almost unknown at American tables, and this is sad, because not only is the "butter" of lightly boiled urchins deliciously rich and "iodine-y," whether eaten hot or cold with a sprinkle of lemon juice, but it is said to have restorative powers. The "butter," which actually is the roe, is much favored in Europe as is the marvelously savory fish dish, *Oursinado* of Provence, which can easily be made wherever sea urchins can be found.

Fillets of Fish with Sea Urchin Sauce (Oursinado)

SERVES 6

2 pounds fish fillets (bream, sunfish, whiting or conger eel)
1 onion and 1 carrot, scraped and minced
Salt and pepper
1 cup white wine
Bouquet garni
1 cup water
6 egg yolks
2 tablespoons butter at room temperature
6 slices of French or Italian bread cut ½-inch thick*
3 dozen sea urchins

Poach the fish fillets in the wine and water seasoned with the onion, carrot, bouquet garni, salt and pepper. When the fish is cooked through (don't overcook), remove it from the pan. Reserve the liquor. Keep both hot.

Boil the sea urchins in water to cover for 4 or 5 minutes. Drain well and extract the "butter" by cutting holes in the concave sides of the shells and letting all the liquid escape. You can then spoon out and mash the urchin butter to produce a purée. Beat the egg yolks and the soft (cow) butter together and add this to the purée, along with about 2 tablespoons of the reserved fish broth. Whip this mixture with a wire wisk over hot water (use a double-boiler or equivalent) until it is thick and creamy.

Lay the bread slices in the bottom of a deep platter and steep them with some of the remaining (hot) fish liquor, but be sure not to use more than the bread will absorb. There should be no liquid in the bottom of the platter. Pour the cream of urchins over this and set the dish in a medium (350°) oven for a few minutes to reheat. Then send it to the table with the fish on a separate hot platter.

* Use only crusty European type white bread for this dish. Commercial American bread disintegrates into a soggy mass.

Snails, Octopuses, and Squid

There is no logical reason why anyone should consider the octopus less appetizing than, for example, the crab, or to dislike snails while accepting clams on the half shell. But it is the nature of man to be illogical and to distrust the unfamiliar. Most Americans, for instance, look with dubiety if not open horror at the octopus, the snail, the sea anemone, squid, or other food that is thought of as "peculiar" or "foreign" even when, like these four, they are not foreign at all but actually plentiful in the United States and largely ignored. They can be bought, however, in almost all European markets of American coastal cities and are usually offered already cleaned, ready to cook.

We agree that all are tough and chewy. Like lobster, hard-shell clams, tripe, celery, even pineapple, their special contribution is unique flavor that gives the eater an experience in tasting. Europeans — particularly, perhaps, Mediterranean people — seem to enjoy a wider range of gustatory satisfactions than the somewhat self-handicapped American. We hope, therefore, that any reader of these pages who is stirred toward an adventure in the kitchen will remember that one bite does not a gourmet make. A new dish should be given more than a single chance. Often the unknown taste is, like sin, first abhorred, then tolerated, and finally, embraced.

Snails (Escargots)

The snail must, for most people, be most marvelously sauced, although the truly dedicated snail-fancier professes to find him irresistible when simply grilled in his shell over a good bed of wood embers. He is then pried out and eaten, merely dipped in salt. But most diners, when they order snails, expect six or a dozen gastropods in their pretty shells, brimming with a fragrant sauce composed of butter, shallots, garlic, parsley, salt and pepper. This is the *Escargot à la Bourguignonne* of world-wide fame, and one eats him, and then, unabashedly, hoists the shell and drains the luscious sauce to which he has contributed so much distinction.

Because this so-called Burgundian snail has become a world citizen, we give the standard recipe below along with one from Provence. In either case, pretreatment is mandatory.

Live snails can be found in most European markets in the United States or can be procured by special order. They are also available in cans but, unfortunately, the canned form tends to be tough or tasteless or both. The best practice is to get them in the market place where they are offered already purged. They should then be soaked for 48 hours in tepid water to cover, with 1 tablespoon vinegar and 2 tablespoons salt (per quart). This "marinade" should be drained off and replaced several times. The snails are then ready for the next process which is to drain and then plunge them into a boiling court bouillon which includes a slice of fresh fennel (or 1 teaspoon fennel seeds), a strip of orange peel, 1 teaspoon vinegar, salt and pepper (per quart of water).

Cook over moderate heat 1½ hours for the large, striped snails, 35 minutes for the little gray ones (*les petits gris*). This concludes the pretreatment.

Snails à la Bourgignonne

Half a dozen snails is no more than a whet to a snail lover, so order at least 12 per person. Pretreat them as indicated above. With the point of a knife, put a little snail butter (page 14) into each shell. Tuck the snail back in, and crown him with more of the mixture. Sprinkle the filled shells with a thin layer of very fine bread crumbs, and then arrange them — buttered-side up, of course — on a shallow, heatproof platter. Set this in a moderate (325° to 350°) oven for about 7 minutes or just long enough to melt the butter. Don't overcook.

Octopuses (Poulpes)

These leggy creatures are found from time to time in American fish markets, and particularly during the Christmas season. Since cleaning them is a somewhat gruesome process, it is advisable to have this done at the market.

The general rule for octopuses is "The smaller, the better," and even the smallest (about 1 pound) may need a whack or two of a mallet by way of tenderization.

Octopus Stew (*Poulpe en Daube*) SERVES 6

Pound the octopuses and cut them into bite-size pieces. Marinate these for several hours in dry white wine to cover, along with the assorted fresh herbs, salt and pepper.

Sauté the minced onion and carrot and the diced bacon in the olive oil. When lightly browned, add the tomatoes and the whole onion stuck with cloves. Put the octopus pieces into the pot and strain the marinade over them, adding the garlic, the *bouquet garni,* and enough white wine and boiling water (half-and-half) to cover the contents of the pot. Cover, and let all cook gently for 2 hours if the octopuses are small, at least 4 hours if they are large. Remove from the heat when the thickest pieces yield to the pressure of a finger (Ouch!). Serve very hot.

3 pounds prepared octopus meat
Dry white wine
1 bay leaf
2 sprigs each of fennel fern, parsley, and thyme
Salt and pepper
3 tablespoons olive oil
2 small onions, peeled and minced
1 medium-size carrot, scraped and minced
¼ pound bacon, diced
2 large tomatoes, peeled, seeded, coarsely chopped
1 whole onion, studded with cloves
Bouquet garni
2 or 3 whole cloves of garlic
Boiling water

Octopus à la Toulonnaise

This dish is prepared exactly as in the preceding recipe, but is served differently. Three or four slices of bread per person (French bread, of course) are spread with *Aïoli* sauce (page 24), then a little of the *daube* juice is spooned over this, and these garnished *"tartines"* set around the octopus on a hot platter. A bowl of supplementary *aïoli* accompanies the repast.

Squid (*Seiche*)

Like the octopus, the squid is a cephalopod. He has ten arms instead of eight, an internal shell (cuttle) containing "black ink," and an assortment of names and nicknames in both English and French: Cuttlefish, "Devil Fish," "Ink Fish," "Sleeve Fish," *Encornet, Calmar, Calamary, Seiche* (the most commonly used French name) and, in Provence, *Tautene* or *Tantonnet.* He also has a tiny relative, the *Suppion.* But *suppions* are rare and extremely tricky to handle, for their little pouches of black liquid must be removed without being punctured. The small cephalopods are then washed in several waters, carefully dried, rolled in flour, and dropped into deep hot fat. They present a serious threat to the cook, too, for unless a cover is clapped swiftly on the frying kettle, they spit. They are drained and served with lemon juice.

Almost any lobster or octopus recipe can be adapted to squid. However, the flesh is very delicate and the squid should be cleaned at the fish market where skilled, experienced hands can also extract the "ink."

Squid American Style (Seiche à l'Américaine)

SERVES 6

6 cleaned squid
3 tablespoons olive oil
4 shallots and one clove garlic or
  1 onion, peeled and chopped
½ cup cognac, warmed
White wine to cover (about 2 cups)
2 tomatoes, peeled, seeded and
  chopped or ½ cup tomato purée
2 tablespoons concentrated veal
  broth or unsalted meat extract
1 cup rice
3 quarts boiling water
1 tablespoon salt
1 tablespoon butter
1 tablespoon flour

American cooks will be amused, recognizing this recipe as one originally created for lobster. It was revised and converted to the use of squid by P. Walsdorff of the Walsdorff-Victoria in Cannes, and his chef de cuisine, L. Berthelier, who humorously and aptly called it *"la langouste a l'américaine des économiquement faibles"* — in other words, Poor Man's Lobster.

Blanch the carefully cleaned squid in boiling water for 15 minutes. Cut in pieces, then sauté in the olive oil and, after a moment, add the chopped shallots and garlic (or onion). Flame these by igniting the warm cognac and pouring it into the skillet with the squid and vegetables. Add white wine to cover. Put in the tomatoes (or tomato purée) and the veal broth (or meat extract), and cook over low heat for 1½ hours.

Drop the rice in 3 quarts of boiling water with 1 tablespoon salt. Keep at a rolling boil for 19 minutes. Drain, rinse quickly under the cold water tap to stop the cooking, and then set it in a warm — NOT HOT — oven, with the door left open, to dry.

To serve, make a ring of hot rice inside the rim of the serving dish and pile the squid in the center of this crown. Finish the sauce with *beurre manié* (butter, creamed with an equal quantity of flour). Blanket the squid with sauce and serve very hot.

Stuffed Squid (Encornets Farcis)

SERVES 6

Probably squid is more often served stuffed than in any other form. It is found on bills of fare, in and out of France, stuffed with tomatoes, with sausage, with spinach, stuffed with whatever the supplies on hand and the inspiration of the cook suggest. A typical recipe and variations follow.

Pound the squid well to tenderize. Cut off the tentacles and chop them fine. Then prepare the filling as follows: Brown one of the onions in 2 tablespoons of the oil. Add the chopped tentacles, 3 of the tomatoes, bread crumbs, parsley and garlic, thyme, salt, pepper, nutmeg, and (optional) basil. Brown all this well, then add the beaten eggs. Moisten with enough wine (or wine and water) to produce a manageable mixture. Fill the squid with this and fasten with thread.

Sauté the remaining onion and tomato in the remaining oil. Brown the flour slightly in a small, dry skillet and then stir it into the tomato-onion. Add a little wine to moisten. Season with salt and pepper. Place the stuffed squid in this sauce, in a casserole. Cover, and simmer for about 25 minutes or until the skin of the squid "yields" when pressed. Transfer to a hot serving platter. Remove the thread. Strain the sauce and pour it over the squid.

Variations:

By the addition of cooked, highly-spiced sausage meat (and appropriate modification of the other seasonings), this dish becomes *Squid à la Toulonnaise.*

When spinach, instead of sausage meat, is added, 2 or 3 bonded, freshened (page 12), mashed anchovies are whipped into the stuffing to add a piquant accent.

6 medium-size squid
  (cleaned at the market)
3 tablespoons olive oil
2 peeled, chopped onions
4 peeled, seeded, chopped tomatoes
  (or 1 cup purée)
½ cup soft bread crumbs, soaked in
  milk and pressed out
3 sprigs parsley, chopped
2 peeled cloves garlic
Sprig of thyme
(Optional) sprig of basil
Salt and pepper
Grated nutmeg
2 whole eggs, beaten
1 tablespoon flour
White wine or wine and water,
  half-and-half

XII
Poultry and Game

Chicken and Fowl (Poulet et Poule)

CHICKEN is perhaps the greatest common denominator in international cuisine, for there is scarcely a spot on earth where the traveler could be set down and not find it being prepared in some form or other. Even the scrawniest hen, provided it is fresh, can be made appetizing by a knowledgeable cook. But whether the fat is used or discarded, the more of it a chicken has to start with, the better the results will be.

Braised Fowl with Saffron Rice
(*Poule au Riz au Safran*)
SERVES 4 OR 5

3½- to 5-pound fowl
3 tablespoons olive oil
1 onion stuck with cloves
3 small, peeled, halved tomatoes
Bouquet garni, salt and pepper
½ cup each of white wine and water
2 whole cloves garlic
Rice:
   1 finely minced onion
   2 tablespoons olive oil
   1 cup rice
   Salt and pepper
   Saffron and nutmeg, grated

Using a deep, heavy skillet or Dutch oven with a tight lid, braise a whole, trussed plump bird in hot olive oil with the onion. Then add tomatoes, *bouquet garni,* salt and pepper, white wine and water, and garlic cloves. Cook until just tender.

Remove the chicken and set it aside in a warm (not too hot) place. Strain and save the liquor in the cooking pot.

Sauté a finely minced onion in 2 tablespoons olive oil. Do not let it brown. Add 1 cup of rice, turning it delicately in the onion and oil until it "blonds" nicely. Then add the strained liquor, salt and pepper, and a pinch each of nutmeg and saffron. Cover, and cook over medium heat until the rice is just done but not mushy, being careful not to let it burn on the bottom. Serve the chicken on a hot platter, surrounded by the rice.

Fried Chicken of Arles
(*Poulet Sauté Arlésien*)
SERVES 4 TO 6

2 young 2-pound chickens
¼ cup olive oil
1 cup white wine
4 tomatoes, peeled and seeded
2 whole cloves garlic
Salt and pepper
Fried eggplant slices (see Eggplant
   Provençale, page 193)

Cut up the chickens and brown the pieces on all sides in hot oil. Remove chicken, and deglaze the pan by pouring the wine into it and, with a wooden spoon over medium heat, rubbing down all the good brown substances into the liquid in the skillet. Then add the tomatoes and garlic. Simmer until this sauce is somewhat reduced. Season with salt and pepper to taste.

Arrange the chicken in the center of a hot platter. Spoon the tomatoes around it and pour the remaining sauce over all. Garnish the platter with fried eggplant slices.

Chicken Durand (*Poulet Sauté Durand*)

Allowing 3 pounds of cut-up chicken for every 4 persons, roll the pieces in flour and fry them in hot olive oil. Drain. Season with salt and pepper (or the flour may be seasoned). Arrange the crisp chicken in the center of a large hot platter and garnish with little mounds of fried onion rings alternating with "cornets" (one per person) of thinly sliced boiled ham filled with rather thick, highly-spiced tomato sauce (page 32). (Recipe of Chef Durand of Nîmes.)

Fried Chicken Gardanne

SERVES 4 OR 5

Cut the blanched salt pork in strips and wrap each piece of chicken in a strip, tucking a sprig of thyme into the "bundle." Fasten with thread or small skewers. Cook these bundles briefly in the olive oil, then add the salt and pepper, garlic, onion, tomatoes, and wine. Cook, covered, over low heat.

When the chicken is almost done, remove the cover from the pan and let the sauce reduce somewhat. Then add the black olives and, without removing the thread or skewers, serve sprinkled with chopped parsley and ringed around with the "croutons" of fried bread.

3-pound chicken, cut up
¼ pound blanched salt pork (page 21)
12 sprigs fresh thyme
4 tablespoons olive oil
Salt and pepper
1 peeled, chopped medium onion
3 cloves garlic
2 peeled, seeded, chopped tomatoes
2 cups dry white wine
½ cup stoned black olives
Chopped parsley
Slices of bread fried in oil

Chicken Niçoise (Poulet Niçoise)

SERVES 4 OR 5

Brown the chicken pieces in the very hot oil along with the small onions and the clove-studded large one. Season with salt, pepper, and saffron. When the chicken is well colored, add the garlic, tomatoes, and the *bouquet garni*. Add the wine or bouillon and cook, covered, over moderate heat for about 15 minutes. To serve, remove the garlic and the *bouquet garni*, add olives, and blend a few drops of lemon juice into the sauce.

3-pound chicken, cut up
3 tablespoons oil (or more)
6 small white onions
1 large onion stuck with cloves
Salt and pepper
Pinch of saffron
2 whole cloves garlic
5 tomatoes, quartered
Bouquet garni of sage, thyme, and a bay leaf
½ cup white wine or bouillon
¼ cup stoned, black olives
Lemon juice

Fried Chicken with Herb Sauce (Poulet Sauté aux Aromates de Provence)

SERVES 4

Cut up a 3-pound chicken and fry the pieces in olive oil. Season with salt and pepper. Take out the chicken and deglaze the skillet with ½ cup white wine — that is to say, pour in the wine and, with a wooden spoon, stir up all the delicious brown bits left from the frying. Then add to the skillet the tomatoes, garlic, anchovy, savory, marjoram, bay leaf, and (if possible) fresh basil. Let this scented mixture simmer for about 10 minutes. Add the stoned black olives. Heat these in the sauce for a minute. Pour the sauce over the chicken and serve at once.

3-pound chicken
¼ cup olive oil
Salt and pepper
½ cup white wine
3 peeled, seeded, chopped tomatoes
1 chopped clove garlic
1 anchovy fillet
Pinch each of savory and marjoram
Bay leaf, crushed
3 sprigs of fresh basil
½ cup stoned black olives

Chicken with Tarragon Vinegar
(Poulet Sauté au Vinaigre)

2½- to 3-pound (not frozen)
   chicken
Salt and pepper
4 tablespoons butter
2 tablespoons tarragon vinegar
2 medium-size tomatoes, peeled
   and seeded
Fried slices of bread
"Walnut" of butter

Cut up the chicken for frying. Salt and pepper it generously. Melt the butter in a heavy iron or copper skillet. Brown the chicken pieces in the butter and when they are well colored, pour in the vinegar and, with a wooden spoon, deglaze the skillet. Crush the tomatoes and add them. Cook over low heat for about 20 minutes.

When the chicken is cooked, arrange it on a hot platter and pour the pan juices over it through a fine sieve. Add seasoning if needed, and a "walnut" of butter, and serve, surrounded by slices of soft bread* fried in butter.

This recipe was given to the authors by Girard Nandron of the famous 3-star Restaurant Nandron in Lyon.

* Soft crumb bread (*pain de mie*) rather than hard-crusted French bread is specified for this dish.

Chicken with Forty Garlic Cloves
(Poulet aux Quarante Gousses d'Ail)

Young 4-pound chicken
Salt and pepper
Bouquet garni
1 cup olive oil
40 unpeeled cloves garlic
Bouquet of fresh herbs (bay leaf,
   celery, parsley, rosemary, sage,
   and thyme)
Flour and water paste
Toast

Yes, *forty!* Remember that the garlic of Provence is mild; ten cloves of the more aggressive American kind would probably be enough. But remember also that garlic cooked for an hour or more in liquid is thoroughly tamed, merely heightening but not pervading the flavors of the other ingredients.

Salt and pepper the interior of a fat 4-pound chicken and pop a *bouquet garni* inside.

Pour olive oil into a large casserole (preferably earthenware) with a lid. Put into this the whole, unpeeled cloves of garlic and a generous mixed bouquet of fresh herbs: rosemary, sage, thyme, and parsley, plus a bay leaf and 1 or 2 stalks of celery.

Set the prepared chicken on this bed and turn it over and over in the already-perfumed oil. Then, with all the oil and the aromatics below and the chicken on top of them, put the lid on the pot and seal it hermetically with a band of flour and water paste. Bake 1½ hours in a 325° oven.

Carry the casserole to the table and lift off the lid at the moment of serving. An agreeable caress of fragrance is released. The chicken is tender and perfumed. Serve with toasted slices of bread which each person will spread with the incomparable purée.

Chicken Fritters (*Fritots de Volaille*)   SERVES 6

This is a dish in the ancient tradition of Provence, and the temptation to make it with Sunday's leftover chicken must be firmly resisted.

Cook a cleaned *fat* fowl in the salted water over low heat in a covered pot, turning the pieces over occasionally. This will take about 1 to 1½ hours. Let the bird cool until it can be handled and then remove the skin, bones and cartilage, keeping the meat of the wings in as large pieces as possible. Breasts and second joints should be cut in half. Marinate the meat for an hour in an earthenware dish with salt, pepper, a pinch of nutmeg, *fines herbes* (page 16), the juice of half a lemon, and 2 tablespoons olive oil.

Lift the chicken from the marinade. Drain well, and dip the pieces in fritter batter (page 12). Fry them in hot fat (as hot as you dare get it). They will turn golden and crusty very fast, so *watch!* Fish them out of the frying kettle, drain on absorbent paper, and serve with fried parsley (page 18) and a rich tomato sauce (page 32).

5-pound fowl, cut up
2 cups salted water
Salt and pepper
Pinch of nutmeg
Fines herbes
2 tablespoons olive oil
Juice of ½ lemon
Fritter batter
Fat or oil for frying
Fried parsley
Tomato sauce

Braised Chicken Vauclusienne (*Poulet Sauté Vauclusienne*)   SERVES 4 OR 5

Salt and pepper the cavity of a cleaned, whole chicken. Truss the bird and put it into a deep, heavy pot with 2 tablespoons olive oil and the bacon. Brown the bird on all sides. Add the chopped onion, white wine, tomatoes, parsley, and garlic. Season with salt and pepper. Cover, and simmer until the chicken is tender. Finish by adding the stoned black olives during the last few minutes of cooking.

Separately, flour the sliced eggplants and fry them in hot olive oil. Drain and lightly salt. Serve the chicken garnished with the fried eggplant.

4- to 5-pound chicken
Salt and pepper
Olive oil
2 tablespoons chopped lean bacon
1 peeled, chopped onion
½ cup white wine
4 peeled, seeded, chopped tomatoes
1 tablespoon chopped garlic
1 tablespoon chopped parsley
2 dozen stoned black olives
2 peeled, sliced medium eggplants
Flour

Chicken Pie with Olives (*Poulet Olivade*)   SERVES 4

Prepare a pastry dough with ¼ pound butter, ¼ cup water, 1 cup flour, a pinch of salt.

While you allow the dough to "rest," cut up 2 very tender young pullets. Color the pieces in a skillet with the oil, along with the bacon

Pastry dough
2 young pullets
1½ tablespoons olive oil
½ tablespoon diced lean bacon
3 small peeled onions
1 tablespoon flour
2 large, peeled, seeded, crushed
  tomatoes
½ pound stoned olives
Sprig of parsley
Salt and pepper

and the onions. Blend in about 1 tablespoon of flour, add the tomatoes, olives, and parsley. Season with salt and pepper. Cook over moderate heat for about 30 minutes. The tomatoes should provide enough liquid for the sauce which should be scant and rather thick so that it doesn't soften the pastry.

Roll out the pastry dough. Put half of it in a flat mold or pie plate. Dampen the rim of the pastry slightly. Spoon the cooked chicken over it and cover with the other half of the dough. Press the edges of the two crusts together. Insert a funnel through the top crust to allow steam to escape during the baking. Set in a 425° oven for 10 minutes. Then lower heat to 350° and bake 20 minutes longer. (Recipe of Dr. Desfarges.)

Duck (Canard)

Duck is rich, delicious — and infuriating to the carver. For generations, recipe writers have been passing along the optimistic claim that a 5-pound duck will serve 4 or 5 persons. It won't, not if they like duck. There's hardly enough meat on one such duck to feed two, although a *wild* mallard is more abundantly furnished. If there is room enough in the roasting pan and the oven, the best solution is to be lavish and roast two ducks.

Roast Duck Stuffed in the Ancient Provençal Way (Canard Farci à l'Ancienne Mode de Provence)

5-pound duck
2 chopped onions
2 tablespoons olive oil
1 egg
Salt and pepper
1 shallot
30 stoned black olives
Chopped mushroom stems
2 or 3 *small*, seeded, chopped peppers
½ cup marc or Armagnac
Madeira wine
3 tablespoons concentrated brown
  gravy or meat glaze
6 quartered artichoke hearts
Sautéed caps of mushrooms
½ cup blanched green olives
Chopped truffles (optional)

Remove a generous cupful of the breast fat of the duck and blanch it in salted, boiling water. Drain the fat, and then brown it in a skillet along with the duck's liver and the onions, both chopped fine. Season with salt and pepper, and stir in the egg. Add the shallot and black olives, chopped together with an equal quantity of mushroom stems and the peppers. Stir in the Armagnac.

Stuff the duck with this mixture 24 hours before cooking it. Then roast it in a 350° oven for about 1 hour and 15 minutes. During the last 10 minutes, baste with Madeira wine mixed with the gravy or meat glaze. Simmer the duck in the pan juices along with the artichoke hearts, mushroom caps, green olives, and truffles if desired.

Teal (Duck) with Olives (Sarcelle aux Olives)

This recipe is one that is enthusiastically favored by the *gardians,* or cowboys, of the Camargue.

Mix the chopped salt pork with an equal quantity of soaked, pressed-out bread crumbs (3½ tablespoons after pressing out). Pit and chop the black olives and add them. Season with salt and pepper and, with a fork, toss the mixture in ¼ cup of brandy. Stuff the duck, sew up the cavity, and roast it on a rack, in a preheated 325° oven, allowing about 18 to 20 minutes per pound. Baste frequently with the liquid in the pan, adding hot water if necessary. If the duck is very fatty, pour off some of the grease from time to time.

3-pound teal
3½ tablespoons chopped salt pork
3½ tablespoons soaked, pressed-out bread crumbs
Salt and pepper
½ cup stoned black olives
¼ cup brandy
Hot water

Guinea Fowl

The meat of guinea fowl (usually guinea *hen* in the United States) has an unusual flavor — half poultry, half game. It is greatly prized in Provence.

Roasted Stuffed Guinea Hen (Pintade Farcie)

ALLOW 1 POUND PER PERSON. ONE HEN SERVES 2 OR 3

Sauté the sausage meat for 10 minutes and drain off excess fat. Crumble the softened bread crumbs into the meat. Stir in the chopped mushrooms. Turn this mixture quickly in hot olive oil, then moisten it with the port or Madeira. Season with salt and pepper. Stuff the guinea hen with this, and sew or skewer the opening in the cavity. Truss the bird and roast it 20 to 25 minutes, breast down, then reduce heat quickly to 325° (leaving the oven door open to speed the process). Turn bird breast-side up, dredge with flour, and shake on a little salt and pepper. Lay the slices of salt pork over the breast, and roast for 30 minutes longer.

* To be absolutely authentic, *cèpes* are called for. These can sometimes be bought, canned, in specialty food shops but are costly.

2½-pound guinea hen
1 cup bread crumbs, soaked and pressed out.
⅓ cup sausage meat, sautéed and drained
Salt and pepper
¼ pound fresh mushrooms*
    (or 2 tablespoons dried, soaked) chopped
3 tablespoons olive oil
½ cup Madeira or port
Flour for dredging
Thin slices of salt pork

Guinea Chick Antonelle (*Le Pintadon Antonelle à l'Idée de Virginie*)

ALLOW 1 POUND PER PERSON

2- to 2½-pound young guinea hen
8 slices (about) of bacon
Salt and pepper
6 small, blanched white onions
¼ pound small mushrooms
½ cup Madeira
2 teaspoons meat extract
½ teaspoon tomato paste
Eggplant slices, peeled and salted
Batter for frying
Olive oil

We dedicate this dish to the memory of Marcel Provence, ardent champion of Provençal traditions of cookery and are indebted to his faithful servant, Virginie, for having preserved the recipe.

Brown 2 slices of bacon (chopped or diced) in an earthenware or enameled-iron cooking vessel. Remove these with a skimmer or perforated spoon and set them aside to keep warm.

Put the guinea chick, trussed and enveloped in bacon (the bacon skewered or tied on), into the pot. Season with salt and pepper, and cook over moderate heat for about 30 minutes, turning the bird from time to time. Then add the onions and mushrooms, and continue cooking, lowering the heat slightly, for about 20 minutes or until bird is tender. Return the browned lardoons of bacon. Deglaze the cook pot by adding the Madeira and "rubbing down" the interior with a wooden spoon. Add to this winy sauce the meat extract and tomato paste.

Serve the guinea chick in the earthenware pot, accompanied by a platter of very small eggplant fritters. (Let eggplant slices stand 30 minutes, dry them, dip in batter, and fry in hot oil.)

Partridge (*Perdreaux*)

Game birds such as "partridge," quail, woodcock, etc., ordinarily must be specially ordered in the United States and are never available fresh in supermarkets. They are therefore found mostly at the tables of hunters and their friends. In Provence, where, alas! even song birds are eaten, game birds are plentiful.

The "partridge" of the United States is, actually, ruffed grouse or one of his relatives, but is adaptable to any recipes suitable for quail or pheasant or woodcock, as well as many chicken recipes.

No-name Partridge (*Perdreaux Sans Nom*)

SERVES 6

It is essential to the fine flavor of this dish to use small, freshly killed partridges.

Open the birds carefully, cleaning and seasoning the cavities. Then truss them. Heat the butter, olive oil, and bacon and lightly cook the minced onion in this hot fat. Add the birds, turning them until they are nicely colored all over. Then moisten with the white wine combined with the brandy. Season with thyme and bay leaf, and blanched garlic cloves. Cook the birds over medium heat for 15 to 25 minutes, the amount of time depending on the size of the birds. Remove the thread. Add the fried bread crumbs to the juices in the casserole. Serve right in the cooking dish with an accompanying platter of fried eggplant slices (see Eggplant Provençale, page 193). (Recipe of Auguste Escoffier.)

3 partridges
1 tablespoon butter
2 tablespoons olive oil
1 tablespoon chopped, lean bacon
2 tablespoons minced onion
½ cup white wine
½ cup (scant) old Armagnac
  or other good brandy
1 bay leaf, crumbled
Pinch of thyme
15 peeled cloves garlic, blanched for
  5 minutes in boiling, salted water,
  and thoroughly drained
3 tablespoons bread crumbs, fried
  in butter
Fried eggplant slices for garnish

Quail

Quail Hyéroise (Caille à la Hyéroise)   SERVES 4

The quails — having been plucked, cleaned, singed, and cut through the stomach (but not through the back) — should first be browned in hot olive oil, then simmered with 1 cup of bouillon (some people prefer ¾ cup bouillon mixed with ¼ cup Madeira wine), seasoned with salt, pepper, and a *bouquet garni*. Eight or ten artichoke hearts and 1 pound button mushrooms may be cooked in the pot along with the quail. Approximate cooking time 15 minutes.

Quail Marcel Provence (Caille Marcel Provence)

Cut the birds open. Spread them on a large platter and sprinkle generously with a mixture of pepper, chopped onion, parsley, bay leaf, marjoram, and olive oil. Let them lie under this scented blanket for 2 or 3 hours or more. Then shake off the excess herbs, roll the quail in salted flour, and broil them on an oiled grill under a moderate flame. During the cooking (which at no time should be fast), baste the little birds with oil and turn them. Quail absorb oil beautifully. It makes their firm, white fat even more delicious.

1 fat quail per person, eviscerated
  and singed
Pepper
Chopped onion and parsley
1 crumbled bay leaf
4 sprigs fresh marjoram (or
  1 teaspoon dried)
Olive oil
Salted flour

Rabbit and Hare (*Lapin et Lièvre*)

Americans whose early reading was the Beatrix Potter books are never going to be entirely happy about eating Peter Rabbit's descendants. Others, more logical if less tenderhearted, won't swallow a chick and strain at a hare. The following recipes for hare and rabbit are interchangeable, except that hare needs longer cooking. They are interchangeable, also, with many lamb recipes and, indeed, in the absence of game, lamb makes a very acceptable substitute, particularly in Civet (see below).

It is advisable to have the rabbit or hare professionally dressed (skinned, leg tendons freed, etc.) at the market. And the meat is improved by being soaked for an hour in water to cover plus 1 tablespoon salt and ¼ cup vinegar or lemon juice. It should then be drained and thoroughly dried with a cloth before being cooked.

Both hare and rabbit are lean (no fat at all) and need generous supplements of oil, butter, salt pork, bacon, or other fat. This, plus slow cooking, is an important factor in the cook's success.

Bundles of Rabbit Brignolaise
(*Lapins en Paquets Brignolaise*)   SERVES 3 OR 4

4-pound rabbit
Bacon
Garlic
3 tomatoes
3 tablespoons olive oil
Salt and pepper

Cut up the rabbit and free the leg tendons (if butcher has not already done so). Wrap each piece around with strips of bacon, tucking a sliver of garlic into each.

Separately, peel, seed, and crush the tomatoes. Put them into a skillet with 3 tablespoons hot olive oil, salt and pepper. Cook over medium heat until the tomatoes are about half done, then transfer them, with their juices, to a baking dish. Place the rabbit bundles on top and bake, covered, at 350° for 30 minutes, then lower heat to 325° and bake for another 30 minutes, uncovering the dish for the last 10 minutes of cooking.

Civet of Hare or Rabbit
(*Civet de Lièvre ou de Lapin*)   SERVES 4, IF RABBIT; 6, IF HARE

This savory wine stew is similar to the jugged hare of England and to Germany's *Hasenpfeffer* in that the meat is marinated for a long time and, during long cooking, develops a rich wine sauce. If anyone is astonished to find this dish counted among those typical of *cuisine provençale*, let him remember that "rabbit stew" turns up wherever there are rabbits and that there are certain details that give the following recipe its Provençal character.

Cut the rabbit or hare in pieces, reserving the blood (which, if the meat is dressed in the market, a knowledgeable butcher will have saved for you). Put 2 cups of the red wine in a large bowl. Season with salt, pepper, minced onion, bay leaf, and the chopped herbs. Add the meat and marinate for at least 8 hours.

Put the chopped bacon and the quartered onion into an earthenware or enameled iron cook pot over medium heat. When the fat has been rendered, drain the pieces of hare or rabbit thoroughly (saving the marinade), pat them dry with paper towels or a cloth, and toss into the hot fat. When the pieces have taken a good brown color, strain the marinade and add it, plus the third cup of red wine. Let this liquor reduce somewhat, then sprinkle in the 2 tablespoons of toasted flour*. Blend well and add the boiling water or bouillon and the *bouquet garni* reinforced with a sprig of thyme. Simmer 1½ to 2 hours or until the rabbit or hare is tender. Add more salt and pepper if needed.

Remove the meat from the pot. Strain the sauce, and bring it again to a boil. Dilute the reserved blood with the vinegar and add it to the sauce. Return the meat to the sauce which should be rich and rather thick. They say in Provence, "Each morsel must carry its own sauce." (If there is not enough rabbit blood, the dish may be completed with pork or chicken blood bought from a butcher.)

* Toasting the flour, by stirring it over low heat in a heavy skillet, removes the raw flavor so often noticeable in carelessly prepared dishes.

1 rabbit or hare
Salt and pepper
1 medium-size onion, minced
1 bay leaf
½ cup mixed chopped fresh thyme, savory, and sage
3 cups red wine
3½ tablespoons chopped bacon (or 3 tablespoons olive oil)
1 onion, peeled and quartered
2 tablespoons flour, lightly toasted
6½ cups boiling water or bouillon
Bouquet garni plus thyme
Vinegar: 1 tablespoon for rabbit; 1½ tablespoon for hare

Fillets of Hare Provençal
(*Filets de Lièvre à la Provençale*)   SERVES 4

Have the butcher cut 4 fillets from the hare. With the aid of a small, sharp knife, lard these with strips of anchovy. Season with salt and pepper (light on salt), sprinkle generously with the minced garlic, and then wrap each fillet in bacon or thin overcoats of blanched salt pork. Cook over gentle heat in a covered skillet with the olive oil for about 45 minutes, basting often. As soon as the meat is tender, transfer it to a hot platter. Blanket with a sauce made by adding to the pan juices the tomato purée, wine, and bouillon beaten either with a little blood from the hare or with egg yolk.

1 hare
Freshened anchovy fillets (page 12)
Salt and pepper
Minced garlic
Bacon or blanched salt pork
2 tablespoons olive oil
3 tablespoons thick tomato purée
¼ cup white wine
½ cup bouillon
A little of the blood of the hare (or 1 egg yolk)

Fried Rabbit or Hare Marseillaise
(*Sauté de Lapin ou de Lièvre à la Marseillaise*)

SERVES 4 OR 5

5-pound young hare, or rabbit
Flour
½ cup olive oil (or more)
Salt and pepper
2 onions, chopped
2 cloves garlic
2 cups white wine
2 cups bouillon
Bouquet garni
3 tomatoes, peeled, seeded and
  chopped
12 small anchovy fillets, freshened
  (page 12)
1 tablespoon chopped parsley or
  fresh tarragon
1 tablespoon vinegar
½ cup stoned black olives
12 slices of fried bread

Cut up the rabbit or hare, roll the pieces in flour, and brown them in 4 tablespoons hot olive oil. Season with salt and pepper. Add the onions, and 1 clove of garlic, left whole. Add the wine and bouillon, the tomatoes, and the *bouquet garni*. Cook at a brisk boil for 40 minutes.

In a mortar, pound the anchovy fillets with the second clove of garlic (peeled), and 3 tablespoons olive oil, plus the tarragon or parsley.

Brown the slices of bread in the remaining oil, adding more oil if necessary.

Arrange the pieces of meat on a hot platter, removing the *bouquet garni*. Add the vinegar to the sauce in the pan and then let this liquid reduce by half. Stir in the anchovy purée and the olives. Pour the steaming sauce over the meat and circle the platter with the "croutons" of fried bread.

Roasted Stuffed Rabbit (*Lapereau Farci*) SERVES 3

2-pound rabbit
1 cup bouillon (optional)
Cooked veal or lean ham
1 tablespoon blanched salt pork
Salt and pepper
½ teaspoon powdered thyme (or
  wild thyme)
4 young carrots, scraped
1 onion, chopped
Bouquet garni
Bacon
1 cup white wine

It is best to use a young rabbit (*lapereau*) for roasting.

Chop the liver (simmer it in a cup of broth first, if it is too hard to handle in its uncooked state) and combine it with an equal quantity of cooked veal or lean ham, chopped, and 1 tablespoon blanched salt pork, diced rather fine. Season with salt, pepper, and powdered or wild thyme. Stuff the rabbit with this mixture and close the opening with thread or skewers. Place the rabbit in a roasting pan just large enough to hold it with the carrots, onion, and *bouquet garni*. Cover with thin slices of bacon and roast at 325° for 1 to 1½ hours, basting occasionally. When the rabbit is tender, remove it from the roaster which can then be deglazed to make a thin sauce: first strain out the fat and vegetables that have caramelized, setting aside the cooked carrots. Pour 1 cup white wine into the pan, set it over low heat, and with a wooden spoon stir the brown bits that adhere to the pan into the wine. Strained or not, this is a good sauce. Serve the rabbit surrounded by the carrots. The sauce is sent to the table separately.

Turkey (*Dinde*)

Christmas Turkey
(*La Dinde de Noël*)

ESTIMATE ¾ POUND PER PERSON

In Provence, as in the United States, the midday dinner on Christmas Day is turkey. The stuffing, however, is very different from that used in the American bird and is less copious.

It is important to select a tender, fat turkey, preferably a female. In France she can be young. In America, as a rule, only the older, heavier birds (upwards of 12 pounds) reward the cook. Turkeys bred "for apartment-size stoves" tend to be tough and taste rather like indifferent chicken.

12- to 15-pound hen turkey
1 chopped onion
¼ pound sautéed sausage meat
¼ pound lean cooked ham
   (preferably Smithfield)
Salt and pepper
¼ cup white wine or bouillon
2 cups shelled fresh chestnuts
Chicken bouillon
Thin slices of fat bacon or pork fat
Soft unsalted butter
Salted flour

The bird should be thoroughly rinsed inside and cleared of any dark substances overlooked when it was eviscerated at the market. Then dry thoroughly, inside and out. Salt the cavity lightly.

Sauté the chopped onion. Stir in the sautéed sausage meat, ham, and the uncooked turkey liver, all chopped together. Season highly with salt and pepper. Moisten with the white wine or bouillon, and cook over medium heat for 10 minutes, stirring occasionally.

Peel the fresh chestnuts and simmer them for 45 minutes in clear chicken broth to cover, adding more broth if necessary, to keep them submerged throughout the cooking time. (Broth should be saved for next day's soup.) Leave the chestnuts whole and add them to the stuffing. Fill the cavity with the stuffing, and sew up or skewer the openings. Envelop the bird in *very thin* slices of fat bacon or pork fat. [Order these in advance from a cooperative butcher because the easiest way to "lard" a bird is with very wide, long, thin strips that can be tied or skewered on.]

The giblets may be larded and threaded on skewers and roasted, or may be broiled on a rotisserie spit.

For crisp skin, the bird should be rubbed with soft unsalted butter, then powdered all over with salted flour. The length of roasting time depends on the weight of the bird. It averages 20 minutes per pound but a thermometer inserted on the inside of the thigh (NOT touching either the pan or bone) is a safer guide. When turkey is cooked, this should register 185°. A 14-pound bird roasted at 300° needs 4 to 4½ hours and should be basted frequently throughout.

The *Provençaux* do not thicken the gravy but merely skim off the fat in the pan and serve the juices in a sauce boat.

Turkey Stew (*Dinde en Ragoût*)

2½ cups turkey meat
2 squares bacon
1 tablespoon olive oil or lard
1 tablespoon minced bacon
1 tablespoon minced cooked ham
Salt and pepper
Bouquet garni
½ cup cognac
2 or 3 peeled, diced carrots
A chopped onion
1 clove garlic, crushed
¼ cup tomato purée
Fried slices of French bread

A little-known Provençal recipe.

This stew is best when made with uncooked turkey although it is adaptable to leftovers. Fortunately for small households, many American markets now offer turkey breasts or turkey legs separately packaged. [**The ham should be, preferably, Smithfield or similar dry-cured ham.**]

The meat should be cut into pieces of equal size and browned, along with 2 squares of smoky bacon, in olive oil or lard. Transfer turkey and bacon from the skillet to a baking dish. Add to them 1 tablespoon each of bacon and ham, minced, salt and pepper, a *bouquet garni,* and ½ cup *eau-de-vie* or cognac.

In the fat left in the skillet, brown the chopped onion, diced carrots, and crushed garlic. Pour the tomato purée over these and let all come to a boil. Then lower heat and simmer for a few minutes, stirring to blend well. Pour this savory mixture over the browned pieces of turkey in the baking dish. Cover very tightly and cook over low heat (just at a simmer) or in a 275° oven for at least 2 hours or a little longer. Test for seasoning, adding more salt and pepper if needed. Serve very hot, garnished with fried slices of bread. (Recipe of Auguste Escoffier.)

Woodcock

Canons' Woodcock (*Bécasses des Chanoines*)

ALLOW 1 BIRD PER PERSON

How this dish got its title nobody seems to know, but we suspect its origin was mischievous since the recipe has also been found listed under "Lenten Woodcock."

The birds are hung until as gamy as suits your taste. Traditionally, woodcock are never eviscerated. They are bathed in olive oil, roasted whole for 15 minutes in an oven preheated to 350°, and cut in half. These morsels are then rolled in a frying pan with lemon juice and a little mustard, and seasoned with salt and pepper. The "trail" (intestines) are chopped, and a generous half cup or more of champagne (which woodcock dote on) added. This liquor is heated, ignited, and poured over the meat. The sauce should be simmered to reduce slightly before serving.

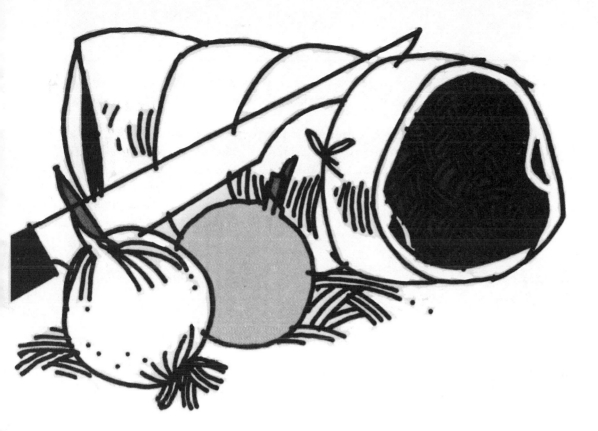

XIII. *Meat*

Broiled Meat

IN PROVENCE, the preferred method of broiling meat — rib steak, Delmonico, or "club steak," lamb or mutton chops, lamb steak, pork chops — is to dip in oil and then grill over a fire made of vine shoots or wood embers. Before the meat is completely cooked, there are thrust under it several well-dried bay leaves or sprigs of thyme which will, of course, ignite and "flame" the meat with their fragrances. At the moment when the meat is served, it is sprinkled with a few drops of olive oil.

Pork chops are additionally glorified by being "pinked" with bits of sage. This is done by making tiny incisions in the chops, with the point of a sharp paring knife, and then pressing bits of sage into the incisions.

With the average gas stove, broiling is apt to be unsatisfactory. A surer method is to pan-broil as follows: Get a heavy iron skillet extremely hot, rub it with a piece of fat from the meat, and then brown the meat fast on both sides, turn down the heat and, cook (uncovered) to the desired doneness. Check by making a small incision in the meat from time to time. *Caution:* Steak and loin lamb chops should be removed from the skillet while still slightly undercooked as the meat continues to cook itself for a while in its own stored heat.

Beef (Boeuf)

Beef Stew of Arles
(Estouffade de Boeuf Arlésienne)   SERVES 4 OR 5

2½ pounds beef round
½ cup diced bacon
3 tablespoons olive oil
2 tablespoons flour
3 medium-size onions, quartered
Salt and pepper
3 cups white wine, 1 cup water
3 whole cloves garlic
Bouquet garni
4 large tomatoes, quartered
½ cup each of stoned green and
    black olives
½ cup minced parsley

Try out the bacon in the olive oil, then remove the crisp lardoons. Cut the beef into 10 or 12 pieces and roll these in the flour. Brown in the "bacony" oil, then add the quartered onions and let these brown lightly. Season with salt and pepper. Stir in the wine and water, a little at a time. Add the garlic and the *bouquet garni.* Cover, and leave to simmer (never boil!) for 2 hours.

Now remove the *bouquet garni,* skim the fat from the sauce, and add the tomatoes, the two kinds of olives, and the reserved bits of crisp bacon. Cook over low heat for 1 hour longer. Serve powdered with minced parsley.

Beef Birds (Paupiettes à la Provence)   SERVES 6

2½ pounds top round
1 cup minced, cooked meat
2 freshened anchovy fillets (page 12)
Salt and pepper
2 tablespoons olive oil
1 scraped, minced carrot
1 small, peeled, minced onion
¾ cup white wine
¾ cup bouillon

"Alouettes sans Têtes" (Headless Larks), *"Paupiettes," "Roulade," "Petites Ballotines,"* or whatever else this dish may be called, it is still our well-known American friend, "Veal Birds," except that in this recipe it is made with beef.

The piece of top round should be cut into very thin slices about 4-inches square. This should result in about 18 slices, enough for six people. The filling is made by combining a generous ½ cup each of cooked minced pork and veal or 1 cup of any cooked, minced meat (sausage or ham do nicely) and 2 desalted fillets of anchovy. Chop all together. Season to taste with salt and pepper. Spread a layer of this mixture on each slice of beef, roll it up and fasten with thread.

Put 1 tablespoon of the olive oil into a skillet plus the minced carrot and onion. Place the "birds" on top, salting very lightly. Raise the heat and brown the birds all over. If the vegetables start to brown too quickly, remove them with a slotted spoon and return them to the skillet after the meat has taken on a nice, rich color. Then pour in the white wine and bouillon. Stir to blend. Cover the skillet and cook over moderate heat for 1½ hours. Watch carefully, and lower the heat under the skillet if the sauce starts to evaporate fast. The sauce should, however, be well reduced.

Note: This dish may be made with veal slices, in which case, a few chopped mushrooms are added to the filling.

Boiled Beef I
(Boeuf Bouilli Sauté Provençale)   SERVES 6

This Provençal dish is a variation of (or, more likely, the origin of) the celebrated *Boeuf Miroton,* one of the great specialties of Parisian cuisine. It is, in any case, an inspired treatment for leftover, cooked beef.

12 thin slices cold boiled beef
3 tablespoons (about) olive oil
1 cup (about) bouillon
2 onions, minced
2 tablespoons flour
Toast points

Grease an oblong ovenware dish with some of the oil and lay the slices of beef in it, overlapping slightly. Moisten with a little well-seasoned bouillon, about 2 teaspoons per slice; the meat should not float in the liquid. Set the dish in a preheated 325° oven.

While the beef is heating, color the minced onions in olive oil. Add flour, in proportions of 1 tablespoon flour to 1 tablespoon oil, and make a brown *roux.* Stirring constantly, add 1 cup hot bouillon for each 1-to-1 quantity of *roux.* Simmer for several minutes. As soon as the onions are well blended into the sauce, pour the whole over the slices of beef. Leave in the oven for several minutes longer to heat through. Serve surrounded by toast points.

Boiled Beef II à la Ratatouille
(Boeuf Bouilli à la Ratatouille)

This recipe for using leftover boiled beef (or any other sliceable meat, for that matter) is one that would probably suggest itself if the larder also contained a bowl of *Ratatouille* (page 193), for it consists merely of garnishing an ovenware dish with the *ratatouille,* laying the meat slices over it and topping it with an additional layer of the *ratatouille*. In short, making a sandwich which is then lightly sprinkled with oil, dusted with fine crumbs, and glazed under the broiler.

Braised Beef (*Boeuf en Daube*)   SERVES 6 OR MORE

2½ pounds "butcher's stew meat"
¼ cup olive oil
¼ cup (scant) diced fresh pork fat*
3 quartered onions
1 whole onion stuck with cloves
2 scraped carrots, halved
1 tablespoon tomato paste
4 cloves garlic
Bouquet garni
A slice of orange rind
Salt
1 teaspoon peppercorns
1 calf's foot, split lengthwise
Red wine to cover

Boeuf en Daube is one of the most ancient of the Provençal dishes which have traveled to the far corners of the provinces. It differs in minor details from place to place but should never be made from a single piece of meat. To be authentic, you must have *"daube du boucher"* which is a mixture of choice lean and fat pieces taken from several different parts of the carcass and including some that is gelatinous. This variety results in a savory blend of the qualities inherent in the diverse cuts of meat.

The name of the stew derives from the type of utensil in which it is cooked. This, in olden days, sat on legs so that it could be thrust right into the coals, and had a cover high enough so that live coals or wood embers could be set on top without burning the contents of the pot, yet cooking them at low heat all night. In today's kitchens a Dutch oven or similar large, heavy pot with a snug lid has to serve.

Cut the meat into pieces of equal size weighing about ¼ pound each. Into the bottom of your *daubière* put the oil and pork fat, onions, carrots, tomato paste, garlic, *bouquet garni,* orange rind, salt, and peppercorns. Lay the calf's foot on this bed of vegetables and surmount with the pieces of beef. Add enough good red wine to just cover the contents of the pot.

Cover, and start the cooking over quick heat until the boiling point is reached. At this moment, lower the heat quickly. After the boiling is reduced to no more than a steady simmer, continue cooking (never any faster) for about 6 hours. The success of the traditional *boeuf en daube* depends on the evenness of the low-heat cooking.

La daube is usually preceded or accompanied by a dish of macaroni and is always served on hot plates. When reheated (again always over low heat), it is even better. It then becomes something that, in Provence, is considered a veritable beef confection.

* Fat salt pork or ham fat may be substituted if first blanched.

Jellied Braised Beef (*Boeuf en Daube en Gelée*)

Beef stew, prepared "en daube" as above, when refrigerated in its own juice, jellies and constitutes an exquisite cold entrée (known, sometimes, as *Cold Boeuf à la Mode*). All you have to do is to bone the calf's foot and put it, with the beef, in an earthenware casserole and pour the juice through a strainer over the meat. Some like to add ½ cup of wine or brandy at this point. Let it cool for 2 or 3 hours and unmold it just before serving. Cut in slices, it is usually served with a seasonal salad.

Braised Beef with Olives (*Boeuf Braisé aux Olives*)

SERVES 5 OR 6

Here is a recipe for a braised beef that doubles one's appreciation of the famous red wine, Châteauneuf-du-Pape, for, in this dish, the "violet" aftertaste of that good wine is rapturously wedded to the slightly bitter flavor of the olives with wonderful results.

With a sharp, narrow, thin knife, make 6 to 8 incisions in the surface of the round of beef. Roll the bacon strips in the parsley-garlic-pepper mixture and push the strips into the incisions. Heat the olive oil in a deep earthenware or enameled iron pot and brown the meat on all sides. Add the calf's foot, the carrot, and one of the onions. When all has taken a good color, drench it with the wine. Add salt, allspice, mustard, garlic, the *bouquet garni,* and the second onion, studded with the cloves. Cover and turn the heat very low.

While the meat is simmering, desalt the olives by soaking them for an hour or longer in cold water to cover. Then drain them and remove the stones.

At the end of 3 hours of simmering, add the Madeira and olives to the braising beef in the pot. At this point also, for those who prefer a slightly thickened gravy, the surface fat should be skimmed off and the flour-bouillon paste stirred in. Continue cooking over low heat until the meat responds tenderly to the pressure of a fork — probably about 1 hour longer. Then transfer the meat to a hot platter.

To serve, make a bed of olives on a long, heated serving dish. Carve the beef in slices and lay these over the olives. Cover all with the sauce.

3 pounds beef round (left whole)
9 ¼-inch strips bacon
¼ cup parsley and garlic, minced, peppered, mixed
3 tablespoons olive oil
1 calf's foot, skinned and cleaned
1 carrot, scraped and cut in rounds
2 whole onions
4 whole cloves
1 bottle Châteauneuf-du-Pape
Salt and pepper
Pinch of allspice
½ teaspoon dry mustard
Bouquet garni plus thyme
2 cloves garlic
½ cup Madeira
1¼ pounds green olives
(Optional) 1 **tablespoon** cornstarch or potato flour, mixed to a thin paste with bouillon or water

Beef Fillets and Tournedos

In the United States a fillet is always the tenderloin of beef, lamb, pork, or (rarely) veal. In France, it may also be a piece of meat taken from the sirloin. In either case, it is a long, narrow, boneless portion. *Tournedos* (sometimes called *médaillons*) are made only with true tenderloin. They are round, rather thick slices weighing about ⅓ pound each.

If sirloin strips rather than the more costly tenderloin (or "filet mignon") are used in the following recipes, care must be taken in selecting the meat. If it is a bright and glossy red, it will be tough. Desirably aged beef is rather dark on the surface and even slightly molded before being trimmed. And the best beef is speckled all through with fat, the more small flecks the better. The misleading term, "marbled," is best forgotten since to most one-time marble players, it brings to mind "aggies," which were *streaked.* Outside layers of fat can be cut away, but although not all beef with a lot of fat is good, *all* good beef has a lot of waste fat.

Fillets that are to be cooked whole should be larded with strips of bacon or salt pork and basted during the cooking with the drippings in the pan.

In Provence, the name of a fillet or *tournedos* dish is more or less determined by its final garnish. The little rounds of beef are oiled and broiled, arranged on a hot platter and variously embellished. Almost all have tomato in some form. Pretty much at the discretion of the cook, the tomato can be sliced and fried, baked, or made into a sauce. With fried slices of eggplant the dish becomes *Beauvallon. Mirabeau* has half a tomato as in *Tomatoes Provençale* (page 202) plus broiled mushrooms. *Provençale* is topped by a large, fat olive (black or green) wrapped in a fillet of anchovy, and flanked by fried eggplant or tomato. When the grilled beef rounds sit on slices of fried bread and are ringed with stuffed mushrooms (page 196) they become *Sainte-Baume.*

Roasted whole fillets served in tomato sauce with *chipolatas* (oniony sausages) or braised chestnuts and little glazed onions are called *"à la Caraque."* If, in addition to tomato and eggplant, they have fried onion rings, they become *St. Rémy.*

A typical treatment for *tournedos* follows.

Tournedos of Beef with Anchovies (*Tournedos de Boeuf en Brochette aux Anchois*)

ALLOW ⅓ TO ½ POUND PER PERSON

It is best to use real beef tenderloin for this dish. Cut it in *tournedos* (about 3½ ounces each). The rounds should be of equal diameter. Thread them on skewers alternately with thin squares of bacon and tuck a tiny piece of garlic inside each pair. Season lightly with salt mixed with powdered rosemary and a little white pepper. Tie these little reconstructed "roasts" to their skewers firmly and broil them, basting frequently with olive oil in which anchovy fillets have been "melted."*

When the meat is *"à point,"* that is, has been cooked just the right amount (about 8 minutes, 4 on each side), it should be beautifully browned outside and still pink and juicy inside, and marvelously savory. It may equally well be pan-broiled in a very hot, heavy iron skillet.

* This oil and anchovy mixture should be put into a small bottle that has a tight cork so that it may be vigorously shaken up before each basting.

Steak Côte d'Azur
(*Entrecôte Côte d'Azur*) SERVES 1 HUNGRY, 2 NOT

An entrecôte is just what its name implies, a piece of beef taken from *between the ribs*.

Combine olive oil, lemon juice, the garlic clove, peeled and mashed. Grind the peppercorns and add these with the rosemary powder and tarragon mustard (or Colman's dry mustard mixed with ½ teaspoon powdered tarragon). Blend well.

Rub the steak with this mixture and set it aside for an hour to absorb the flavors. Then broil over (or under) high heat, 5 minutes on each side. Serve sprinkled with olive oil or lightly spread with softened butter and mustard.

½ cup olive oil
Juice of 1 lemon
1 clove garlic
6 peppercorns
2 tablespoons powdered rosemary
1 tablespoon tarragon mustard
1 pound steak (entrecôte)
(Optional) butter

Delmonico, Club, or other Steak à la Rhodanienne
(*Grillade de Boeuf à la Rhodanienne*) SERVES 2 OR 3

Broil the meat as in the preceding recipe but without pretreating and serve it with a sauce made as follows: Color the minced onion in the olive oil over medium heat, and add the anchovy. Transfer to a saucepan, and add the vinegar, garlic, bay leaf, thyme, cloves, paprika, or allspice, salt and pepper. When the liquid has somewhat reduced, add the flour, stirring until smooth. Then add the bouillon or water, a little at a time. Cook over very low heat for 30 minutes. At the moment of serving, stir the minced pickles and the capers into this sauce.

2½ pounds steak
2 tablespoons olive oil
1 medium-size onion, minced
1 freshened anchovy fillet, minced
½ cup wine vinegar
3 whole garlic cloves
1 bay leaf and sprig of fresh thyme
3 whole cloves
¼ teaspoon paprika or allspice
Salt and pepper
1 tablespoon flour
1 cup bouillon or water
2 small pickles, minced
1 tablespoon capers

Delmonico or Rib Steak with Anchovies
(*Entrecôte Anchoise*)

Allowing ¾ pound of steak per person, rub the meat well with olive oil and broil it. Then season with salt and pepper and brush lightly with *anchoïade* (page 48). Decorate with crossed pairs of small anchovy fillets (tinned) and serve, ringed with stoned black olives.

Rhône Bargemen's Beef
(*"Grillade" des Mariniers du Rhône*)   SERVES 4

1½ pounds beef round
2 teaspoons vinegar
1 tablespoon cognac
3 or 4 tablespoons olive oil
½ onion, chopped
1 clove garlic, chopped
5 sprigs parsley, minced
½ cup water (generous)
Salt and pepper
1 tablespoon butter
1 tablespoon flour

Although called a *"Grillade,"* this dish is not a grill at all but is a kind of sauté of beef.

Cut the beef in slices and then cut the slices in squares. Flatten these with the flat side of a cleaver (or have the butcher do it) as for scallopini. Put these slices into a skillet with the vinegar, cognac, and olive oil. Add the onion, garlic, and parsley. Pour in the water and season with salt and pepper, stressing the pepper. Cover the skillet snugly and cook over fairly brisk heat for about an hour, stirring and shaking the skillet from time to time. Five minutes before serving, roll a "walnut" of butter in the flour and toss it into the skillet to thicken the sauce, being careful to stir well. Serve very hot.

Lamb (*Agneau*)

In France, the flavor of lamb varies with the region in which it grazed. Certain mountain meadows, rich in herbs, produce one kind, the salt meadows *(les prés salés)* one quite different, and the experienced cook adapts his seasonings accordingly. In the United States, no such distinctions are made. There is spring lamb and there is lamb. Occasionally, there is mutton but not very often or, at least, not so labeled. Possibly it is because of their uninspiring diets that American lambs grow up to become mutton of such uninviting "barnyardy" quality.

The recipe titles followed by M in this section are those that, in the French edition, specified mutton but that are also suitable for American lamb.

Lamb with Anchovy or Garlic Sauce
(*Agneau, Sauce aux Anchois ou à l'Ail*) M

Any piece of broiled, pan-broiled, sautéed, or roasted lamb can be glorified by the addition of anchovy or garlic sauce made with the drippings. Either results in something truly Provençal.

To make *Anchovy Sauce,* bone and chop 3 freshened (page 12) anchovies. To the drippings left in the roaster, grease skimmed off, add the anchovies, pepper, ½ cup chopped parsley, and the juice of ½ lemon. Stir with a wooden spoon over medium heat.

For *Garlic Sauce,* pound 12 peeled cloves of garlic in a mortar with ½ teaspoon salt, ¼ teaspoon pepper, a pinch of thyme, and a crumbled bay leaf. Mix well and add 3 tablespoons good wine vinegar. Strain this mixture through several thicknesses of cheesecloth, wringing the cloth hard to extract all the garlic juice. Then with this perfumed vinegar, deglaze the roaster or skillet, mixing in all the good brown meat glaze that adheres to the sides and bottom.

Breast of Lamb with Artichokes
(*Poitrine d'Agneau aux Artichauts*) M   SERVES 6

Cut breast of lamb in pieces and sear these fast in hot olive oil along with the onions. Sprinkle with the flour and, stirring constantly, add white wine and bouillon, mixed a little at a time. Season with salt and pepper plus a *bouquet garni.* Bring to a boil, then lower heat until the liquid merely simmers. Cover, and simmer 1½ hours, adding, during the last 15 minutes, the medium-size cooked, quartered artichokes (with the chokes removed, of course).

When a more substantial dish is wanted, small new potatoes are added 15 minutes before the stew is finished, but *never* when mutton is substituted for lamb.

4-pound breast of lamb
4 tablespoons olive oil
6 peeled, medium-size onions
2 tablespoons flour
¾ cup white wine
¾ cup bouillon
Salt and pepper
Bouquet garni
6 cooked artichokes

Breast of Lamb Aixoise
(*Poitrine d'Agneau à l'Aixoise*)   SERVES 4

Have the butcher cut a breast of lamb into squares. In a skillet cook the pieces in hot oil just until they have taken on a good color. Season the lamb with salt and pepper, and transfer the contents of the skillet to a saucepan. Add 2 or 3 peeled whole garlic cloves and a *bouquet garni* and cook the lamb over low heat, without basting, until it is tender. Remove the meat from the pan and keep it warm. Add to the pan 1 generous cup of fresh Tomato Sauce (page 32) and cook the mixture, stirring with a wooden spoon to blend in the flavorful brown particles until it boils up. Pour the very hot sauce over the lamb.

Stuffed Breast of Lamb
(Poitrine d'Agneau Farcie) M

SERVES 6

4-pound breast of lamb with a
   pocket cut in it
¼ pound sausage meat
½ cup soft bread crumbs
1 clove garlic, chopped
¼ cup chopped parsley
Pinch of dried marjoram
Salt and pepper
1 egg yolk, beaten
3 carrots, scraped and halved
3 small leeks
1 small head of cabbage, quartered
1 white turnip, peeled and quartered
1 large onion stuck with cloves
Water

Cook the sausage meat over medium heat, draining off the fat as it is yielded. Soak the bread crumbs in water and press the water out. Mix garlic and parsley and combine with the crumbs and sausage meat. Season with salt and pepper and the pinch of marjoram, and bind with the beaten egg yolk. Stuff the opening with this mixture and sew it up. Put the stuffed breast into an earthenware or enameled-iron casserole that has a tight lid. Add water to barely cover the meat. Simmer, snugly covered, for about 1 hour. Then lay the cleaned vegetables around it in the broth. Cover again, and simmer 30 minutes longer or until the vegetables are cooked but not mushy.

The broth (skimmed of fat if necessary) is served as a first course. The meat is served in slices on a hot platter with the vegetables as garnish.

Note: This is the recipe for the dish as it is made today. But the authentic traditional version is based on *l'épeautre* which is *spelt* (*Triticum Spelta*), a type of wheat that used to be grown in Alpine areas. Alas! *l'épeautre* is almost never cultivated these days. But if you chance to come upon some, be sure to cook it for your breast of lamb.

Breaded Lamb Chops with Herbs
(Côtelettes d'Agneau Panées aux Aromates) M

Allow 1 double lamb chop or 1 mutton chop per person. Dip chops in beaten egg white, then in crumbs which have been seasoned with salt, pepper, and a mixture of powdered thyme, savory, coriander, and rosemary in proportions of 1 teaspoon mixed herbs to 1 cup of crumbs. Fry the breaded chops in hot olive oil or shortening. Transfer them to an ovenware serving dish and set this in a warm (not hot) oven while making the sauce.

To the oil and flavorsome crumbs left in the skillet, add well-seasoned tomato sauce to taste. At the moment of serving, pour this sauce around the chops on their hot platter.

Gardiano of Lamb (Gardiano d'Agneau) SERVES 4

This simple recipe surprisingly produces a dish of lamb in a sauce of unusual texture and is an interesting variation of lamb stew.

Sear 4 large loin or shoulder lamb chops in 2 or 3 tablespoons olive oil. Put into the skillet 1 large, peeled, thinly sliced potato, salt and pepper, and ½ cup chopped parsley. Add boiling water to cover, and simmer until the potato has completely melted into the sauce. That's all there is to it.

Provençal Shepherds' Lamb Chops (Côtelettes d'Agneau à la mode des Bergers de Provence) M ALLOW 1 OR 2 CHOPS PER PERSON

This somewhat forgotten recipe was once a favorite of Provençal shepherds, especially when, following an accident or at the time of moving the herd, they were obliged to kill an animal. As will be seen, the sauce that accompanies the grilled meat is very simple and suits the rural life of the Haute Provence shepherds.

Broil the chops (over wood embers if possible) or pan-broil. Toast a slice of bread for each chop.

Meanwhile, prepare a sauce as follows: Brown the flour in a skillet with the olive oil. Add the onion, garlic, and parsley. Season with salt and pepper and let all cook over gentle heat for a few minutes, stirring to prevent the mixture sticking to the pan. Stir in the water. Allow to thicken slightly, and just before serving, add the white wine. Simmer for 2 or 3 minutes. Lay the hot broiled chops on the slices of toast and pour the sauce over them.

1 or 2 chops per person
Bread
2 tablespoons olive oil
2 tablespoons flour
1 medium-size onion, peeled and minced
1 clove garlic, peeled and chopped
¼ cup (or more) chopped parsley
Salt and pepper
1 cup water
½ cup white wine

Sautéed Lamb Chops Jean-Louis Vaudoyer (Côtelettes de Mouton Jean-Louis Vaudoyer) M

We dedicate the recipe for this traditional (although sadly neglected) dish to the eminent scholar, knowledgeable gastronome, Provençal by adoption, who has so magnificently honored, in two famous books, *Les Beautés de la Provence*. The dish, itself, is simple enough but, when presented as suggested below, looks impressively professional.

Allow 1 double lamb chop (or single mutton chop) per person with an extra chop or two for grace. Brown them in a small quantity of olive oil (about 1 teaspoon per chop), then lower heat and cook, turning occasionally, until the desired degree of donenees is reached. Ideally chops should be brown outside, pink and juicy but not raw within.

Arrange the chops on an earthenware or other flameproof platter. Top each chop with a tablespoonful of *Sauce Béchamel à l'Huile* (page 34) which has been lightly "agrémentée" with a caress of garlic juice and thickened with the yolk of an egg. Set the platter under the broiler for a few seconds to glaze. Garnish each chop with a stuffed olive, an anchovy fillet, and (optional) a grilled mushroom.

Boned Leg of Lamb Provençale
(*Gigot d'Agneau à la Provençale*) M SERVES 6 OR MORE

Stuffing:
1 cup bread crumbs
¼ cup milk
¼ cup *petit salé,* minced
½ cup minced parsley
1 clove garlic, minced
Salt and pepper
1 whole egg

5-pound leg of lamb (*gigot*), boned
2 slices bacon or lean salt pork, diced
2 minced carrots or small white turnips
3 small onions, left whole
½ cup white wine
1 cup bouillon
Bouquet garni
Salt and pepper
3 medium-size eggplants
2 medium-size onions, minced
4 peeled, seeded, crushed tomatoes
2 cloves garlic, peeled and chopped
4 small, sweet green peppers (optional)
3 tablespoons olive oil (or more)
1 sprig each of thyme and fennel fern

Because of the large number of ingredients, this recipe looks, at first glance, rather formidable. Actually, it is a "meal in one" and requires no more effort than many another everyday menu.

Have the butcher bone the leg of lamb (but be sure he gives you the bone to make a little broth with later). Replace the bone with a stuffing made as follows: Soak the bread crumbs in the milk and press out. Mix in the *petit salé* (see Salt Pork, page 21), parsley, 1 clove of garlic, minced, salt and pepper, and the egg.

Stuff the *gigot* and tie with string to hold in the stuffing. Cook the bacon slices or salt pork in a heavy pot. Remove them and brown the *gigot* all over, slowly, in this fat. Add the carrots or turnips and small whole onions. Let these color (but not brown). Add wine, bouillon, *bouquet garni,* salt and pepper. Lower heat and simmer, covered for 3 to 3½ hours.

Meanwhile, peel the eggplants, slice them crosswise and salt them. Lay these aside for an hour to allow the bitter juice to bubble to the surface. Rinse slices and dry them well. Fry them in the olive oil with the 2 minced onions, the tomatoes, chopped garlic and (optional) seeded, cleaned, sliced peppers, adding more olive oil if needed. Season with salt and pepper, a sprig of fresh thyme and one of fennel top (fern). Serve the *gigot* in its own juices, flanked with vegetables.

Leg of Lamb with Garlic Sauce
(*Gigot d'Agneau Sauce à l'Ail*) M SERVES 6 OR MORE

Don't let the title of this excellent dish alienate anyone who fears that the flavor of the garlic would be too pronounced. It should be remembered, always, that garlic is thoroughly tamed when long-cooked in liquid or moisture.

Lard the leg of (unboned) lamb with nubbins of fat cut from unsliced bacon or salt pork. (Make small slits on the surface of the meat, 3 or 4 inches apart, and poke small pieces of the fat into them.) Melt 4 squares of bacon in a deep heavy pot or Dutch oven and brown the larded meat all over in this. Add the white wine and bouillon or water. Season with salt and pepper and (optional) cognac. Cover snugly, bring to a boil. Lower heat quickly and when the liquid is just barely simmering, cook for 3 hours or until meat is tender, turning it over occasionally.

Separately, boil the 20 cloves of garlic in salted water until soft. Drain well and purée them, or use electric blender. When the lamb is cooked, transfer it to a hot platter. Strain the juices in the pot and add these to the garlic purée. Serve this sauce separately in a gravyboat.

5-pound leg of lamb
Fat bacon or sliced pork
½ cup white wine
½ cup bouillon or water
Salt and pepper
(Optional) 2 tablespoons cognac
20 whole cloves garlic

Noisettes of Lamb Roumanille
(*Noisettes d'Agneau Roumanille*)

A *noisette* is a piece of lamb taken from the saddle. It is round in shape and weighs about 3 ounces: a tenderloin.

For 6 *noisettes,* heat 3 tablespoons olive oil and when it is just smoking hot (but not burning), put in the *noisettes* and cook them fast, 4 minutes on each side. Season with salt and freshly ground black pepper, and set aside to keep warm.

Adding more oil to the pan, fry 6 slices of eggplant that have been salted and left to stand for an hour to drain their bitter juices, and then wiped dry. Separately fry 6 rounds of bread and prepare a mornay sauce (page 34).

Arrange the *noisettes,* each on its own "crouton," on a flameproof platter, and blanket in hot Mornay Sauce. Set the platter under the broiler for a few minutes to glaze the surface of the sauce attractively. Top each *noisette* with an olive rolled in a fillet of anchovy, and serve on the platter, bordered with the fried eggplant slices.

6 noisettes of lamb
Olive oil
Salt and pepper
6 slices eggplant
6 round slices bread
6 olives
6 fillets anchovy

Rack of Lamb Bas-Alpine
(Carré d'Agneau Bas-Alpine)

This dish that is so simple and so savory was one of the triumphs of the Master Chef, Féraud, who was formerly the owner and chef of the Hôtel du Belvédère at Moustiers-Sainte-Marie. We reproduce the recipe in memory of that loyal custodian of Provençal culinary traditions.

Rub a 4-pound rack of very white lamb with olive oil and then roll in a mixture of dry bread crumbs and finely minced parsley, seasoned with salt and pepper. Put the rack in an oiled roasting pan and cook in a 325° oven for about 1½ hours, basting occasionally. At the end of the 1½-hour period, shake a little salt and pepper over the surface of the meat and continue cooking 20–30 minutes longer. Then transfer meat to a hot platter and deglaze the roasting pan with a cup of white wine. Pour this glaze over the lamb which you then serve with a little lightly browned butter poured over it.

Rack of Lamb Roasted with Herbs
(Carré d'Agneau aux Senteurs de Provence)

This recipe was given to the authors by the chef of Le Prieuré restaurant in Villeneuve-les-Avignon where it is a specialty of the house. The method of roasting may be equally well applied to a *gigot* or other cut of lamb if the amounts of oil and butter and the roasting time are proportionately adjusted.

2-pound rack of lamb
2 tablespoons olive oil
4 tablespoons butter
Salt and pepper
Fresh thyme, rosemary, and savory
   (or ¼ teaspoon *dried*)

Rub the meat with the olive oil and half the butter. Salt and pepper it generously and set it to roast in an open pan in a preheated 350° oven. After 30 minutes, lift the meat and slide half the herbs under it, strewing the rest on top. Add remaining butter to the hot pan. Baste the meat well with the melted fat and juices. Return it to the oven and roast it 15 minutes longer. Then turn off the heat and let the meat "repose" (still in the oven) for another 15 minutes.

Skewered Lamb (Agneau à la Broche)

ALLOW 3 2-INCH CUBES OF LAMB AND 2 KIDNEYS PER PERSON

Cut the lamb (preferably boned loin) in 2-inch cubes for threading on a rotisserie spit or on skewers as for shish kebab. Allow 2 kidneys (gristle removed) for every 3 cubes of lamb. Marinate both lamb and kidneys for 3 hours in olive oil seasoned with salt, pepper, thyme, and a small grated onion in an earthenware casserole. Then thread the lamb, alternately with the kidneys, on spit or skewers and broil. Turn frequently if a revolving spit is not used. When the meat is two-thirds cooked, impale a cherry tomato and a small green pepper on each skewer and complete the broiling. Before serving, sprinkle liberally with fresh lemon juice. Serve, still skewered, with a bowl of rice, seasoned with salt, pepper, and butter.

Lamb Steaks of Arles
(Côtelettes d'Agneau Arlésiennes)   SERVES 4

For 4 steaks grind in a mortar: 1 tablespoon thyme, ½ teaspoon peppercorns, 1 scant teaspoon salt, 1 tablespoon rosemary (or use the powdered rosemary sold in supermarkets and elsewhere). Rub the steaks well with this mixture and add any of it that is left over to the grill pan. Broil the steaks 4 or 5 minutes on each side. Just before serving, top each steak with a blob of anchovy cream (anchovy fillets pounded in a mortar with olive oil).

Braised Lamb Steaks
(Tranches d'Agneau Braisées) M   SERVES 4

This much neglected dish deserves to be restored to its former place of honor for it ranked high enough in Provençal cuisine to be cited by Mistral in his immortal "Poème du Rhône."

Lard ¾-pound (or larger) steaks and *pique* them with garlic — that is, make tiny incisions in the surface and bury bits of garlic in the cuts. Sauté chopped bacon in olive oil (about 1 tablespoon each per steak) in a non-metal casserole. Remove cooked bacon with a slotted spoon and then brown the steaks in the fat, turning them to color both sides. Season with salt and pepper and a pinch of nutmeg. Add the bay leaf, carrots, turnip (scraped and coarsely cut up), celery cut in 3-inch lengths, scallions (in season), and the tomato or tomato purée. Simmer all this for a few moments, then add the white wine. Turn the chops over in this mixture several times. Then cover very tightly and simmer for 2½ hours, making sure the liquid never comes to an active boil. [*Listen* to it. **Don't remove cover.**]

After 2½ hours, lift the lid from the pot and put in the cooked drained beans and artichokes. Cover again, and simmer for 30 minutes longer.

4 ¾-pound lamb steaks
Garlic
Bacon, chopped
Olive oil (about 4 tablespoons)
Salt and pepper
Pinch of nutmeg
1 bay leaf
3 carrots
1 white turnip
3 stalks celery
4 scallions (in season)
1 large tomato (or ½ cup tomato purée)
1 cup dry white wine
½ cup white beans, soaked overnight and parboiled
8 small, tender, cooked artichokes (page 12)

Lamb Stew of Avignon
(Daube Avignonnaise) M

3 POUNDS SERVES 5 OR 6

3 pounds boned lamb
2 cups white wine (generous)
1 tablespoon olive oil
Salt and pepper
2 scraped carrots, chopped
Bouquet garni
1 medium-size onion, peeled and
  chopped
2 garlic cloves, peeled and chopped
½ cup chopped parsley
Strip of orange rind

Put the boned lamb into an earthenware (or other non-metal) casserole and pour over it a marinade consisting of the rest of the ingredients. Mix well. Let the casserole stand for 6 hours, turning the meat over in the marinade occasionally. Then proceed as for *Boeuf en Daube* (page 154), except that the cooking time may be reduced.

The lamb may be left in one piece or cut into individual servings. The marinade is strained and the liquid poured over the meat at the start of the cooking period. The contents of the pot is brought to a boil, then reduced to a simmer, covered, and left over low heat for 3 or 4 hours, depending on the tenderness of the lamb.

Pork

Pork Chops in Cases
(Côtelettes de Porc en Crépine)

ALLOW 1 CHOP PER PERSON

For each chop:
1 scant tablespoon olive oil
Salt and pepper
Minced parsley
½ strip bacon
1 ounce pork liver (skinned)
½ single small, peeled clove garlic
Membrane
Beaten egg
Crumbs

This specialty, for which stuffed pork chops are wrapped in membrane (such as sausage casings are made from), is a cousin to the haggis of Scotland. The recipe may alarm the average American cook at first sight and the procedure does require vigilant attention, but the trouble will be rewarded by the excellence of the result. Nowadays, American gastronomy is becoming international very fast and many a supermarket provides ingredients for making foreign dishes. However, if pork membranes (see page 175) are unavailable, the chops may be snugly wrapped in aluminum foil instead. The appearance won't be authentic, but the taste of the chops will be similar.

Marinate the chops for several hours in olive oil seasoned with salt and pepper and mixed liberally with chopped parsley. Then roast them on an oiled pan in a 350° oven for about 25 minutes. Remove and allow to cool.

Sauté (but do not brown) ½ strip of bacon per chop. Remove and reserve. Lightly cook a 1-ounce piece of liver per chop in the bacon fat left in the pan. Chop the bacon and liver together with ½ small, peeled garlic clove and 1 tablespoon fresh parsley per chop. Season with salt and pepper. Spread a layer of this "hash" on each chop and wrap in membrane. Dip in beaten egg and then in crumbs and broil on an oiled rack. [If foil has to be substituted for the membrane, make a bed of crumbs in each piece of foil, then dip the chop in beaten egg, lay it on the crumbs, and sift another layer of crumbs over it. Do not wrap the laden meat in the foil but arrange the open packages on a flat, shallow baking pan and broil, turning the chops once.]

Loin Pork Chops Broiled with Sage
(Côtes de Porc Grillées à la Sauge)

ALLOW 1 CHOP PER PERSON

Score the chops very lightly with a sharp knife. Rub a little coarse salt, freshly ground pepper, and crumbled sage (or powdered sage) into the surfaces. Oil very lightly and broil or pan-broil. Serve the chops ringed with Tomatoes Provençale (page 202).

Loin of Pork with Lima Beans
(Porc Frais aux Haricots Blancs)

SERVES 6

Brown the loin roast of pork (preferably center cut) in a heavy skillet with the bacon, turning the roast to color it well all over. Put it, fat side up, in an earthenware casserole.

Meanwhile, blanch the lima beans in rapidly boiling salted water. Drain well but reserve the cooking water. Spoon the beans around the meat in the casserole and pour in enough of their liquor to just cover the contents of the pot. Season with salt and pepper, a bay leaf, and a sprig of sage. Put the casserole in a preheated 325° oven and cook for 2 hours, turning the vegetables with a spoon from time to time as skin forms on the surface of the liquid. When the pot liquor is almost completely evaporated, the top layer of beans dry and even slightly roasted, the dish is ready. Serve it right in its casserole.

5-pound loin of pork
4 tablespoons chopped bacon
2 pounds fresh lima beans, shelled
Salt and pepper
1 bay leaf
2 sprigs fresh sage
  (or 1 teaspoon dried)

Veal

Veal, ubiquitous staple on the European menu, has never been particularly popular in the United States. The American cook doesn't understand it and (or perhaps the word should be *there-*

fore) American butchers don't have to. Behind the housekeepers and butchers a long history of responsibility-dodging goes way back to the breeders whose calves aren't fed right because "there isn't any demand for milk-fed veal." Calves need to be fed by their mothers if Americans are ever to have any veal that is not dry meat, dark in color and disappointingly tough and fibrous (what the French call *coriace*). When people consistently say no to any veal that isn't young and pale pink (almost white), the demand will create supply, as demand almost always does.

It should be borne in mind that even the best veal is so lean that supplementary fat is indispensable. Also, veal contains a good deal of water which must be allowed to cook away before the meat can start to brown properly. "Good veal" and "slow cooking" are, therefore, inseparable. In fact, the caliber of cooks may almost be judged by their attitude toward veal. The "cook-if-I-must" type begrudges the extra time it requires. The others love it for its hospitality to subtle sauces.

Breast of Veal à la Brignolaise (*Carré de Veau à la Brignolaise*) SERVES 6

4-pound quarter of veal
Salt and pepper
3 tablespoons drippings or other fat
2 tablespoons (about) bouillon
1 pound little white onions
Bouquet garni
Sprig of fresh basil
Water
1 cup stoned, ripe olives

Have the butcher cut a piece of veal across the full width of the breast and trim it neatly. Braise the meat in the drippings or other fat with only just enough bouillon for extra moisture. Season with salt and pepper.

Peel the little white onions and cook them separately over medium heat, with the *bouquet garni,* the sprig of basil, and just enough water to keep them from burning. Put them with the cooking liquor through a food mill (or use a blender). Simmer 1 cup stoned ripe olives in a little water for 10 minutes.

Serve the veal garlanded with olives on a hot platter, the braising liquor in a gravyboat, and the onion purée in a separate serving dish.

Stuffed Breast of Veal (*Poitrine de Veau Farcie*)

Follow the directions for preparing Stuffed Breast of Lamb (page 160) but roast the meat instead of simmering it. Also, unlike the lamb version, Stuffed Breast of Veal may be served cold with a salad.

Veal Loin Chops with Basil
(Côtes de Veau au Basilic)

ALLOW 1 CHOP OR ½ POUND CUTLET PER PERSON

Rub the chops [or veal cutlets] with a little olive oil, butter, bacon fat, or other fat, and broil or pan-broil them. Season them with salt and pepper only *after* they are cooked. Blend together 2 tablespoons butter, 1 tablespoon olive oil, and 1 tablespoon finely minced fresh basil (or 1 teaspoon dried basil in the lamentable absence of fresh). Top each hot chop with a good dollop of this herb butter.

Veal Chops Provençale
(Côtelettes de Veau Provençale)

Rub the chops vigorously with the clove of garlic and then sauté them in olive oil. When well browned, moisten with wine. Add the onion, combined with the parsley and rosemary. Season with salt and pepper. Cover, and simmer until the juices in the pan are almost completely gone. Deglaze the pan with the bouillon or hot water, and then stir in the egg yolk. Dip the chops in the egg white and then in fine bread crumbs. Place them in a flameproof pan. Spoon the sauce around the meat and glaze (2 or 3 minutes) under the broiler.

1 veal chop per person
1 clove garlic, cut in half
1 tablespoon olive oil per chop
½ cup dry white wine
1 medium-size onion, peeled and chopped
½ cup chopped parsley
1 sprig fresh rosemary (or ½ teaspoon dried)
Salt
Freshly milled black pepper
2 tablespoons bouillon or hot water
1 egg yolk, beaten
1 egg white, beaten
Fine bread crumbs

Garlic Veal Cutlet (Aïllade de Veau)

Slice the veal, then cut it in pieces about 2 inches in diameter. Brown these on both sides in olive oil. Add the bread crumbs and garlic, then the tomato sauce (or tomato paste simmered for 10 minutes in 1 tablespoon olive oil to remove the sharp taste). Season with salt and pepper. Add the white wine. Simmer for 1 hour. Serve with rice.

⅓ to ½ pound of veal (cutlet or rump) per person
Olive oil
12 peeled cloves garlic
1 tablespoon soft, fine bread crumbs
½ cup fresh tomato sauce (page 32) or diluted tomato paste
Salt and pepper
¾ cup white wine

Veal Cutlet Provençale
(Fricandeau de Veau à la Provençale)   SERVES 6

2 pounds veal cutlet

2 teaspoons blanched salt pork (page 21), diced

2 or 3 medium-size mushrooms, minced

1 teaspoon minced onion

1 teaspoon minced parsley

1 peeled clove garlic

Pinch of curry

Thin, broad slices of bacon

Bouquet garni

1 carrot, scraped and chopped

1 peeled onion, chopped

1 stalk celery, chopped

Salt and pepper

½ cup cognac or champagne

Ratatouille (page 193), spiced with clove

Grated cheese (Parmesan)

Remove the bone from the center of a fine veal cutlet. Replace the bone with a filling made by finely chopping together a small piece of salt pork, a spoonful each of minced onion, mushroom, parsley, and garlic, a pinch of curry. Season with salt and pepper. Skewer the bacon slices over both sides of the cutlet to keep the stuffing in place. Put the chopped vegetables plus the *bouquet garni* into a deep skillet or casserole. Add more salt and pepper (if needed). Lay the meat on this bed of vegetables and pour the cognac or champagne over all. Stir to blend. Simmer for a few minutes, spooning the liquid in the pan over the meat and vegetables to moisten all thoroughly. Cover the casserole very snugly and continue the cooking, over low heat, for a least two hours. At the moment of serving, surround the cutlet with the ingredients in the *braisage*. Serve the clove-spiced *ratatouille* separately, topped with a little grated Parmesan.

Riblets of Veal à la Gardiane
(Tendrons de Veau à la Gardiane)   SERVES 6

Tendrons from a 3-pound breast of veal

4 or 5 tablespoons olive oil

Salt and pepper

2 whole cloves of garlic

4 or 5 tiny onions, peeled and lightly browned

¼ pound mushrooms, minced

½ cup white wine

1 tablespoon (generous) tomato purée

6 each of green and black olives

Tendrons are long pieces of veal cut the full width of the breast, from the ends of the ribs at the point where the chops begin to the sternum. They usually weigh about ½ pound each or a little less.

Brown the tendrons well in olive oil. Season with salt and pepper. Garnish with the garlic and the lightly browned little onions. Add the minced mushrooms, wine, and tomato purée. Stir well. Set over low heat to simmer for about 1½ hours. Then add the olives and simmer a few minutes longer. Serve very hot, accompanied by saffron rice.

Stew of Mixed Meats Bas-Alpine
(Entrée de Viandes à la Bas-Alpine)

SERVES 4

Cut the mixed meats in 1½- to 2-inch cubes and brown them in the olive oil in a heavy pot, along with the diced bacon. When all is richly colored, remove the meat from the pot and, in the same oil, brown the onion and flour. Dilute the tomato purée with water and add it to the onion-flour *roux*. Turn up the heat under the pot, stirring to mix well. When the sauce comes to a boil, put back the pieces of meat. Add the garlic and the *bouquet garni*. Season to taste with salt and pepper. Reduce the heat and cook, at barely a simmer, for 1½ hours. Add the olives and simmer for another 30 minutes. Serve very hot.

2 pounds boneless beef, veal, and
   lamb (or mutton), mixed
2 tablespoons (about) olive oil
3 slices lean bacon, diced
1 peeled, chopped onion
1 tablespoon flour
3 tablespoons tomato purée
1 tablespoon (about) tepid water
Bouquet garni
1 peeled clove garlic
Salt and pepper
½ cup stoned, blanched green olives

XIV. *Variety Meats*

Brains

Crépinettes of Brains (Crépinettes Reine-Jeanne)

Allow a generous ¼ pound of meat per person. (Calves' brains will weigh about 1 pound, lambs' brains about ¾ pound). Trim the brain neatly and drop it into salted boiling water with 1 tablespoon vinegar. Boil, but not too rapidly lest the brain disintegrate, for 5 minutes per quarter pound. Drain, dry well, and cut into bite-size pieces. Stir these into a very thick Béchamel Sauce (3 tablespoons butter, 3 tablespoons flour, 1 cup bouillon or milk). Add 2 or 3 tablespoons each of diced ham, minced, cooked onions, and lightly cooked truffles, sliced.

Cut a pork membrane (page 166) in squares and fill these with the meat mixture. Tie each *crépinette* bundle firmly with thread (in somewhat the shape of a hobo's bandana-wrapped "luggage"). Dip each bundle in beaten egg white and then in bread crumbs. Fry these in oil or butter Serve with lemon slices.

Kidneys

Veal Kidneys with Stuffed Mushrooms (*Rognons de Veau Provençale*)   SERVES 4

2 large veal kidneys
4 (or more) tablespoons olive oil
½ pound large mushrooms
2 cloves garlic, peeled
Salt and pepper
Parsley

Remove all the skin from the kidneys. Cut them in half, lengthwise, and remove as many of the tendons as can be cut out without losing all the attached kidney fat. It is important to have some of the fat left *on*.

Pepper the kidney halves lightly and brown them, cut-side down first, in 2 tablespoons olive oil, using fairly brisk heat. The kidneys should not be overcooked but should be still faintly pink inside and not dry. Set them aside on a hot, heatproof platter to keep warm.

Separate the caps from the mushroom stems. Mince separately the stems, the garlic and the parsley.

In another skillet, over medium heat, sauté the mushroom caps in 1 tablespoon olive oil (adding more if needed), turning them over and over until, although still firm, they are no longer white. Set these aside to keep warm.

Add the remaining oil to the skillet in which the kidneys were cooked and sauté the minced mushroom stems for 2 or 3 minutes, then add the minced garlic. Stir to mix well and cook over low heat 1 or 2 minutes longer. Then stir in the minced parsley. Season with salt and pepper to taste.

Fill the mushroom caps with this mixture and place them around the kidneys. Set the platter in a hot oven for 2 minutes before serving.

Liver (Foie)

During the past several decades the nutritive values of liver have had such unanimous endorsement by doctors and dieticians that, in the United States at least, many people unconsciously think of it as therapy rather than as the delicious food it *can* be. "Can be" . . . too seldom *is*. Most of those who like it like only calf liver, which is a pity. And there are two rarely mentioned but valid reasons for *dis*liking it: (1) It isn't properly treated *before* being cooked. (2) It isn't cooked at the right temperature.

To be good, liver *must be skinned* and all bits of fiber cut out with a small pair of scissors — an untidy and exasperating business but making the difference between a delectable slice and a tough "fist." Liver must also be seared *very quickly* on both sides in foaming hot butter over brisk heat and taken from the heat while still pink inside.

Lamb liver is every bit as delicate as the now luxury-priced calf liver. And good steer liver, skinned, defibered, and soaked for an hour or two in milk, becomes a very acceptable and thriftier substitute. Pork liver is harder to tame — except in Provence where olive oil, herbs, and wine make quite a different thing of it.

Liver Ancestral Style
(*Foie de Porc à la Manière des Ancêtres*)   SERVES 4

This old (*very* old) recipe, indigenous to the Avignon region, is for a dish usually made with pork liver. It may, of course, be adapted to calf or lamb. For its restoration we have to thank M. Henry, proprietor of the Hôtellerie du Manoir at Port-Cros.

Skin the liver and cut out any gristle. Cut in pieces about 3 inches square. Wrap each square in a piece of pork membrane. [**Sold in pork stores and some supermarkets; it is sometimes called caul.**] Place the "packages" side-by-side in an ovenware dish. Salt and pepper them, and douse with the wine and vinegar. Add bay leaf, garlic, and butter or oil. Set the dish in a cool place for 24 hours. Then roast the meat in a 350° oven for 1 hour. Serve scorching hot.

1 pound pork (or other) liver
Pork membrane (page 166)
Salt and pepper
1¼ cups red wine (generous)
1 tablespoon vinegar
1 bay leaf
4 crushed, unpeeled cloves garlic
3½ tablespoons butter or olive oil

Liver Arlésienne
(Foie de Veau ou de Mouton à l'Arlésienne) SERVES 6

1½ pounds liver (veal or lamb)
5 peeled, minced medium onions
3 tablespoons olive oil
Salt and pepper
1 tablespoon flour
1 peeled, minced clove garlic
1 bay leaf
¼ cup white wine

Cook the onions in the oil over medium heat until clear but not brown. Skin the liver and remove gristle. Cut in thin slices and lay these in the pan over the onions. Season with salt and pepper. Sift the tablespoonful of flour over them. Add the garlic and bay leaf and pour in the wine. Bring to a boil. Lower heat and simmer, covered, for 20 minutes. Serve on a hot platter.

Broiled Liver (Foie Grillé) SERVES 6

1½ pounds liver
Olive oil
Salt and pepper
Parsley
Fine bread crumbs
Lemon slices or tomato sauce

This dish is usually made with lamb liver and is delicate and delicious, and needn't be marinated. Beef or pork liver should be first skinned and then soaked for an hour in milk.

Skin the liver. Cut in slices ¼-inch thick. Season the slices and dip them in olive oil and then in minced parsley mixed, half-and-half, with fine, dry crumbs. Broil 2 minutes on each side. Serve with lemon slices or tomato sauce.

Note: The liver may be sautéed in very hot butter just as easily and with more control of the cooking. Heat ½ tablespoon butter for each slice of liver and cook only as many slices at one time as the skillet will hold, *flat,* without crowding. When the butter froth begins to color lightly, put in the liver. Cook about 2 minutes on each side, or until an incision made with a sharp knife blade shows the center of a slice to be no longer raw. (The juice should still run pink.) When transferred to a hot platter the meat will continue to cook itself for a few minutes. Deglaze the pan with ¼ cup red wine. Add 1 tablespoon butter and pour this sauce over the meat.

Crépinettes of Pork Liver Vauclusienne

1 pork membrane (pages 166 and 175)
2 pounds pork liver
½ pound (scant) bacon
¼ cup stoned black olives
1 peeled onion, 1 peeled clove garlic
A small bunch of parsley
¼ pound raw spinach leaves, washed
Salt and pepper
Pinch of grated nutmeg

Scrub and soak a pork membrane. Cut it into pieces about 5 to 6 inches in diameter. Chop all other ingredients together. Dispose this stuffing on the pieces of caul and fasten the "bundle" with thread. Cook these *crépinettes* in a double boiler for 30 minutes.

Liver with Herbs (*Foie de Porc aux Herbes*)

Sauté skinned "de-gristled" slices of liver (in this case, pork liver is the usual choice) in oil (see page 17). Just before transferring liver from pan to hot platter, put a sprig or two of sage in the pan. Serve powdered with chopped fresh basil and garlic, mixed.

Tripe (*Tripes*)

There are several kinds of tripe. In France these are used both together and separately. But in the United States, where tripe is viewed with suspicion by most Americans, the kind known as "honeycomb" is the best bet for any purpose. A few stores sell pickled tripe which is unsuitable for use in the following recipes. Luckily, fresh tripe usually comes already blanched. It should, however, be further pretreated by being brought to a boil in water to cover with 1 tablespoon salt, and then simmered for *at least* an hour.

Honeycomb Tripe Provençale (*Gras-Double Provençale*)

SERVES 6

Cut the tripe in 3-inch squares. In a heavy pot, color the onion and salt pork in the olive oil. Add the pieces of tripe and a generous cup of white wine. Season with salt, pepper, and *bouquet garni*. Simmer for 1 hour. Then thicken the sauce with 2 well-beaten egg yolks. Add the basil or, lacking this, 1 tablespoon chopped parsley. Serve strewn with grated cheese.

1½ pounds pretreated honeycomb tripe
1 medium-size peeled, chopped onion
2 tablespoons blanched, minced salt pork
2 tablespoons olive oil
1 cup white wine (generous)
Salt and pepper
Bouquet garni
2 well-beaten egg yolks
1 tablespoon chopped fresh basil (or ½ teaspoon dried)
Grated cheese

Tripe Niçoise (Tripes Niçoises)

SERVES 3 OR 4

1 pound tripe, pretreated
1 medium onion, peeled and minced
¼ cup olive oil
5 tomatoes, peeled, seeded, coarsely
   chopped
1½ cups white wine
Salt and pepper
Bouquet garni
2 whole, peeled cloves garlic
Grated cheese

Cut the tripe into strips. Brown the onion in the oil in a heavy sauce-pan. Add the tripe and simmer at very low heat, covered, for 2 hours. Then add the tomatoes, wine, salt and pepper, *bouquet garni,* and the 2 whole cloves of garlic. Cover, and continue cooking over low heat for 4 hours longer.

At serving time, strain the sauce, pour it back over the meat, and sprinkle with the grated cheese.

XV

Vegetables

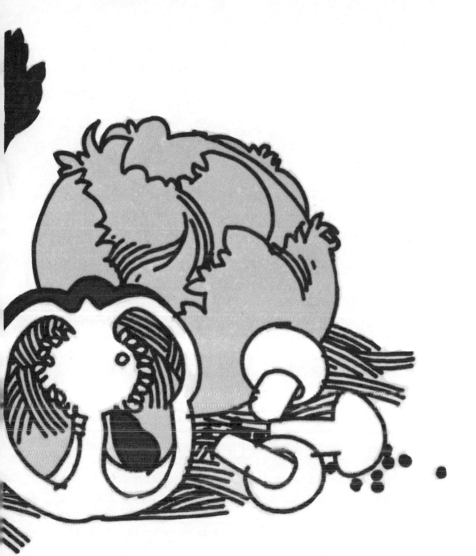

Artichokes (Artichauts)

THE PETALED CONE that started as a thistle and was cultivated into a classic vegetable is still considered "fancy food" in the United States, but is as commonplace in France as a bean in Boston. There must be easily a hundred ways of cooking and saucing it . . . and probably more in Provence than anywhere else. If it is rather bothersome to eat, the artichoke addict is not in the least discouraged. Once "hooked" he is incurable. Examples of temptation follow.

Artichokes Barigoule
(*Artichauts à la Barigoule*) ALLOW 3 OR 4 PER PERSON

3 or 4 tiny artichokes per person
3 tablespoons olive oil
2 medium-size onions peeled
  and sliced
2 carrots scraped and diced
(Optional) 1 tablespoon blanched
  chopped salt pork
½ cup dry white wine
½ cup water
Salt and pepper

To be successful, this dish must be made with small, very young, very tender artichokes such as those, for instance, which in Provence are called *"Mourre-de-cat"* (from the game, *Mora* or "How many fingers do I hold up?")

Pull off any hard, outside leaves and snip the tips of the others. Cut a slice off the bottom of each artichoke. Put 2 tablespoons of oil in the bottom of a heavy, non-metal casserole. Add the onions and carrots plus (optional) salt pork. Arrange the artichokes, upright, side by side, over the bed of vegetables. Season lightly with salt and a good shake of pepper. Sprinkle with the third tablespoon of oil. Turn the heat high for a minute or two, and pour the wine and water (mixed) over the artichokes. Cover the pot. Lower the heat and simmer for 1¼ to 1½ hours. The sauce should be well reduced.

Note: In a variation of this recipe, the tips of the artichokes are strewn with soft bread crumbs mixed with chopped garlic and chopped parsley before cooking. The garlic touch must be light, however, not to mask the delicate flavor of the artichokes.

Artichokes Cannoise ALLOW 1 OR 2 PER PERSON

1 or 2 medium-size artichokes
  per person
1 medium-size onion, peeled and
  chopped
4 ounces lean ham, minced
2 tablespoons olive oil
4 medium-size mushrooms, chopped
½ cup white wine
¼ cup tomato purée
Salt and pepper

Remove and discard the chokes and the hard, outside leaves of the artichokes. Quarter and blanch the artichokes in boiling water.

Meanwhile, brown the onion and the ham in the olive oil. Add to these the mushrooms, white wine, and tomato purée. Let this mixture simmer until somewhat reduced. Season highly with salt and pepper. Arrange the cooked artichokes on a hot platter and pour the sauce over them. (Proportions given for sauce should dress 4 to 6 artichokes.)

Artichokes with Fava Beans (*Barbouiado*) SERVES 6

In the absence of fresh fava beans (and they're usually absent), frozen ones may be substituted. Several brands are now available in large supermarkets.

If fresh favas (also called "broad beans") are used, they must, of course, first be shelled, then cooked, and then the inner shell removed . . . a rather tedious process, except for dedicated favophiles.

Remove the stems and cut the tips of the tiny artichokes (tender and young ones). Quarter them. Brown the minced onion lightly in olive oil. Toss in the artichokes and shelled raw limas or the favas, frozen or cooked fresh. Add water to one half the depth of the vegetables in the pot. Season with salt and pepper plus a pinch of grated nutmeg, or a piece of cinnamon bark which adds an element of pleasant surprise. Simmer covered until cooked through.

12 tiny artichokes
2 tablespoons olive oil
1 medium-size onion minced
1 cup shelled fava or lima beans
Water
Salt and pepper
Nutmeg or cinnamon

Hearts of Artichokes au Gratin
(Fonds d'Artichauts au Gratin)

For this dish large artichokes may be used. Drop them into boiling salted water (in a *non-metal* pot), and when it boils again, lower the heat, cover the pot with a cloth, and boil (just above a simmer) for about 50 minutes. Then "liberate" the hearts and drop them in cold water with 2 tablespoons of either vinegar or lemon juice in it. This keeps hearts from darkening unattractively. Drain well and then fill with an onion purée: minced onion cooked in butter over low heat, covered, until very soft, thickened with 2 of the egg yolks. Season with salt and pepper, brush with the third egg yolk, and bake in a 375° oven until lightly browned.

1 large artichoke per person
Boiling salted water
Cold water
2 tablespoons vinegar or lemon juice
Thick onion purée
3 egg yolks beaten
Salt and pepper

Artichokes with Little Peas
(Artichauts aux Petits Pois)   SERVES 4

Trim, quarter, and blanch the small artichokes and sauté them in 3 or 4 tablespoons of olive oil. Remove from pan. Brown scallions or small white onions in the oil remaining in the skillet, adding the butter. Add the shelled small peas, about ½ pound of scraped new potatoes, and water. Stir in the cooked artichokes. Season with salt, pepper, and 2 lumps (or 2 teaspoons) sugar. Simmer covered for 1 hour.

4 small artichokes
4 tablespoons olive oil
12 scallions, trimmed, or 8 tiny
    white onions, skinned
2 tablespoons butter
1 cup tiny peas, shelled
½ pound new potatoes, scraped
2 cups water
Salt and pepper
2 lumps sugar (or 2 teaspoons)

Artichokes Marseillaise
(*Artichauts à la Marseillaise*) SERVES 6

12 small or 6 large artichokes
1 shallot
2 or 3 sprigs parsley
6 cloves garlic
2 tablespoons olive oil
12 stoned green olives
6 anchovy fillets
1 cup (scant) white wine
Pepper

Discard the hard outer leaves and cut the artichokes in half, top to bottom. Carefully remove chokes.

Lightly cook a peeled, chopped shallot, the parsley, chopped, and the peeled, mashed cloves of garlic in olive oil. Add the artichokes, olives, anchovy fillets cut in pieces, and white wine. Season with pepper (but not salt because of the anchovies). Cover and simmer for 1½ hours.

Artichokes in Pepper Sauce (*Artichauts Poivrade*)

2 or 3 tiny artichokes per
   person
Olive oil
Vinegar
Salt
Freshly milled pepper

Only the tiniest young artichokes are suitable for this dish, especially those of the type called *"proumié griou"* in Provence, which is to say, the first to grow. They are eaten raw with a sauce made of 4 parts olive oil, 1 part vinegar, salt and a very generous amount of freshly ground peppercorns. Be sure not to add onion, garlic, or mustard. To appreciate the delicious flavor of this "flower in bud," nothing must cover it by way of strong seasoning.

Artichokes Provençale
(*Artichauts à la Provençale*) SERVES 3

9 small or 6 medium-size artichokes
1 cup fine bread crumbs
¼ cup milk
¼ cup chopped parsley
1 clove garlic, peeled and minced
Salt and pepper
1 medium-size onion, chopped
2 carrots, scraped and cut in discs
Bouquet garni
2 or 3 tablespoons olive oil
½ cup (plus) bouillon

Cut off the tips of the leaves and remove the toughest ones. Cut the base of each artichoke straight across so it can sit down firmly without tipping. Make a mince of the fine bread crumbs, soaked in milk and pressed out, and the parsley mixed with the garlic, salt and pepper.

Slip small spoonfuls of this stuffing between the leaves of the artichokes, putting the largest portions in the center ones. Put a layer of chopped onion in the bottom of a nonmetal casserole. Strew over it 1 or 2 scraped carrots cut in discs. Add a small *bouquet garni* and place the filled artichokes, close together, on this bed. Sprinkle generously with olive oil and place the casserole over moderate heat. After the contents have begun to heat, add ½ cup (or a little more) of bouillon. Cover very tightly. Reduce the heat. Simmer for 1½ to 2 hours depending on the size of the artichokes.

Stuffed Artichokes (*Artichauts Farcis*)   SERVES 4

Trim the artichokes as for Artichokes Provençale (page 184). Cut each in half and remove the choke. In its place stuff a mixture of the sautéed sausage meat (or minced cooked ham or bacon), minced onion, bread crumbs soaked in milk and pressed out, garlic, parsley, salt and pepper, all this bound with the beaten yolks of the eggs. Reshape the artichokes and tie them with string. Moisten with a generous half cup of white wine mixed with the tomato sauce. Sprinkle with oil. Cover, and bake in a 375° oven for about 45 minutes.

4 large artichokes, blanched
1 cup sausage meat, ham or bacon
4 tablespoons peeled, minced onion
1 cup bread crumbs
¼ cup milk
Small clove garlic, peeled and minced
2 tablespoons chopped parsley
Salt and pepper
2 egg yolks, beaten
½ cup white wine
3 tablespoons tomato sauce
Olive oil

Artichokes Toulonnaise (*Artichauts à la Toulonnnaise*)   SERVES 6

Remove and discard the chokes and the tips of the leaves of the 12 young artichokes. Season the artichokes well with a mixture of the salt, pepper, nutmeg, and bay leaf.

In a non-metal casserole cook the bacon, garlic, and onion. Put in the artichokes. Add the hot bouillon, plus the white wine and wine vinegar. Cover, and simmer for 3 hours.

12 young artichokes
2 tablespoons salt (or less)
1 teaspoon freshly ground pepper
¼ teaspoon grated nutmeg
1 bay leaf, pulverized
2 tablespoons bacon, finely minced
1 whole clove garlic
1 small onion, peeled and minced
⅔ cup hot bouillon
⅓ cup good dry white wine
2 tablespoons wine vinegar

Beans (*Haricots*)

Lima Beans with Savory (*Fèves à la Sariette*)   SERVES 4 TO 6

Shell and cook the beans in boiling, salted water to (more than) cover, along with half the savory. Cooking time will depend on the size and freshness of the beans — average time 15 minutes. The beans should not be mushy. Drain well. Stir in the butter, season to taste with salt and pepper and, at the last moment, add the rest of the savory. [Savory is *the* bean herb.]

2 pounds* fresh lima beans
Boiling salted water
Small bunch of fresh savory (or 2 teaspoons dried)
3 tablespoons butter
Salt and black pepper

* Two pounds of fresh lima beans will serve 5 or 6 persons if the beans are fully podded. Otherwise 2½ to 3 pounds will be needed.

String Beans with Aïoli
(*Haricots Verts à l'Eigressado*)   SERVES 6

This is a vegetable not to forget when there is a bit of *Aïoli* (page 24) left over. It is very, very Provençal and couldn't be more simple.

Trim and blanch 1½ pounds of string beans. Drain well and chill thoroughly. Then coat them generously with *aïoli*.

String Beans Provençale
(*Haricots Verts à la Provençale*)   SERVES 6

1½ pounds green string beans
Salted water for blanching
2 tablespoons olive oil
2 medium-size onions, peeled and sliced crosswise
½ small clove garlic, peeled
3 tomatoes, peeled, seeded, and coarsely chopped
Chopped parsley
Chopped fresh basil

Trim string beans and blanch them in boiling, salted water. Do not let them completely cook. They should still be slightly crisp. Drain well.

Meanwhile, cook the onions in olive oil in a non-metal pot. When they are soft and yellowed but not browned, add the garlic and tomatoes. Cover, and simmer until this has become a smooth, thick purée.

Add the blanched string beans to the sauce, turning them over in it with a spoon, so that all are well coated. Cook over gentle heat for 12 minutes. Serve in a deep, hot dish, powdered generously with chopped parsley and (if possible) fresh basil.

Wax Beans Moustièrenco
(*Haricots Blancs à la Moustièrenco*)   SERVES 4

1 pound wax beans
Water to cover
Bouquet garni
1 stalk celery
1 whole onion, stuck with cloves
Salt and pepper
1 onion, peeled and chopped
1 tomato, peeled and chopped
3 tablespoons olive oil
2 tablespoons drippings
1 clove garlic, peeled and minced

Trim the wax beans and blanch them in water to cover generously, with a *bouquet garni,* a stalk of celery, and an onion stuck with cloves. Drain them, remove celery and *bouquet garni*. Season with salt and pepper, and add an onion and a tomato which have been peeled, chopped, and lightly cooked in the olive oil. Add 2 or 3 tablespoons of drippings from a roast of pork (or substitute bacon fat). Simmer over low heat for about 20 minutes. Before serving, add 1 finely chopped clove of garlic but do not let this cook.

Note: **This recipe adapts well to dried white beans but these must, of course, be soaked first (see page 187) and parboiled.**

Dried White Beans Provençale
(Haricots Blancs à la Provençale)
SERVES 4

Soak beans overnight. Drain thoroughly. Put them in a casserole with the olive oil, bacon, onions, garlic, and the tomato or tomato purée. Add the bouillon, salt, and pepper. Cover the casserole and bake for 4 hours at 300°. The sauce should be well reduced. Strew with parsley before serving. Some people add, at the last moment, a few dots of Anchovy Butter (page 14). Canned beans may be used if well drained and well rinsed.

2 cups dried white beans
½ cup olive oil
2 slices bacon
3 small onions, peeled and quartered
1 whole clove garlic, peeled
1 large tomato or ¼ cup purée
1½ cup bouillon
Salt
Freshly milled pepper
Parsley for garnish
(Optional) anchovy butter

Red Bean Casserole
(Haricots Rouges en Daube)
SERVES 6

The procedure for this dish is the same as for Dried White Beans Provençale except that 2 cups of red wine replace the bouillon, blanched salt pork replaces the bacon, and the onions are left whole and studded with 2 or 3 cloves.

2 cups dried white beans, stuck with cloves
½ cup olive oil
Blanched salt pork
3 onions
1 whole clove garlic, peeled
1 large tomato or ¼ cup tomato purée
2 cups red wine
Salt and freshly milled pepper
Parsley for garnish
(Optional) anchovy butter

Cabbage (Choux)

Green Cabbage, Stuffed and Steamed
(Chou Vert en Fassum)
SERVES 6

This dish, said to be Greek and dating back to the founding of Antibes, is a famous specialty and excellent. The cooking procedure is not as complicated as it may seem at first glance. It calls for a *"fassumier,"* which is a kind of net, but several layers of cheesecloth will serve. Try it, for it is a dish you will adopt.

1½- to 2-pound head of cabbage
Boiling, salted water
6 ounces lean salt pork
Pork spleen (optional)
½ cup bread crumbs
2 tablespoons water
¼ cup rice
Salt and pepper
2 tablespoons olive oil
(Optional) ½ cup shelled young peas
Bouillon or water to cover
1 clove garlic
3 sprigs parsley
Bouquet garni

Remove the less attractive outside leaves and the stem of the head of cabbage. Discard these and blanch the cabbage in a large potful of boiling, salted water for 10 or 12 minutes. Carefully pull the leaves apart without detaching them. Remove the hard core and chop it very fine with the lean salt pork and (optional) a bit of pork spleen, the soaked, pressed-out bread crumbs, and the rice. (One may, in season, add also ¼ cup fresh, shelled young peas.) Season with salt and pepper plus 2 tablespoons good olive oil.

Line a deep, earthenware pot with the *"fassumier,"* allowing the edges to overlap the rim of the pot. Reassemble the cabbage on this, beginning with the largest leaves. Fill the center with the mince. Tie up the *filet,* knotting it at the top. Cover with water or bouillon. Add a clove of garlic, 2 or 3 sprigs of parsley, and a *bouquet garni.* Cook over low heat (at a simmer) or in a 325° oven for 2½ to 3 hours. Remove the *filet* and serve cabbage in a salad bowl.

Stuffed Cabbage Marseillaise (*Chou Farci à la Marseillaise*) SERVES 6

1 large head of cabbage
2 tablespoons blanched salt pork, diced
2 tablespoons cooked ham or sausage meat, minced
2 medium-sized onions, peeled, chopped, and sautéed
½ cup soft bread crumbs
2 tablespoons water
1 clove garlic, peeled
Small bunch parsley, chopped
Salt and pepper
3 tablespoons olive oil
2 egg yolks or 1 whole egg, beaten
½ cup (about) bouillon

Separate the leaves of a tender head of white or curly (Savoy) cabbage. Mince and blanch the heavy, outside leaves and blanch the remaining cabbage, being careful to keep it intact. Drain it and lay it on a cloth. Remove and chop the heart.

Prepare a stuffing, thus: Dice the blanched salt pork. Add the chopped, cooked ham (or sausage meat that has been sautéed for a few minutes and drained) and the finely chopped, sautéed onions, the chopped cabbage heart, the bread crumbs soaked in water and pressed out, the garlic and parsley chopped together. Season with salt and pepper. Mix well and then sauté lightly in 2 tablespoons of olive oil. Remove from the heat and add the beaten egg yolks or 1 whole egg, beaten.

Garnish each leaf of the cabbage head with this mixture, then tie the head up like a package, and set it in an oiled baking dish. Moisten with a little bouillon and then with a light sprinkle of olive oil. Brown in a 350° to 375° oven for about 15 minutes.

Celery (Céleri)

Celery Provençale (Céleri à la Provençale)

SERVES 4

Trim and thoroughly clean the celery. Cut it in 4-inch lengths and boil in salted water for about 20 minutes. *Drain well.* Place in an earthenware casserole. Season with salt and pepper. Sprinkle lavishly with grated cheese. Dot with butter. Cover the dish and set it in a 375° oven until cheese and juices have melted together — about 30 minutes.

1 pound bunch celery
Salt and pepper
3 tablespoons butter
¼ cup grated cheese

Chard

Chard au Gratin Vauclusienne

SERVES 4

Cut 1 pound of chard into 3- to 4-inch lengths and remove the heavy ribs and fibers. Blanch in salted water (page 13). Drain thoroughly. Lay the chard in a rather shallow, well-oiled casserole. Season with a little salt and grated nutmeg. Dust with grated cheese and chopped parsley. Cover this completely with thick cream which has been whipped with the yolks of 2 eggs over medium heat until somewhat thickened. Sprinkle with crumbs and glaze in a hot oven.

1 pound chard
Salt
Grated nutmeg
Grated cheese
Chopped parsley
¾ cup heavy cream
2 egg yolks
Bread crumbs

Chard Pie (Tarte de Blettes)

SERVES 6

Here is the recipe for a dish, originally Italian, which has become one of the great specialities of Nice. It is an odd dish, hardly ever made any longer in family kitchens but eaten a great deal, nevertheless, because it is sold in the market places of Nice and in the little shops of Vieux Nice.

Wash the leaves of the chard in copious amounts of water. Spread them on a towel and when they are thoroughly dry, roll them up and shred them as fine as possible with a sharp knife (but don't put them in a blender or grinder). Make a pastry dough with the flour, salt, lard (or butter), and the sugars, plus just enough water (3 or 4 tablespoons) to make a workable dough. Spread pastry in pie plate as for any pie. Prick the bottom all over with the floured tines of a fork. Fit another pie plate over the pastry and half-fill this with rice or dried beans to weight it down. Bake at 400° for about 8 minutes. It will then be only half cooked but the surface will be dry enough so that damp filling won't

Filling:
1 pound large-leaved chard
¼ pound grated Gouda cheese
Salt and pepper
2 or 3 tablespoons currants
1 whole egg, beaten
Pastry:
1¾ cup flour
½ teaspoon salt
6 tablespoons lard or butter
Water
1 egg
1 tablespoon brown sugar
1 tablespoon granulated white sugar

make it soggy. Take from oven. Remove top plate. Discard rice or beans. Lower oven heat to 375°.

Combine chopped chard with the cheese, currants, beaten egg, salt and pepper. [Do not beat the egg until just before it is to be used or it will lose its "rising" power.] Fill pie shell and bake (oven will have dropped its temperature to 375°) for 25 minutes.

Chick-peas (Pois Chiches)

Now *here's* a vegetable sadly neglected in the United States, perhaps because too few people know how good it is when well prepared . . . and how nutritious.

Most American supermarkets carry canned chick-peas. These save one long step in preparation. However, it is best to drain the liquor they are packed in and rinse the peas under cold water to eliminate the slight "canned" flavor. The peas may then be simmered briefly in a previously cooked tomato or meat sauce.

Dried chick-peas must be soaked overnight in twice their quantity of water plus 1 tablespoon baking soda. Next morning, rinse them well, and blanch them starting with cold water (9 cups water to 2 cups peas) and 1 peeled onion, 1 clove of garlic, salt, and a bay leaf. Cook only until tender.

In Provence, chick-peas are served most often as a salad which is always slightly warm but not hot.

Note: Don't discard the bouillon in which the peas were cooked. It makes a good base for soup.

Chick-pea Salad
(Salade de Pois Chiches)   ALLOW ½ CUP PER PERSON

Chick-peas, cooked as indicated above, are served warm, dressed in any of the following ways:

1. Quite simply, with oil, vinegar, and onion rings
2. In a *Vinaigrette* Sauce (page 30)
3. Supplemented with bits of tuna fish or diced herring fillets
4. With scallions and capers
5. With oil and vinegar dressing, mixed with grated *poutargue*

(page 219), powdered with grated nutmeg and minced parsley and served with a special mayonnaise (See Chick-pea Salad à la Martégale, (page 220).

Eggplant (Aubergines)

Eggplant Pertuis (Aubergines à la Mode de Pertuis)

1 POUND OF EGGPLANT SERVES 6

We put this recipe first, though out of alphabetical order, because it is the simplest of all ways of treating this everywhere plentiful vegetable. It is, in fact, the pure essence of eggplant and can become an addiction, say the *Provençaux*.

Grill unpeeled, medium-size eggplants very close to the heat. (Some people even put them right on the embers of an outdoor grill). When they are cooked, split them in half. The insides will still be white as a lily. Sprinkle with salt, a grind of pepper, and a generous amount of olive oil. That's all there is to it and it is excellent.

Anchovy-stuffed Eggplant (Aubergines aux Anchois)

SERVES 6

Use 12 very small eggplants. Trim and cut them in half, lengthwise. Salt and set aside, cut-side down, to drain for 30 minutes. Then fry, cut-side down, in the hot olive oil. Remove from pan, reserving the oil. Excavate the pulp, taking care not to break the outside skin. Mash the pulp with anchovy fillets (about ½-inch of fillet per eggplant), the bread crumbs, crushed cloves of garlic, salt and pepper. Brown this mixture in a little of the oil in which the eggplants were fried. Fill the shells and bake at 375° for 30 minutes.

12 very small eggplants
4 tablespoons hot olive oil
Anchovy fillets
2 peeled, crushed cloves garlic
½ cup of bread crumbs
Salt and pepper

Eggplant and Tomatoes (Bohémienne)

SERVES 6

Bohémienne and *Ratatouille* are sometimes confused: they are completely different preparations. *Ratatouille* (page 193) is indigenous to Nice and the ingredients include, in addition to eggplant, zucchini and green peppers. *Bohémienne* is from the Avignon region and is based on eggplant and tomatoes *only*.

1 pound eggplant
1 pound skinned, seeded tomatoes
5 tablespoons olive oil
2 desalted anchovy fillets (page 12)
1 tablespoon flour
½ cup milk

Peel and slice the eggplant. Salt and drain as in preceding recipe. Fry the slices in 3 tablespoons of the olive oil, along with the tomatoes (slightly crushed). While the mixture is cooking, it should be mashed with a fork.

In a separate skillet, sauté the anchovy fillets in the remaining 2 tablespoons of olive oil until they are dissolved. Stir in the flour over low heat and then add the milk, slowly (still over low heat), until sauce is thickened and smooth. Mix sauce and vegetables. Turn the whole into a baking dish and put in a 400° oven until heated through and browned.

Eggplant "Cake" (Gâteau d'Aubergines) SERVES 4

1 pound eggplant
Olive oil
½ cup soft bread crumbs
Milk
2 tablespoons chopped parsley
1 peeled clove garlic, mashed
3 desalted anchovy fillets (page 12)
2 egg yolks, beaten
2 egg whites, beaten
Salt and pepper
Tomato sauce (page 32)

Peel the eggplants and cut them in half, lengthwise. Salt the cut sides and set, salted side down, to drain for about half an hour. Then wipe them dry and fry in olive oil. Soak the bread crumbs in milk and press out. Mix crumbs with the parsley, garlic, and anchovy fillets. Chop the eggplant and add it to this mixture along with the beaten egg yolks. Then fold in the whites (beaten to a snow). Season with salt and pepper. Pour into an oiled, heatproof baking dish and bake at 350° for about 30 minutes. Serve with tomato sauce.

Eggplant Escoffier (Aubergines Escoffier) SERVES 4 OR 5

4 eggplants
Olive oil
2 tablespoons chopped onion
Snip of peeled garlic
3 tomatoes, peeled and seeded
Salt and pepper
3 or 4 tablespoons bread crumbs
2 or 3 tablespoons meat juice*

Peel medium-size eggplants, cut them in slices, lengthwise, salt and pepper them and set aside, cut-side-down, to drain for 30 minutes. Then dry the slices and fry them in olive oil.

Meanwhile cook the chopped onion in oil until soft. Add the peeled, seeded, and chopped tomatoes, a snip of garlic, salt and pepper. Cook all this gently for 15 minutes. Then chop two of the fried slices of eggplant and add them to the sauce, plus 3 or 4 tablespoons of bread crumbs and, if possible, 2 or 3 tablespoons of meat juice (preferably from a stew).

Pair the remaining slices of eggplant with this filling in between. Lay these "sandwiches" on a heatproof platter. Sprinkle them lightly with olive oil, and put them in a 350° to 375° oven for 20 minutes.

This dish may be served hot or cold.

* Broth or gravy from a roast or a stew can be used, or meat extract (page 18).

Eggplant au Gratin
1 POUND (ABOUT 3 EGGPLANTS) SERVES 4

Trim eggplants and cut them in very thin slices, crosswise. Salt the slices and set them aside for 30 minutes to drain. Then blanch them in salted water for 10 to 15 minutes. Drain well, and dry with a cloth. Oil a heatproof dish. Make a layer of eggplant in the bottom, then a layer of thick, highly seasoned tomato sauce (include a little garlic). Top with another layer of eggplant and finish with sauce. Dust generously with grated cheese, sprinkle lightly with oil, and set in a preheated 375° oven for 25 minutes to cook through and brown.

1 pound of eggplant
Salted water
Salt
Tomato sauce, highly seasoned
  (page 32)
Grated cheese

Eggplant Provençale
(Aubergines à la Provençale)
SERVES 4 or 5

Trim eggplants and slice crosswise. Salt and allow to drain for 30 minutes. Then fry the slices in very hot olive oil. Transfer to a serving dish and keep them hot, reserving the oil in which they were cooked.

Chop together 3 peeled, seeded tomatoes, a sprig of fresh basil, and 1 peeled clove of garlic. Blend in 3 tablespoons chopped parsley. Simmer this mixture in the reserved oil until it is reduced to a smooth purée. Pour over the eggplant slices and serve very hot.

3 medium-size eggplants
Salt
Olive oil
3 tomatoes, peeled, seeded
Sprig of fresh basil
1 clove garlic, peeled
3 tablespoons chopped parsley

Ratatouille Niçoise
SERVES 6

This summer dish is becoming more and more popular. The ingredients are usually available and it is good hot or cold.

Slice and salt eggplants. Set on paper towels to drain off the somewhat acrid juices. Cut zucchini in slices ¼ inch thick. Remove seeds and veins from peppers; cut in narrow strips. Slice tomatoes, remove seeds with point of a small knife, and drain off juices. Peel and mince onion and garlic. Dry eggplant slices thoroughly, fry lightly in 2 or 3 tablespoons olive oil. Drain on paper towels. Add 2 tablespoons oil to skillet and sauté zucchini; drain and reserve.

Cook the minced onion and garlic in remaining oil in a heavy enameled (or other non-metal) casserole over moderate heat until soft but not brown. Then add green peppers, tomatoes, salt and pepper, and *bouquet garni*. Lay the fried zucchini and eggplant on top, cover the pot, and simmer 20 to 25 minutes. Then tilt out the excess juices into a small saucepan and cook over brisk heat until reduced to about ¼ cup. Pour this back into the casserole. Raise heat and cook, watchfully, uncovered

2 medium-size eggplants, peeled
Salt and pepper
6 tablespoons olive oil (more if needed)
3 small green peppers
4 (unpeeled) medium-size zucchini
4 tomatoes
1 medium-size onion
2 cloves garlic
Bouquet garni
(Optional) A few stoned black olives

10 minutes or more. There should be very little juice in the finished *ratatouille*. Garnish with (optional) black olives.

Leeks (Poireaux)

Leeks (Poireaux)

SERVES 6

12 leeks
1 beaten egg
Flour
Olive oil
Salt and pepper
¼ cup minced parsley
Sprig of fresh thyme
1 bay leaf
Few drops of wine vinegar

Leeks are called "Asperges du Pégot" — The Shoemaker's Asparagus — in Provence, and the leek is a fine vegetable however it is cooked. The recipe given below was acquired through the kindness of an elderly relative of the pastor of a small parish on the banks of the Rhône. It is a simple, rustic dish with a delectable flavor.

Clean, trim, and blanch 12 leeks (about 2 inches or a little less in diameter). Dip them in beaten egg and then roll them in flour. Start these in hot olive oil in a covered skillet, adding salt, pepper, minced parsley, a sprig of fresh thyme (or 1 teaspoon dried), and a bay leaf. After about 10 minutes, lower the heat. The leeks should be tender in about 20 minutes longer. Serve them sprinkled with a few drops of wine vinegar.

Lentils (Lentilles)

Lentils Ventresco (Lentilles à la Ventresco)

Lentils
1 onion, peeled and chopped
6 tablespoons chopped salt pork
1 tablespoon flour
2 cups bouillon
Bouquet garni
1 clove garlic
2 tablespoons tomato paste
Salt and pepper

Allow ½ cup of lentils per person. Soak them overnight in cold water. Drain well. Cook the peeled, chopped onion with the chopped, blanched salt pork. Stir in the flour and allow this to brown (not too dark). Add the bouillon and lentils, a *bouquet garni,* a whole clove of garlic, tomato paste, salt and pepper. Cook over low heat until the lentils are soft. Proportions of sauce should be enough for 2 cups of lentils. More broth may be added if moisture evaporates too fast.

Mushrooms (Champignons)

Many kinds of mushrooms go into French dishes and many kinds are sold, the most flavorsome being the rich, black *morilles* gathered in the spring. The United States has many types also, but only one or two are grown commercially. People (with good reason, alas) are afraid of mushrooms because some kinds are poisonous. But it is a pity, for the puffballs that grow wild (and enormous) in the fall are delicate, creamy, delectable. Morels, too, could be sponsored to advantage. Meanwhile, except for an occasional windfall in a foreign market, Americans must make do with the familiar round-headed, smooth white commercial mushrooms. These are available everywhere and are suitable for any of the recipes that follow.

Broiled Mushrooms
(*Champignons des Pins Grillés*)

ALLOW 4 LARGE MUSHROOM CAPS PER PERSON

September through October is the season for pine mushrooms in Provence where it is the custom *"d'aller aux champignons"* in gay groups of townspeople. Those who aren't interested in this sport, however, can buy them in the market.

Remove the stems and wash the caps of large mushrooms. Dip the caps in olive oil and set them on a grill over a good bed of embers, (or under a broiler, if indoors). Salt and pepper them while they are cooking. Serve sprinkled with garlic and parsley minced together.

A variation: the caps are filled with snail butter (see page 14) and baked in an earthenware platter in a 350° oven until the butter is hot and bubbly — but no longer. Mushrooms should not be overcooked.

Mushrooms
Olive oil
Salt and pepper
Garlic
Parsley
Snail butter

Provençal Mushrooms
(*Champignons Provençals*)

¾ POUND SERVES 5 OR 6

Wash, drain, and cut the mushrooms in half lengthwise. Set them to marinate in olive oil to cover, seasoned with salt, whole peppercorns, and a snip of garlic.

At serving time, sauté over brisk heat long enough to color nicely. Serve on thin slices of toast or on bread fried in oil. Sprinkle with minced parsley and a few drops of lemon juice.

Mushrooms
Olive oil
Salt
Peppercorns
Garlic
Toast
Minced parsley
Lemon juice

Stuffed Mushrooms (*Champignons des Pins Farcis*)

ALLOW 2 OR 3 LARGE CAPS PER PERSON

12 to 18 mushrooms
Olive oil
½ cup of bread crumbs
2 tablespoons water
2 cloves garlic, peeled
2 tablespoons minced parsley
Salt and pepper
1 hard-boiled egg
Fine dry crumbs

Clean 12 to 18 mushrooms of equal size. Remove the stems and chop them. Brown the caps in oil. Then add to the chopped stems the bread crumbs, soaked in the water and pressed out, the minced cloves of garlic, the parsley, salt and pepper, and a hard-boiled egg, mashed. Mix well. Fill the caps and place them (filled side up, of course) in a flat, ovenware dish. Sprinkle with oil, dust with fine dry crumbs and bake at 375° until mushrooms are cooked and lightly golden (about 15 minutes).

Onions (*Oignons*)

Onions Stuffed with Garlic (*Oignons Farcis à l'Ail*)

SERVES 6

6 large onions
6 cloves garlic
Salt and pepper
Olive oil
Buttered bread crumbs
Toast

Peel and blanch the onions and garlic cloves. Hollow out the centers of the onions. Pound the extracted pulp of the onion in a mortar with the cooked garlic, salt, pepper, and enough olive oil to make a manageable paste which you stuff into the onion "shells," reserving a little. Place them in an oiled, ovenware dish. Strew with buttered crumbs and set in a 400° oven for about 10 to 15 minutes. Serve with toast points, spread with the reserved purée.

Potatoes (*Pommes de Terre*)

New Potatoes with Artichokes (*Pommes Nouvelles aux Artichauts*)

SERVES 6

2 pounds little new potatoes
6 artichokes
1 medium-size onion
6 tablespoons olive oil
Salt and pepper
Bouquet garni
2 whole cloves garlic

Prepare artichokes as for a *Barigoule* (page 182). Peel or scrape the new potatoes, leaving them whole. Cook chopped onion in 2 tablespoons olive oil. Place the artichokes firmly on their bottoms, arranging them around the inside rim of a skillet. Put the potatoes in the center. Sprinkle with 3 or 4 tablespoons of olive oil. Season with salt, pepper, a *bouquet garni* and the cloves of garlic. Cover and cook over low heat, basting from time to time with the *Barigoule* juices in the pan. The sauce should be well reduced by the time the potatoes are cooked. Retire the *bouquet garni* and the garlic. Serve the potatoes on a hot platter, surrounded by the artichokes.

Draçenoise Potatoes
(Pommes de Terre Draçenoise)
SERVES 6

Boil potatoes in their jackets just to the point where they are cooked but still firm and intact. Drain well and chill. Then pare and slice the potatoes crosswise.

Heat the olive oil in a skillet. Lay the potato slices in it. Season, going light on the salt and pepper. Sprinkle with grated nutmeg and the grated peel of half a small lemon. Brown the potatoes lightly on both sides, being careful not to let them stick to the pan. Before serving, add minced parsley mixed with a minced clove of garlic, the freshened anchovy fillets (page 12), and lemon juice.

2 pounds potatoes
4 tablespoons olive oil
Salt and pepper
Grated nutmeg
Grated lemon peel
¼ cup minced parsley
1 small clove garlic
2 freshened anchovy fillets
2 teaspoons lemon juice

Potatoes with Cucumbers
(Pommes de Terre aux Concombres)
SERVES 6

Peel and slice potatoes. Combine these in a skillet with olive oil, salt and pepper, a sprig of fresh basil, a bay leaf, and peeled, seeded tomatoes. Add water to just cover. Put a lid on the pot and cook for 20 minutes over brisk heat.

To serve, peel 2 chilled, young cucumbers, quartering each one, lengthwise. Salt and pepper these and combine them with the potatoes. The taste of the hot potatoes and the fresh, raw cucumbers together is a happy surprise.

1 pound potatoes
3 tablespoons olive oil
Salt and pepper
Sprig of fresh basil
1 bay leaf
2 medium-size tomatoes
Water
2 chilled cucumbers

Tian of Potatoes Aptésienne
(Tian de Pommes de Terre Aptésienne)
SERVES 6

Peel and slice the potatoes and onions and arrange them in alternating layers in a casserole, lightly salting and peppering each layer. Add 1 or 2 bay leaves, and a pinch of chopped basil. Fill the dish almost to the top layer with bouillon. Sprinkle a few drops of olive oil over the surface. Bake, covered, in a 375° oven for 30 minutes. Then remove the cover and bake 15 minutes longer to brown the top.

1 pound potatoes
3 medium-size onions
Salt and pepper
1 or 2 bay leaves
Pinch of chopped basil
Bouillon
Olive oil

Sweet Potatoes (Patates Douces)

Allow 1 or 2 per person. The *Provençaux* like sweet potatoes and serve them in the simplest possible form, either baked in their skins and eaten with salt and olive oil, or boiled, peeled, and escorted to the table by a bowl of *Aïoli* (page 24), which admirably suits them.

Rice (Riz)

Risotto Toulonnaise

1 onion, chopped
3 tablespoons olive oil
1½ cups raw rice
3 cups hot water or chicken broth
Salt and pepper
Sauce Toulonnaise

Color the peeled, chopped onion in olive oil. Add the raw rice, stirring it in the hot oil for 2 or 3 minutes. Then add the hot water or broth and continue stirring until the liquid comes again to a boil. Turn down heat, season with salt and pepper, cover the casserole and set it in a preheated 350° oven. Bake for 20 minutes by which time the moisture should be completely absorbed and the rice cooked and fluffy. Serve accompanied by *Sauce Toulonnaise* (page 33).

Risotto Nissardo

2 tablespoons of tomato paste
Pinch of saffron
½ cup diced button mushrooms
2 tablespoons olive oil
¼ cup diced ham
¼ cup stoned small black olives
5 or 6 cooked artichoke hearts
Tomato Sauce (page 32)

Cook 1½ cups rice as in the preceding recipe. Exception: after the first 10 minutes in the oven, the tomato paste and saffron should be stirred in.

Separately, cook the diced button mushrooms in olive oil. Add diced ham, stoned small black olives, and cooked artichoke hearts cut in smallish pieces. Combine with the rice when it is cooked. Shape the risotto in a dome on a hot serving dish and blanket it in rather thick tomato sauce.

Spinach (Épinards)

Spinach Cannoise (Épinards Cannoise)   SERVES 4

Blanch the carefully washed spinach in a large quantity of boiling water for 4 or 5 minutes — no longer. Drain well in a colander, pressing the spinach hard to extract all the water. Chop it coarsely.

Separately, in an earthenware casserole, cook the sliced, medium-size mushrooms in olive oil or butter. Blend the flour and heavy cream in a small saucepan over low heat to thicken. Add this to the mushrooms. Combine spinach and mushrooms. Spoon a scant ½ cup of Madeira or port over the vegetables. Powder generously with grated cheese and set in a hot (400°) oven for 10 minutes to brown.

Leftovers make a delicious addition to a soufflé or filling for a main course lunch dish.

2½ pounds spinach
Boiling water
½ pound mushrooms
3 tablespoons olive oil or butter
1 tablespoon flour
3 tablespoons heavy cream
½ cup Madeira or port
Grated cheese

Squash (Courges)

Tian of Squash Vauclusienne
(Courge au Gratin Vauclusienne)

SERVES 6

Here is a delicious, too little known dish which comes to us from Vaucluse where it is called *"Le Tian de Courge."* A *tian* is the oblong, red earthenware dish in which it is usually served.

Pare and dice the squash. Cook the dice in 4 tablespoons olive oil or butter (no water!), adding more if needed. When the squash is soft, purée it in an electric blender or put it through a sieve or food mill.

Separately, prepare a thick Béchamel Sauce (page 12), season with salt, pepper, and (important) grated nutmeg. Blend in the squash purée plus 2 beaten eggs. When all is smoothly mixed, pour it into a shallow, buttered casserole. Dust with crumbs, dot with butter, and bake in a 350° oven for about 45 minutes.

3 pounds squash, preferably yellow
5 tablespoons olive oil or butter
Béchamel Sauce
Salt and pepper
Grated nutmeg
2 beaten eggs
Bread crumbs
Butter

Stuffed Squash (or Zucchini) Blossoms
(Fleurs de Courgettes Farcies)

This is an agreeable culinary fantasy of Provence. It is also prepared in Italian households in the United States when (usually in summer) the foreign vegetable markets offer attractive bunches of squash flowers for sale.

Blanch the flowers very quickly in boiling salted water and, with great care, spread them with either a mince such as that used for stuffed eggplant (page 191) or a sauce with a seasoned spinach base. Fold over the heads of the flowers so as to form little packages. Oil a baking dish and place the stuffed squash in it. Moisten with a little white wine and water, half-and-half, or meat drippings. Set the dish in a 350° oven for about 10 minutes.

Gratin of Zucchini (*Courgettes au Gratin*) SERVES 6

2 pounds zucchini
Water
Salt and pepper
Butter
1 whole egg
4 tablespoons light cream
Grated cheddar cheese

Peel and mince zucchini. Put it in a skillet with a pinch of salt and just enough water to keep it from sticking. Stir frequently and cook only until all the rendered moisture has completely evaporated. Then season with butter, salt and pepper, and the whole egg beaten with the light cream. Turn into an ovenware dish, sprinkle with grated cheese, and brown in a 375° oven.

Zucchini Niçoise (*Courgettes Niçoises*) ALLOW 3 SMALL ZUCCHINI PER PERSON

Small green zucchini
Tomato sauce, well seasoned
Fresh basil

This dish, served cold on a hot day, is wonderfully refreshing.

The little green squashes should be so young that their seeds are hardly seeds at all yet. Scrape, rather than pare them, and cook in a thick, well-seasoned tomato sauce (page 32) for about 30 minutes. Sprinkle with chopped, fresh basil just before serving.

Stuffed Zucchini (*Courgettes Farcies*) SERVES 4

2 medium-size zucchini
Eggplant filling
Oregano
Bread crumbs
Olive oil

Cut 2 medium-size zucchini in half, lengthwise. Hollow out the insides, chop rather fine, and put them aside. Prepare a filling as for Anchovy-Stuffed Eggplant (page 191) and combine it with the chopped squash. Add a pinch of oregano. Fill the shells, powder with bread crumbs lightly mixed with olive oil and put them in a shallow, oiled baking dish. Brown 15 minutes in a 375° oven.

Tomatoes (*Tomates*)

How much more evocative and poetic than the word "tomato" is the name *"pomme d'amour"* given by the *Provençaux* to the beautiful rosy vegetable.

Love apples should be eaten when the weather is hot and sunny. As soon as the nights begin to cool and the cold rains come, tomatoes become acid.

If tomatoes that are to be stuffed are drained of their juice before they are filled, the finished product will be more shapely and taste better. Another technique for hot stuffed tomatoes is to put 1 teaspoon of dry raw rice in the bottom of each tomato cup. The rice will be deliciously plump and scented by the time the tomatoes are cooked and will have absorbed the excess juice so that the vegetable can bake without boiling.

Tomatoes Antiboise

SERVES 6

Take a large slice off the stem end of the tomatoes, and hollow out the pulp with a spoon, being careful not to spoil the shape of the tomatoes. Season them inside with salt and pepper, then turn them, open-side down, to drain. Drain the pulp in a colander. Then chop it and mix it with the tuna fish (the best is the kind that is packed in olive oil), the tinned, mashed anchovy fillets, minced parsley, the ½ cup soaked, pressed-out bread crumbs, salt, pepper, thyme, and fennel.

Fill the drained halves with this mixture, sprinkle with a few drops of oil, and broil them. [Watch carefully not to scorch them.]

6 tomatoes
Salt and pepper
1 cup tuna fish
3 anchovy fillets
4 tablespoons minced parsley
½ cup bread crumbs
¼ teaspoon thyme
1 teaspoon dried fennel
Olive oil

Broiled Tomatoes

ALLOW 1 TOMATO PER PERSON

Cut firm, smooth tomatoes in half, crosswise, and seed them. Season with salt and pepper and dust with a stingy bit of powdered thyme. Give each half a splash of olive oil and broil (preferably over wood embers). When they are cooked, top each half with a well-crushed anchovy or a blob of anchovy butter (page 14).

These tomatoes make a fine garnish for any kind of grilled meat or fish.

Tomatoes, medium size
Salt and pepper
Powdered thyme
Olive oil
Anchovies

Tomatoes Calendal

ALLOW 2 TOMATOES PER PERSON

Choose small tomatoes of equal size. Decapitate and excavate, keeping the shapes intact. Season inside with salt and pepper, and then place the tomatoes, cut-side down, in a skillet containing the hot olive oil. Cook 5 minutes, then turn right-side up and cook a few minutes more. Arrange on a platter, sprinkle with olive oil and put in the refrigerator to chill.

At serving time, fill the tomato cups with crumbled tuna fish, anchovy fillets, and grilled, skinned green bell peppers, cut in small dice, all dressed with highly seasoned mayonnaise. They may also be garnished with finely chopped hard-boiled egg yolks and, in the center of each tomato half, a "lozenge" of chopped parsley.

Small tomatoes
Salt and pepper
½ cup hot olive oil
Tuna fish
Anchovy fillets
Green bell peppers
(Optional) hard-boiled egg yolks
Chopped parsley

Tomatoes Stuffed with Broiled Mushrooms
(Tomates Farcies aux Champignons Grillés) SERVES 4

Tomato cups (4 medium or 8 small)
¾ pound button mushrooms
3 tablespoons olive oil (or more)
4 tablespoons tomato sauce
1 egg yolk, beaten
Salt and pepper
Bread crumbs
Olive oil

In these stuffed tomatoes the contrasting flavor of tomato and mushroom creates a dish of great distinction.

Prepare tomato cups (as in the preceding recipe). Peel and dice button mushrooms and cook them in the olive oil (adding more if necessary). When they begin to smell "mushroomy," and the juices are somewhat reduced, remove from the heat, add the thick tomato sauce, the beaten yolk of an egg, salt and pepper. Mix thoroughly.

Fill the tomato cups with this mixture. Dust with bread crumbs, sprinkle lightly with olive oil, and bake in a greased, non-metal baking dish at 400° for about 15 minutes.

Tomato Casserole (Tomates en Charlotte) SERVES 4

Olive oil
1 yellow onion
3 tomatoes
Salt and pepper
Spanish (red) onion
3 boiled, peeled potatoes
Grated cheese

Lightly color a medium-size, peeled, finely minced onion in ½ cup olive oil. Spread one-third of the hot, oniony oil in the bottom of an earthenware (or other non-metal) baking dish. Cover with a layer of tomato slices (about 1 medium-size tomato), season with salt and pepper and 1 teaspoon grated red (Spanish) onion. Cover the tomatoes with a layer of boiled (but still firm), peeled, sliced potatoes. Season lightly with salt and pepper plus a thin sprinkle of grated cheese. Make a second layer of onion, tomato slices, red onion, and potato. Finish with a layer of tomatoes and cooked, minced onion. Sprinkle with remaining oil and bake 30 minutes in a 350°-oven.

Tomatoes Provençale SERVES 4

4 large tomatoes
Salt
3 tablespoons hot olive oil
Bread crumbs
2 tablespoons parsley
2 cloves garlic
1 tablespoon olive oil

Cut the tomatoes in half perpendicularly (down through the stem). Carefully remove the seeds. Salt the tomatoes and cook them, cut-side down, in 3 tablespoons hot olive oil (adding more if necessary). When the juices have evaporated, turn them over and cook for a few minutes longer. Transfer them to a non-metal baking dish in which the peeled, minced cloves of garlic and the parsley have been cooked in 1 tablespoon olive oil for 2 to 3 minutes. Spoon this fragrant sauce over the tomatoes and set the dish under the broiler for 4 or 5 minutes to brown, being careful not to let the tomatoes get scorched.

Optional: A few bread crumbs may be mixed with the cooked parsley and garlic. What must *not* be done and what is *not Provençal,* is to sprinkle the tomatoes with *un*cooked parsley and garlic.

Truffles are, for most Americans, pure fantasy. Fresh ones are unobtainable and the kind sold in food specialty shops, four to a five-dollar jar, barely hint at the true truffle flavor. And, in any case, they aren't something the average housekeeper is going to dress any dish up with very often (if ever). But the truffle is part of the culinary treasure of the great truffle-producing Vaucluse country of Provence, and so . . . for the record:

Truffles Provençale (*Truffes à la Provençale*) SERVES 6

Peel 6 fine, fat black truffles and cut them in rather thick slices. Rub the inside of an earthenware casserole or tureen with the ½ clove of garlic. Put in the sliced truffles, olive oil, good red wine (not too young), and the strong meat juice from, preferably, a veal roast. (Commercial meat extract may be substituted but is, of course, inferior to the fresh.)

6 truffles
½ clove garlic
3 tablespoons olive oil
3 tablespoons red wine
5 tablespoons strong meat juice
Flour-and-water dough

Cover the casserole with a lid that has a vent hole in it. Seal the lid to the pot with a strip of flour-and-water dough. Sink the pot in hot embers up to the edge of the lid. As soon as vapor begins to escape through the little vent hole, the truffles are cooked and ready to be served. Do not remove the cover until everyone is at the table, to be charmed, simultaneously, by the sight and fragrance of this lyrical food.

Note: Presumably, if the truffles have to be cooked, unromantically, indoors, the casserole can be sunk into *hot, hot* water in a larger vessel and then put into a hot oven for 10 minutes or so.

Vegetable Casserole

Vegetables-Cheese Casserole
(*Le Gratin Provençal*) SERVES 6

This casserole of tomatoes, eggplant, onion, zucchini, and cheese makes a wonderfully savory main course for lunch or may be used as a separate vegetable course for dinner.

1 large eggplant
2 medium-size zucchini
2 medium-size onions
4 tomatoes
Boiling salted water
4 tablespoons olive oil
Salt and pepper
Grated Cheese
(Optional) cracker crumbs
(Optional) butter

Peel, slice, and salt a large eggplant, and set it aside to drain. Meanwhile, peel, and slice the zucchini, and peel and mince the onions. Peel, seed, and cut the tomatoes in thick slices.

When the eggplant slices have given up some of their juices, dry the slices and blanch them, along with the sliced zucchini, for 3 or 4 minutes in rapidly boiling, salted water. Drain *thoroughly*.

Cook the minced onion lightly in 3 tablespoons olive oil. Put a layer of this onion in the bottom of an ovenware dish, a layer of zucchini over it, then a layer of the tomato slices, then of the eggplant. Salt and pepper these, and strew with grated cheese, Repeat the process until all the vegetables are neatly nested. At this point tilt out excess juices, if any, and broil them over brisk heat until reduced to about ¼ cup. Pour this back over the vegetables in the casserole, and top all with a final flourish of grated cheese. Sprinkle with olive oil and bake in a preheated 350° oven for about 30 minutes.

XVI
Desserts and Preserves

Cakes and Pastries

PROVENÇAL CUISINE is not very rich in prepared sweets, or at least not any longer. The explanation is twofold. The region abounds in luscious fruits from April to November. And, during the winter months, these delicious fruits are eaten dried: figs, raisins, almonds, etc., even melons. Second, the sweet baked specialties of Provence are not often made at home nowadays because such excellent ones are available in the pastry and confectioner shops where ancient traditions are scrupulously followed in the production of fête-day goodies. It is, therefore, only by way of documentation that we list, below, the names of some of the sweets that were made in olden times in Provence.

Le Bescuchelloo: a dry cake of light dough.

Le Biscotin: a small rusk (like Zweibach).

Les Chichi-Fregi: of Italian origin, these are fried chick-peas and are still sold in shops.

Le Crespeu: an egg pastry fried, like fritters, in oil.

L'Échaudé: a pastry, shaped like a hollow croquette, that is first poached in water, then suspended (like a thimble) over a twig, and baked in the oven. A slightly different version of échaudé is called *Le Brassadeu.*

L'Estevenoun: the traditional cake for St. Étienne's (St. Stephen's) Day.

Les Fougassons: little, flat butter pastries. The best are made in Vence.

La Navette: a Candlemas Day sweet made in Marseille.

L'Oreillette: a little pillow-shaped pastry.

Les Pignoulats: pine-nut cookies.

La Pompe à l'Huile: the traditional crown-shaped cake eaten on Christmas Eve. It is made with yeast, brown sugar, flour, oil, eggs, grated lemon and orange rinds, and, when taken from the oven, is sprinkled with orange flower water. [According to *Larousse Gastronomique,* it is also sprinkled "copiously" with mulled wine (page 230) when it is eaten. Beakers of the cooked wine accompany it].

For British and American readers at home, and expatriate *Provencaux* (if any such exist), herewith a handful of recipes to try for remembrance' sake or anticipation.

Fried Cakes of Arles (Bugnes Arlésiennes)

The recipe for this very ancient Provençal confection (or some version of it) traveled up the Rhône past Valence, reached the Dauphiné, then Lyon and the Saône, Bresse, and the Franche-Comté with such success that each of the provinces claims it as its own. [As for the name — bugne was very likely the great-great-grandfather of the bun].

Sift the dry ingredients together and heap them in a large bowl or onto a board or marble slab. Make a depression in the center and put into this the egg yolks and rum. Work these gradually into the flour, adding just enough water to make a dough that will hold together. Knead the dough until it is smooth. Then break off one piece at a time and roll it into a little ball the size of an egg. Roll out these "eggs" into thin ovals. Next, with a pastry wheel, pierce them crosswise, being careful not to pierce the outside edges. Drop these pastries, a few at a time, into very hot (370°) deep fat or oil. When they are nicely golden, remove them from the fat with a slotted spoon. Drain them well and cool slightly. Powder with sugar. To serve traditionally, pile the *bugnes* lightly in a flat-bottomed basket.

2½ cups sifted flour
Pinch of salt
⅜ cup granulated sugar
4 tablespoons butter
3 egg yolks
⅓ cup rum
Water
Oil for deep frying
Confectioner's sugar

Pine-nut Crescents
(Croissants aux Pignons)   MAKES ABOUT 3 DOZEN

Cream butter and sugar together until very soft. Then carefully blend in the ground almonds, salt, vanilla, and flour. The dough will be rather firm. Cut off pieces about the size of prunes and roll them into little cigar-shaped pieces about ½-inch thick. Roll these in the chopped pine nuts and then bend them to half-moon shape. Place these 1 inch apart on greased baking tins. Bake at 350° for 15 to 20 minutes. (The crescents should not be brown.) Cool about 5 minutes, then strew with a little granulated sugar or brush with heavily sweetened milk.

1¼ pounds unbleached almonds, ground fine
1 cup butter
½ cup sugar
1 teaspoon vanilla
½ teaspoon salt
2 cups sifted flour (or a little less)*
1 cup (about) pine nuts, chopped
A little extra granulated sugar
Sweetened milk (optional)

* For reasons never adequately explained, cake and other baked foods need more flour on some days than on others.

Dry Almond Cakes
(Croquets aux Amandes)   MAKES ABOUT 2 DOZEN

Cream sugar and butter together. Add orange flavoring, the whole egg, and the chopped nuts. Combine with the flour sifted with the salt.

Cut the dough in half. Roll each half into a "rope" about ¾-inch thick and shaped rather like a long sausage that has been slightly flattened along its two sides. Brush with the egg white thinned with a few drops of water. Place the "ropes" on a greased cookie sheet. Bake for about 25 minutes at 375°. Remove from oven. Cool slightly. Cut in slices about ¾-inch wide. (Adapted from the recipe of J. B. Reboule.)

½ cup butter
1 cup sugar
1 tablespoon orange flower water (page 48) or 1 teaspoon grated orange rind
1 whole egg
1¼ cup roasted almond meats, chopped
½ teaspoon salt
1½ cups sifted flour
1 egg white
A few drops of water

Twelfth Night Cake or The Cake of the Kings (Gâteau des Rois)

In Provence, where all the ancient traditions are still honored, Candlemas Day still has its *navettes,* Shrove Tuesday (*mardi gras*) its fritters. Cakes at Easter are decorated with eggs and matrimonial bangles, and "dove" bracelets are worn for Pentecost. Christmas has its *vin cuit* (Mulled Wine, page 230) and the always popular cake called *La Pompe* from the word for ceremony or, because it emerges from the oven covered with lumps, *Gibassier,* from the same root as gibbous, meaning hunch-backed. No yearly fête, though, is anticipated with more delight than that of the Twelfth Night "Kings," which goes on for a month or even longer. The "king" is received at home and in public places and the ceremony is the occasion for charming reunions and much gaiety. It has always been a festival in which, says *Larousse Gastronomique,* "many come together to dine and elect a king by lot or vote. Their sons then make haste to follow their example, holding sumptuous banquets. Finally, the head of the family, the good master, causes to be brought forth, according to his means . . . a cake in which has been hidden a silver coin. He cuts and distributes the cake, keeping back portions for the Infant Jesus, the Virgin and the Magi. These he gives to the poor in their names. Whoever receives the piece containing the coin is recognized as king and all the guests shout for joy."

Nowadays, a bean is the token king plus (sometimes) a little porcelain "subject," and whoever becomes king or queen must be the next host and offer the next cake (unless he's at the dentist for repair of a broken tooth).

We have checked half a dozen recipes for Twelfth Night cake. All differ in some respect from all the others and the contrasts are as great as two eggs and twelve, as baking times of "two hundred degrees Fahrenheit or less" and 450°. But, essentially, the cake is a *brioche,* and *brioche,* whatever recipe it is made by, is a tricky cake to make. So, although the writers have a profound distaste for imitations of authentic regional specialities, they suggest to the average (or even better-than-average) cook that using a simple yeast coffee-bread dough can save a lot of uncertainty, not to speak of butter and eggs. It can be fruited, decorated, glazed, "beaned," and "subject-ed" at will.

Provençal Spinach Pie
(Tarte aux Épinards Provençale)

Line a 9-inch pie pan with the short pastry dough. Prick the dough all over with a sharp-tined fork. Line this pan with another pan of the same size and weight this down with 1 cup dried beans. Bake 10 minutes in a 400° oven. Remove the bean-filled pan. The pie shell will then be half cooked and dry on the surface. This dryness prevents the filling from soaking into the pastry and spoiling the texture of the finished pie.

When the pastry has cooled, combine the custard filling (*Crème Patissière,* page 15), cooked spinach, lemon rind, vanilla, and salt. Spread this evenly over the pastry in the pie plate. Cover with thin slices of preserved melon or tangerine segments. Cut the remaining pastry dough into narrow strips and "braid" these across the top of the pie in a latticework design. Brush with egg yolk and bake at 375° for about 25 minutes.

Spinach Pie may be served hot or cold.

Pâte brisée (page 19) for a 9-inch pie
1 cup *Crème Patissière*
1 cup cooked, seasoned, chopped spinach
1 teaspoon grated lemon rind
½ teaspoon vanilla
Pinch of salt
Preserved tangerine or melon
Egg yolk

Quince "Bread" (Le "Pan-Coudoun")

In Provence, quinces are prepared in the following way: Unbaked bread dough is bought from a baker. Quinces are wiped off, and their centers hollowed out and refilled with powdered sugar. Each is then wrapped in the dough which is pricked all over with a fork and put into a 350° oven and baked for about 40 minutes. They emerge as savory cakes.

Note: Unless the quinces are at their peak of ripeness, it may be advisable, before coring them, to poach them in water to cover, for 15 to 20 minutes.

Fruits and Preserves

Escoffier Figs
(Figues à la Manière d'Escoffier)

A simple treatment for producing a delicious dessert of fresh figs is to rinse and dry them, powder with sugar, and bake at 350° until the sugar has caramelized (being watchful to prevent burning). Chill and serve with sweetened whipped cream, flavored to taste with vanilla, anise, cardamom . . . or nothing.

Preserved Figs (*Confiture de Figues*)

6 HALF-PINT JARS

2 quarts fresh figs
4 cups granulated sugar
1 cup water
Juice of 1 lemon
1 teaspoon anise seeds (optional)

Wash figs and remove stems. Stir sugar and water over low heat until sugar is dissolved. Drop in figs, flavor with the lemon juice and anise seed. Let the mixture stand overnight. Then bring to a boil. Reduce heat at once, and cook, barely simmering, for about 2 hours. Transfer the figs to hot sterilized half-pint jars. Fill jars with the syrup to within ½-inch of the tops. Cool, seal, and store (or eat!).

Melon à la Saint-Jacques

The famous dessert melon of Provence is the Cavaillon, named for a little town in the Vaucluse, and is sometimes affectionately called *un charentais* (brandy). Any American melon of the cantaloupe type may be substituted but it must be perfectly ripe. Cut the melon in half. Take out the seeds, and remove the meat with a "baller" (the little kitchen tool used for making potato balls). Put the pretty tinted spheres in a bowl and chill them. Powder lightly with sugar and moisten with muscatel (Muscat de Frontignan is used in Provence) or port, or — even better — with the excellent wine of the Rasteau (Côtes du Ventoux).

Tomato Jam (*Confiture de Tomates*)

5 pounds tomatoes
4 pounds sugar
Pinch of salt
Rind of 1 lemon
(Optional) ¼ pound chopped walnut meats

Pour boiling water over the tomatoes or drop them into a pot of boiling water. This will loosen the skin which must be removed. Put the peeled tomatoes into a non-metal saucepan with the sugar and pinch of salt. Bring to a boil, stirring attentively to prevent caramelization. Then lower heat and simmer for 1 hour. Stir in the lemon peel which must be freed of all its white inside pulp, and be cut in small slivers. Bring to a boil again and immediately lower heat (as before) and simmer 1 hour longer. Add the nut meats, if used; pour into jars and seal as usual.

Watermelon Conserve (*Confiture de Pastèque*)

The watermelons of Provence come in assorted colors. Some have red flesh, others white or yellow.

Slice the watermelon. Remove the outside skin and seeds. Dice the melon slices. Mix watermelon dice and sugar in proportions of 3 cups sugar to each 2¼ pounds of fruit.

Let the mixture stand until the sugar has absorbed all the juice yielded by the fruit. (The sugar will, by then, have dissolved). Pour the fruit and juice into a jam kettle. Add the lemon rind which should be freed of its white inside pulp and be cut in small thin lozenges. Cook over gentle heat for about 1½ hours, stirring frequently. To test, remove a spoonful of the syrup from the kettle and, when it has cooled sufficiently, pinch a little between thumb and forefinger. If the syrup adheres, the conserve is sufficiently cooked. Jar and seal as usual.

1 watermelon (about 7 pounds)
6 pounds sugar (approximately)
Rind of 1 lemon

Watermelon and Orange Conserve
(*Confiture de Pastèque et d'Oranges*)

Prepare watermelon conserve as indicated above.

Carefully peel, seed, and slice 6 large navel oranges. Poach the slices in water for a few minutes. Then weigh them and add an equal weight of sugar and the chopped rind of 1 lemon. When sugar has completely dissolved, boil the fruit mixture over low heat for 1 hour. Then combine the two conserves and cook them together for 10 minutes more.

Watermelon à la Provençale
(*Pastèque à la Provençale*)

Make a deep circular incision around the stem of a perfectly ripened watermelon. Lift out and reserve this natural cork.

Shake the melon gently to spill out its ripe seeds, and then fill it with a good Tavel wine, Châteauneuf-du-Pape or other Provençal wine. Cork the melon with its stem, and seal this with a little wax. Set in a pailful of ice (or in the bottom of your well!) to chill for an hour.

At serving time, uncork the melon and pour the wine, through a strainer, into a large pitcher to be portioned out in port glasses. Cut the melon in slices and serve it on a platter along with the pitcher of wine.

XVII

Too Provençal to Travel

THIS CHAPTER will be of only academic interest to readers outside Provence. But incurable cookbook readers can't be easily discouraged by the supposed nonavailability of ingredients mentioned in a recipe. If American and British waters can't provide *nonats,* say, or *rascasse,* the determined adventurer will, somehow, find an obliging sea food merchant who can suggest reasonable facsimiles . . . or at least something to work with. And if nothing of the sort is to be had, the reading can generate sunny dreams of Provence and a secret promise to go there one day.

The Artichoke's Daughters
(*Les Filles de l'Artichaut*)

In Provence, early in the spring when the cultivation of artichoke beds begins again, the young shoots called *"filles"* are culled. Their roots and the few little leaves that have grown on them are cut off. Then these "daughters" are boiled for 45 minutes in salted water and eaten with *Vinaigrette* Sauce (page 30), or covered with Béchamel Sauce (page 12), powdered with grated cheese, and browned in a hot oven.

Caillettes Pugetoise

SERVES 6 TO 8

2 pounds pork liver, skinned
½ pound sweetbreads
½ pound fresh pork fat
Salt
Freshly ground pepper
7 cloves garlic, peeled and chopped
2 tablespoons minced parsley
Pork caul (pages 166 and 175)

This very simple dish is one of the most popular hors d'oeuvres on the Provençal menu. Excellent versions are also prepared in country butcher shops. The most renowned are those of Solliès-Pont, Puget-Ville, and Le Luc in the Var.

Cut liver, sweetbreads, and pork fat in narrow strips. Mix with salt, pepper, garlic, and parsley. Leave in a bowl, covered, in a cool place for 24 hours to season.

Soak the caul (*crépine*) in warm water until it is supple. Then spread it out and fill it with the stuffing, making sure that liver, fat, and sweetbreads are evenly distributed. Roll up the caul like a fat sausage 4 to 5 inches in diameter. Fasten firmly with thread, and roast at 350° for about 1½ hours. Let the *caillette* chill in its own juice. This dish keeps well for several days.

Pieds et Paquets

SERVES 6

1 tripe
Filling:
  ½ cup chopped parsley
  2 cloves garlic, peeled and minced
  3 tablespoons fat lamb intestines
  4 tablespoons minced lean bacon
  Salt, pepper and nutmeg

This dish of tripe and lambs' feet is one of the most famous examples of *Marseillaise* cuisine. It takes a long time to prepare and even longer to cook, but no one should visit Provence without sampling it. And, although Mr. Waverley Root (in his *The Food of France*) says, "the feet seem to have disappeared from the combination," the authentic recipe is still followed in some Provençal kitchens (especially in Toulon), and here it is.

One tripe will weigh 8 or more pounds and will make 12 or more "packages." Both tripe and feet are best prepared for cooking by the butcher. Cut the tripe into 3-inch squares and make a small incision in one corner of each square. Then prepare a filling as follows: Mix together the chopped parsley, *minced* garlic, minced lean bacon, and (thoroughly cleaned) intestines. Season generously with salt, pepper, and a little nutmeg (about ½ teaspoon). Place a spoonful of filling on each square of tripe. Roll up the squares and fasten them by pulling three of their corners through the incision in the fourth corner (or they may, instead, be tied up with thread although this makes them look less professional).

In an earthenware pot or a "daubière" (a special stew pot found in Provence), melt the 4 tablespoons of minced *fat* bacon or *petit salé* (page 21). Add the chopped onion and, after having browned this lightly, the carrots, sliced crosswise, chopped tomatoes, whole onion studded with a few cloves, whole garlic cloves, salt, pepper, and the other ½ teaspoon nutmeg.

Arrange the lamb feet on this bed of vegetables with the "packages" on top. Drench with the wine and bouillon. Bring to a boil and cook briskly for 3 or 4 minutes, then cover tightly, lower the heat, and simmer for 7 or 8 hours, (adding liquid if necessary). *Pieds et Paquets* are always served on very hot plates.

Note: In Provence a deep soup plate is sometimes substituted for the conventional pot lid. Its purpose is to facilitate a kind of basting action. A Dutch oven with a "drip" cover serves the same way.

4 tablespoons minced fat bacon or *petit salé*
1 chopped onion
2 scraped carrots
3 chopped tomatoes
1 whole onion, peeled and studded with cloves
2 whole cloves garlic, peeled
1 lamb's foot per person
1¼ cups dry white wine
1¼ cups bouillon or water

Limaces

The *limace* has been called "the quintessence of snail." He thrives only in Provence, it seems, and is a gastropod much smaller than an ordinary snail, and his flesh is much more delicate. By preference, he lives in stone walls, in meadows, on vine roots, and particularly among fennel plants which give him a most agreeable perfume.

Limaces are pretreated like snails — that is to say, fasted, and then cooked for 30 minutes in a highly spiced court bouillon plus a bit of orange peel, and then drained.

Limaces à la Sucarelle

Let yourself be tempted by this incomparable dish if you ever have a chance. You will be astonished and delighted.

Allow about 30 *limaces* per person, soaked in 2 cups of vinegar with 2 tablespoons salt for 10 to 12 hours. Then cook them in water seasoned with salt, a large *bouquet garni,* and several sprigs of fresh fennel fern. They must simmer for at least 2½ to 3 hours. Drain them and make two punctures in each shell opposite its opening.

Prepare a sauce as follows: In an earthenware or other non-metal saucepan put 2 tablespoons olive oil, 1 cup rather lean sausage meat, 4 peeled, chopped onions, 2 or 3 peeled, seeded, crushed tomatoes, 3 cloves of garlic peeled and chopped together with an equal quantity of parsley. Let this cook over moderate heat for 7 or 8 minutes. Add 1½ cups dry white wine and a *bouquet garni.* Simmer for a minute or two and then put in the *limaces,* and just water enough to cover the contents of the saucepan. Let all this simmer for about 1 hour. Thicken the sauce with 2 tablespoons crumbs. Serve very hot.

One eats *limaces* prepared this way by sucking them right out of their shells, which is made easy by the punctures. Hence the name *"sucarelle"* (from *sucer*).

Limaces Persillade

The cooked *limaces* are marinated in a highly seasoned *Vinaigrette* Sauce (page 30) plus a generous quantity of chopped parsley, and served cold.

Nonats (ou Nounat) et Poutina

"The richness of the Nice markets is the outward token of the richness of its food," says Waverley Root in *The Food of France.* "The crowded fishmongers are a reminder of the crowded Mediterranean. It seems something of a miracle that it remains crowded, given the existence of a certain Niçois specialty, *poutina et nounat.* These are barely hatched fish, taken at the time when they emerge from their eggs, so that fish and roe are often mixed together. By a special dispensation the Nice area is absolved from the usual conservation regulations which elsewhere protect fish at this time. They are taken in special nets in April and May, and are boiled and eaten with olive oil and lemon juice, or cooked in omelettes . . . or fritters."

The *poutina* and *nonats* are sometimes spread out on a cloth, sprinkled with vinegar, dried, powdered with flour, and tossed into a skillet where minced onions are browning in olive oil. When the poutina is golden, it is removed from the pan, seasoned with pepper, and served on very hot plates accompanied by slices of lemon.

Soupe à la Poutina

This Provençal specialty is made as follows: To serve 2 or 3 persons, lightly cook 1 leek, 1 stalk of celery, and 2 peeled onions, all coarsely chopped, in olive oil. Add 1 crushed clove of garlic and 4 cups water, a pinch of saffron and 4 or 5 ounces of *poutina*. Bring to a boil, and add ¼ cup coarse vermicelli. Cook for 10 or more minutes or until the pasta is just done but not mushy.

Poutargue

Poutargue, a kind of "Provençal caviar," is a specialty of Martigues, near Marseille. It is one of the oldest preparations still in use, for it was known to the people of Crete at the time of Minos and was taken to Provence by Phocaean navigators. *Poutargue,* which is mullet roe, pressed and dried, is today an essentially Provençal product. It is usually cut into narrow strips and seasoned with pepper, olive oil, and lemon juice. Or it may be grated into a sauce of oil, pepper, and lemon juice, and spread on lightly toasted slices of French bread.

    Poutargue is used also to provide accent in an otherwise bland salad such as *Haricots Blancs en Salade à la Poutargue* and *Salade de Pois Chiches à la Martégale* (see the two following recipes).

White Bean Salad with Poutargue
(Haricots Blanc en Salade à la Poutargue)

Soak 1 cup dried white beans overnight in water to cover. Drain, add fresh water to cover and 1 teaspoon salt. Simmer until soft but not mushy. Drain well. Season with salt (lightly) and pepper, olive oil, lemon juice, and (to taste) grated *poutargue* (see preceding recipe). Canned white beans may be used for this dish if well rinsed in cold water and thoroughly drained before seasoning is added. They will not, of course, have to be cooked.

    The *poutargue* may, alternatively, simply be grated over an already-mixed salad.

Chick-pea Salad à la Martégale
(Salade de Pois Chiches à la Martégale)

1 cup dried (or canned) chick peas
Water to cover
1 clove garlic
1 small onion, peeled and chopped
Salt and pepper
½ teaspoon dry mustard
3 tablespoons *fines herbes* (page 16)
1 cup olive oil
Lemon juice
4 tablespoons olive oil
1 tablespoon vinegar
2 small green peppers
Nutmeg
Chopped parsley
1 tablespoon *poutargue* (see page 219)
Anchovy fillets and black olives

Soak the dried chick-peas overnight and then cook in lightly salted water to cover until soft but not mushy. If canned peas are used, they need only be rinsed thoroughly in cold water. Drain and set aside.

Rub a salad bowl with the garlic and mix in it the onion, pepper, salt (very little salt), mustard and *fines herbes*. Add the cup of oil, a few drops at a time, stirring continuously, to make a mayonnaise which you finish with a few drops of lemon juice. Remove this sauce from the salad bowl and set it aside.

In the emptied (but not washed) salad bowl, put the additional 4 tablespoons olive oil, the vinegar, pepper, and a mere hint of salt. Add the chick-peas and (in season) green peppers which must be seeded and cut in narrow strips. Grate the *poutargue* over the vegetables and mix it with the peas, being careful not to bruise them. Add a flourish of grated nutmeg and strew with chopped parsley.

In the center of your salad bowl, pose a generous whirl of the golden mayonnaise, and then garnish with the anchovy fillets and black olives.

Pieds de Veau Sauce Provençale

Cook the calves' feet in a court bouillon fortified with a *bouquet garni,* an onion studded with cloves, 2 or 3 carrots, 2 tablespoons flour (blended separately with a little of the broth before being stirred in), salt and pepper.

As soon as the feet are tender, bone them and serve hot with Provençal Sauce, hot or cold (page 30).

Rascasse Grilleé

It is generally believed that the fish *rascasse* is good only for bouillabaisse. This is a mistaken idea. Grilled *rascasse* is delicious.

Buy fishes about the size of a man's hand and, when they are cleaned, have the stomachs cut completely through, lengthwise, so that the fish can be spread open like a book. Marinate them in olive oil with sprigs of sage, fennel, and thyme (wild thyme if possible).

Place the fish on an oiled rack, their opened part toward the embers (or gas broiler flame or electric unit). While they cook, baste them gently with a stalk of thyme or bay leaves which are kept soaked in olive oil during the cooking period. When the fish are almost cooked, turn them over and lightly broil the skin side. Sprinkle with garlic and parsley minced together and remove from the broiler when this garnish has been just barely toasted. (Recipe of Dr. Raoulx.)

XVIII
Regional Wines and Homemade Liqueurs

IF, WITH THE EXCEPTION of Châteauneuf-du-Pape and a very few others, the lovely wines of Provence and Nice are little known outside their own regions, the explanation is simple. First, most of them are delicate and, thus, poor travelers. Second, even those that can survive a long journey unaltered seldom have a chance to leave home, except inside a Provençal or knowing tourist. People drink most of them all up right on the spot.

Of the wines discussed below, those marked with stars are available, periodically, in the United States, and wine merchants hope to have more. As for the strictly indigenous *crus,* the list is too long for the adventurer in Provence to carry in his head.

Friends hearing that he is "going" will insist that he "must try" such and such a one, but, in the end, it will be his own discoveries that will be the most exciting. And, surprisingly, some of these may be *vins ordinaires,* so called. Because, says connoisseur Waverley Root, "very drinkable beverages are served, anonymously, in carafes." For superior wines of whatever type, he recommends "the vintages of *Château de Saint-Martin, Château de Sainte Roseline, Domaine des Moulières, Domaine de la Croix,* and *Clos Cibonne.*" But to each traveler his own.

The Côtes du Rhône

"The most distinguished wines of Provence are those that fall under the heading of *Côtes-du-Rhône,*" says Waverley Root in *The Food of France.* But the classification is, he points out, "more a handy way of lumping together a number of different vintages that do not fall into other well-defined wine-growing areas than anything else, for if these growths have the shared characteristic of appearing on the banks of the Rhône, they have little else in common . . . . Many of them fall outside the Provence area, but may be considered there as conveniently as anywhere."

In ancient times, the valley of the Rhône was the great highway by means of which Mediterranean civilization penetrated Gaul, long before the Christian era. The Phocaeans, founders of Massalia (now the Marseille country) very likely brought the first vine shoots there — the *shyra* of oriental origin. It is there, probably, that one must go to find the birthplace of the Côtes du Rhône wines.

In this extensive wine-growing district, Provence is an important area, stretching to the south of Orange all the way to the Mediterranean. It has, as its crown jewel, the famous Châteauneuf-du-Pape, universally renowned for its virility and warmth.

★ Châteauneuf-du-Pape

Several miles to the south of Orange, where Provence begins, is seen against the horizon a lordly silhouette, dominating a village that clings to the slopes of a steep hill; it is Châteauneuf-du-Pape. Below the base of the tower — a surging foam of green rising in waves that beat against the very tower itself — are the wonderful vineyards, fertile descendants of those created by the popes of Avignon, carefully preserved in the incomparable glory of their papal wine. For, in this hot and tranquil country, choice, golden vines ripen to make the splendid "must," yielding a wine that sometimes develops up to 15 percent of alcohol. It is a wine with a strong scent of raspberries and an astonishing flavor; some 1500 acres of vines are protected by the *Appellation Contrôlée.**

Châteauneuf-du-Pape needs no eulogy (although we just gave it one). It is the great wine that best suits the special character of Provençal cuisine. Glowing in its cardinal purple, warm from the abundant sunlight, rich with the aroma of the moors, it concentrates in its heart all the blessings promised by the azure skies. It crowns, like *un feu d'artifice,* the list of wines that escort the most sumptuous courses, and harmonizes to perfection with roasts, grills, game of every sort, and even cheeses. Châteauneuf-du-Pape is one of the great glories of Provence, and of France.

The extraordinary white Châteauneuf-du-Pape, mentioned by Waverley Root in *The Food of France,* is seldom found outside its own bailiwick, Châteauneuf-du-Pape itself, and is never exported. It is a wine hard to describe. A young American with no wine-tasting vocabulary explained his reaction to it this way, "You sort of *feel* the taste on your tongue and, if you close your eyes, it tastes red."

The Wines of Lirac

The dry white wines and the *rosés* of Lirac have been known since the 1700's and have long carried the *Appellation Contrôlée* identification. They have a highly developed bouquet because of the proximity of the wild marshlands that surround the vineyard. The red and racy Liracs have a scent and savor so distinguished among Vaucluse wines that a number of connoisseurs have stated that Liracs are wines of a special type without counterpart.

★ Tavels

The wines of Tavel (near Avignon), lively and limpid, comprise some of the most honored *crus.* They are a lovely, clear, golden ruby color,

---

* The term, *Appellation Contrôlée,* seems to be rather widely misunderstood. It is mistaken for a sort of official recognition of superiority whereas it is nothing of the kind. The words mean what they literally say: "controlled designation." In other words, *Appellation Contrôlée* means that the wine in the bottle behind the label came from the region, vineyard, etc. claimed for it and from nowhere else. These areas are strictly defined and limited and no wines produced elsewhere may carry the names (which, consequently, are a kind of registered trademark).

and have a superlative bouquet similar to the fragrance of young strawberries. The most famous source of these respected wines is the Château d'Aqueria. Fortunately, the Tavels are abundant and can be successfully exported. Among those that are available in the United States, from time to time, are Coupe de Soleil, and Flûte-Raphia.

Dear to Louis XVI, Tavels have also been praised by Brillat-Savarin, Balzac, Monselet, and many another gastronome. For the Tavels, like their neighbors, the Liracs, in their sprightly aroma equal other fine wines while bearing no marked resemblance to any of them. In coloring and distinction, they are superior even to some of the great *crus,* and leave a suave aftertaste which richer and more astringent wines do not.

Light to drink, although high in alcohol, Tavel wine is as agreeable in winter, when it knows how to bring a ray of sunshine into the somberest day, as in summer when, properly chilled, it is the perfect complement to a hot-weather menu. Tavel is persuasive enough to make more and more converts among connoisseurs.

★ The Wines of Ventoux and Lubéron

East of the Rhône, in the area that extends from Vaison-la-Romaine to the slopes of the Mont Ventoux and southward to the borders of the Montagne de Lure, important vineyards produce, under the name "Côtes du Ventoux," some highly esteemed wines. These are the product of Grenache, Clairette, Syrah, Roussette, and Mourvèdre vines from which wines of high alcoholic content (sometimes 12 or 13 percent) are developed. Though less robust than the Côtes du Rhône, they are agreeably fruity. The list of the principal (and increasingly valued) *crus* is long. It includes the Bedouin, Seguret, Clairanne, Rasteau, Vénasque, Vacqueras, and Flassans.

Farther south, the Côtes du Lubéron wines of very similar characteristics are produced. These are the Bonnieux, Lacoste, Oppède, Mirabeau, Cadenet, Loumarin, La Tour d'Aigues, and others.

Côtes de Provence

From Aix to the Var valley, little green vineyards are hooked to the steep mountainsides, held there by walls of dry stones, strung with vines that clutch the thin soil, here composed of coarse sand and flint, there of whitish or clay-tinted earth. Finally, like the background of a painting, the scented mountains of Sainte-Baume, of the Pré-Alpes, the Maures, and of the Estérel range; this is the country that produces the Côtes de Provence.

These wines have a past rich in history. It is here that the Gauls cultivated the first vines — vines imported from Italy and the Near East by the Phocaeans. In the Middle Ages and during the Renaissance, the vogue for Provençal wines spread far. Tables of kings were furnished with them, and they were already being relished in foreign lands.

So much homage could scarcely leave the vintners unimpressed. To this day, the grapes are selected with the same care from the vines with the melodious names: the *Tibouren, Pécouithouar, Mourvèdre, Clairette de Trans, Oeillade, Cinsault, Grenache* and *Ugni Blanc,* to name only a few.

For some time now, there has been a strong demand for the importation of Côtes de Provence wines and these have crossed many seas. The vintners, restrained by severe disciplines, controlled by the Syndicat des Côtes de Provence, cull more of their vine shoots every day, and thus take every advantage given them by the sun, the admirable situation of their hills, and their soil which, although meager, generates wines of exceptional quality.

The Wines of Bandol

Bandol wines take their names from a little port situated between Toulon and Marseille, although they are produced on the shores of neighboring communities. But, in past centuries, the port of Bandol was the point at which these wines were assembled to be carried far and wide by sailing vessels. Increasing numbers of tourists who frequent this blessed corner of the *Varois* coast can easily visit the vineyards by following the route which leads toward Le Beausset, passing the picturesque villages of Cadière-d'Azur and Castellet.

The wines of Bandol are dry, flowery, and high in alcohol. They age well without becoming Madeira-like, and go extremely well with sea food. The "red" wines are oftener tawny than red and are greatly esteemed as accompaniments to roasts and *civets* (game cooked in wine). As for the *rosés,* these have exquisite flavor and are much in demand.

The quantities of Bandol wines that carry the seal of *l'Appellation Contrôlée* are somewhat limited but, when tourists and summer residents who have tasted them find them elsewhere, they feel transported once more to this magnificent corner of Provence where, under a riotous sun, the vine-covered hills slope to the blue, blue sea.

The Wines of Cassis

Our wine is so famous that Marseille — when she wants to make a present
to a king — asks us to send him some. Oh! if you could taste some of it!
It gleams like a limpid diamond. It smells of rosemary, heather, and
myrtle. It dances in the glass.

— Frédéric Mistral in *Calendau*

Cassis wines were originally made with Muscat grapes, and the dry,
white wines of Cassis (not to be confused with the aperitif) were not
developed until the time of Henry IV of France. Cassis wines today
enjoy the benefit of the *Appellation Contrôlée*. They are dry and warm
like the soil that nourishes them. The judicious selection of vines, the
ideal location of the vineyards, the proximity to the sea, and the irre-
proachable way they are handled account for their world-wide repute.

In the little community of Cassis, so charming and so hospitable to
tourists, situated between the mountain range of Sainte-Baume and the
sea, an area of some 200 acres has been dedicated to the vine, and chiefly
to the production of white wines and dry *rosés*. The white wines (marvelous accompaniments for fish, shellfish, and the famed bouillabaisse)
acquire, in their early years, all their finest bloom, and the special
bouquet, reminiscent of flint. The red wines and *rosés,* rotund and velvety, come to full development only after several years of cooperage,
and they respond joyously to aging. Majestic companions for grills,
roasts, and game, they are especially fine with the wine stews of the
region made of the delicious flesh of mountain rabbits, and scented with
thyme and rosemary.

★ *Gigondas*

In the lower range of the Ventoux, the Dentelles de Montmirail rise in
pure and finely chiseled lines. On the extreme north of this buttress
hangs the picturesque little village of Gigondas. An area of choice for
vineyards because of its limestone soil and Jurassic clay, its hilly posi-
tion gives it an unusual amount of sunshine and protects it from mists
and fog. Comprising only about 650 acres, the vineyards of Gigondas
are planted almost exclusively to Grenaches mixed with some of the
original Cinsault and Clairette stock.

Gigondas wine is always of splendid quality, easily yielding 15 percent. It is heady stuff with a rich and unique bouquet and has a rare
finish which has earned it the protection of the *Appellation Contrôlée*.

The Wines of Palette

A few miles from Aix-en-Provence, at the foot of the last spur of the *massif* Sainte-Victoire, not far from the famous "Wine Road" (Route Nationale No. 7), is the Palette region which, since the reign of King René in the fifteenth century, has produced fine wines. Many factors contribute to their merit: the nature of the soil, the freedom from rain and fog, the fluidity of the air, and the favorable exposure.

The principal *cru* of this area is Château-Simone, a wine of very high quality, brought into being by meticulous selection among noble vines, careful cultivation, and natural maturing in the ancient subterranean cellars, dug from the rock by Grands-Carmes monks, owners of the *Domaine* since the sixteenth century. Château-Simone has a subtle, exquisite flavor and, in its luminous quality, captures the starry heavens of Provence.

From this same region come the grapes from which the vin cuit of Palette is made — a product that since time immemorial has been the delight of Provençal people.

Wines of the Nice Region

The old "shyre" of Nice, where, it is claimed, the most beautiful flowers in the world are grown, is also the birthplace of some unforgettable wines. The reds are high in alcohol — and rather risky for the light-headed — with a vigorous bouquet, full of authority and finesse. The most celebrated of the Nice area wines are the Bellets, red or white (both are served chilled), but perhaps especially the pale, sparkling white Bellet with its distinctively musty flavor of flint and aromatic plants.

The wines of La Gaude, remarkable for their color and authority — the Falicons, Villars, Saint-Laurent-du-Var — were frequently mentioned by Mme. de Sévigné in her *Mémoires*. There are also other white wines which deliciously suit the local dishes such as the famous *Pissaladière* (page 52) and the *Tartes de Blettes* (Chard Pie, page 189). The vineyards of the amiable and smiling wines of Bellet, of l'Escarene, and of Mas-de-la-Garde rise, tier on tier, to the slanting heights that, at Nice, form that wonderful ring, "La Ceinture de Vénus."

Mulled Wine (*Vin Cuit*)

Mulled wine is an almost mandatory accompaniment to fête day cakes such as the *Gâteau des Rois* (page 210) in Provence, and many excellent commercial brands are sold in the wine shops, the most famous of which is the *vin cuit* of Palette (near Aix). But almost everyone who grows his own grapes makes it by the following recipe:

The *mout* (juice which has been pressed from the grapes but is not yet fermented) is set to cook — preferably in a copper vessel — and the froth is continually skimmed off as it rises, until the original quantity of juice has been reduced by one-third. It is allowed to cool and is then carefully decanted and poured through filter paper. When the juice no longer shows any signs of deposit or fermentation, it is bottled.

Once chilled (for serving), the *vin cuit* may be fortified by the addition of half a cup of brandy per quart of wine.

Homemade Liqueurs (*Liqueurs de Ménage*)

Many American families make wine in the autumn when the grapes are ripe and fragrant. And blackberries, currants, mulberries, and other fruits are still (literally) pressed into the service of family wine cellars. But, oddly enough, very few liqueurs (or, as they are so charmingly called in the States, "cordials") are made at home. Yet a little experimentation with scented potables can wonderfully repay the small amount of effort involved. In private households in Provence, the variety of basic ingredients used for home brews is enormous. For example: acacia (mimosa), almond, anise, apricot, blackberry, carnation, cherry, citron, coffee, currant (black, red, or white), fennel, grape, juniper, lemon orange, orange blossom, peach, peach stone, quince, raspberry, strawberry, tangerine, vanilla, violet, and walnut, not to mention mixtures. All kinds of herbs and spices are used to create subtle differences.

The alcoholic content (proof) of such liqueurs depends upon the spirits used. For most ratafias — that is, liqueurs made by steeping fruit, flowers, and/or herbs in alcohol — *Larousse Gastronomique* recommends 70 to 88 percent. The ingredients are combined with the spirits and left, covered tightly, in a warm place, for anywhere from a few days to two months or longer. For some recipes, the sugar is not added until the initial period of steeping is over. The container is then resealed and left for another week or two. The liqueur is then filtered and bottled.

Other homemade Provençal beverages little known in the United States are:

Aspi

A white wine in which lavender has been steeped for several days. When it is served, the lavender is strained out, and the drink fortified with a small quantity of *eau-de-vie* (brandy) in sugar syrup.

Carthagène

Much the same as Aspi minus the sugar syrup but also sometimes made with rose wine.

Eau de Coing, Eau de Sauge, Liqueur de Dames, and Liqueur de Fenêtre
(Quince Liqueur, Sage Liqueur, Ladies' Liqueur, and Window Liqueur)

All names for cordials made by immersing the fruits, fragrant herbs, or other ingredients in brandy and leaving them for a fortnight in a window where they will be sunned all day and cooled all night — a form of steep said to extract the full flavor of the herbs.

Liqueur de Lait (Milk Liqueur)

Milk and brandy, half-and-half, plus sugar (to taste), a cut-up lemon, and a vanilla bean. It is left to steep for a fortnight and then filtered and bottled.

The possibilities of homemade beverages are limited only by the imagination of the brewer. In fact, they so lend themselves to inventiveness that every house may have its specialty. To encourage this gay pastime and boost readers' spirits, we suggest starting with a very easy method for making a ratafia — in this case, orange.

Ratafia d'Oranges (Orange Cordial)

6 navel oranges
1 pound loaf sugar
¼ teaspoon cinnamon
½ teaspoon ground coriander seeds
1 quart brandy

Peel the oranges. Remove and discard *all* the white pith inside the rind. Then chop the rind fine. Squeeze the juice of the oranges into a jar. Add the sugar and spices. Let the mixture sit, stirring it occasionally, until the sugar is dissolved. Then pour in the brandy. Mix well. Cover tightly and leave the infusion in a warm place for 2 months. Then filter it through muslin, bottle and seal.

A votre santé!

Index